SOCIAL
RESEARCH
METHODS

S O CIAL

2nd Edition

RESEARCH METHODS

NICHOLAS WALLIMAN

The Essentials

Los Angeles | London | New Delhi
Singapore | Washington DC

Los Angeles | London | New Delhi
Singapore | Washington DC

SAGE Publications Ltd
1 Oliver's Yard
55 City Road
London EC1Y 1SP

SAGE Publications Inc.
2455 Teller Road
Thousand Oaks, California 91320

SAGE Publications India Pvt Ltd
B 1/I 1 Mohan Cooperative Industrial Area
Mathura Road
New Delhi 110 044

SAGE Publications Asia-Pacific Pte Ltd
3 Church Street
#10-04 Samsung Hub
Singapore 049483

Editor: Mila Steele
Assistant editor: James Piper
Production editor: Victoria Nicholas
Copyeditor: Camille Bramall
Proofreader: Derek Markham
Marketing manager: Ben Griffin-Sherwood
Cover design: Shaun Mercier
Typeset by: C&M Digitals (P) Ltd, Chennai, India
Printed and bound by CPI Group (UK) Ltd,
Croydon, CR0 4YY (for Antony Rowe)

© Nicholas Walliman 2016

First edition published 2006, reprinted 2007, 2009, 2010, 2011, 2012, 2014
Second edition first published 2016

Library of Congress Control Number: 2015944205

British Library Cataloguing in Publication data

A catalogue record for this book is available from the British Library

MIX
Paper from responsible sources
FSC® C013604

ISBN 978-1-4739-1619-7
ISBN 978-1-4739-1620-3 (pbk)

At SAGE we take sustainability seriously. Most of our products are printed in the UK using FSC papers and boards. When we print overseas we ensure sustainable papers are used as measured by the PREPS grading system. We undertake an annual audit to monitor our sustainability.

Contents

Introduction and How to Use this Book

Every course recommends textbooks to read that tend to be both long and complicated, providing great volume and detail of information all of which can be overwhelming to the student. This book provides you with a simple guide to help you to steer a route through the detail by summarizing the main ingredients of the subject, their interrelationships and background. You will gain a clear overview of the essentials of social research methods that will enable you to fill in further detail as required. It will support you in doing a social science research project all the way through from reviewing the literature, to writing up the results, as well as providing good guidance on study skills to help you on the way through your course.

NAVIGATION

This book is in four parts. **Part I** covers the main issues when beginning a research project such as background theory, practical ways to plan and design your project, as well as how to acquire the background material on which to base your studies. It ends with advice on how to write your research proposal. **Part II** presents the choices you have in methods of collecting and analysing the information you need for your investigations depending on the type of research that you are carrying out, and how you can come to conclusions based on the data you have collected. **Part III** provides guidance on how to write up your research in such a way that it is a full record of what you have done and what conclusions you have come to. **Part IV** provides more general advice on study and writing skills to help you to present your knowledge in the best possible way in your essays, assignments and dissertations. At the end, there is a list of references and a glossary of the main terms used in the subject. An index is provided to help you to find the location of subjects in the book.

HOW TO USE THIS BOOK

This book is designed to help you to succeed in your undergraduate or post-graduate level course on social science research methods. This includes research methods appropriate to a wide range of subjects, such as social science, social anthropology, psychology, leisure studies and sport, hospitality, health studies, the environment, business studies, education and the humanities. It is about helping you to pass your exams and to get the most from your coursework assignments, as well as providing a handy summary of research methods if you are a novice researcher.

It is designed and written to provide you with an easy-to-navigate guide to commonly taught curricula in social research methods courses, and the ways of thinking and writing that your supervisors will be looking for when they review your work. This guide to the essentials is not to be used instead of wider reading, but rather as a means of familiarizing yourself with the basics of the discipline when preparing for assignments or planning a dissertation. This book will help you structure and organize your thoughts, and will enable you to get the most from your other textbooks and the reading that you will do as part of your course.

This book is designed to point you in the direction of key ideas about research and to provide a review of the main methods, and give you the briefest of introductions to how they are used in which contexts. It will also point you in the direction of the most important textbooks and readings, and will encourage you to widen your knowledge and research capabilities so as to improve your skills in your chosen subject.

> **Do:** Remember, this is not a book that you need to read from cover to cover. It is a reference book from which you should extract whatever is interesting and useful to you.

Each course is different and has a different focus. I would strongly advise you to look very carefully at the information provided on the curriculum of the particular course you are doing, and compare it with the contents of this book. You then need only to concern yourself with those issues that are relevant. The book is clearly organized into chapters that are split down under headings, so just highlight those sections that you will need to know about, and leave the rest for a rainy day!

INTRODUCING AND EXPLAINING THE FEATURES

In the rest of this Introduction, there is a short overview of the subject, very briefly summarizing the main ingredients of your course. Then there is a section on how to think like a social science researcher, to help to get you into the mindset of experts in the subject and of your lecturers and examiners. Being familiar with how researchers think and being able to use the terminology they employ will help to convince your examiners that you are at home with the subject.

Parts I, II and III of the book are organized into short chapters that take each aspect of research and research methods in turn. It starts with the theoretical and philosophical issues that underpin research in the social sciences, then moves on to the design of research projects. The nature of the raw ingredients of research is discussed, followed by a review of the main research methods and their applications. Again, you should not see these as a substitute for the detailed coverage that you will get from your lectures and textbooks, but they serve as a handy preparation for the lectures and a good revision guide and quick reference source.

Each chapter in Parts I, II and III will contain the following features:

- An explanation of the main issues, practical and theoretical features are discussed for each aspect of research.
- New terms appear in bold and are closely followed by an easy-to-understand definition. These words also appear in the **Glossary** at the end of the book.
- In order to help you in your studies and to point out issues of importance or remind you of common mistakes there are inserted sections called **Do** and **Don't** throughout the text. These provide useful hints in relation to the subjects being discussed. There are also useful **Examples** provided to illustrate actual applications of the matters discussed in the text.
- At the end of each chapter is a section called **Take it further**. This will point you in the direction of further areas of study or more advanced methods not mentioned in the main text. It could enable you to address the more thorny controversies and questions not easily answered by standard approaches.
- In order to help you to be prepared for assignments or tutorials, I provide a section in each chapter called **Ask yourself**, with some questions to ponder arising from the previous explanations, and a short paragraph on how to find appropriate answers.
- To provide guidance for further reading on the subjects discussed in each chapter, there is a **Further reading** section in the form of a short annotated list of sources that you can refer to when you need to find out more up-to-date detail about the subject of the chapter. This will be particularly useful when you have decided on the methods you want to use, and need more guidance and detail about them and their application in your project.

Part IV gives you guidance on how to study and organize your work and get the most out of the teaching you receive, efficient reading and note taking, and how to write and present your work in order to best demonstrate your knowledge when you come to doing essays.

> **Do:** Use the Index to quickly pinpoint what you are looking for, and the Glossary for useful definitions of technical terms.

THINKING LIKE A SOCIAL SCIENCE RESEARCHER

Although you might be doing a degree in healthcare, education, sport science, business studies or other subjects, the common feature will be that you will be dealing with people and their interactions. Hence, social science underlies all of these disciplines and your course on research methods will be based on those of sociology. The key to success in your course is to learn to think like a social science researcher. That is to say, to learn to speak the language of social science research, using the terms and phrases that mark out 'researcher speak' from that of everyday conversation. This book will give you the information and tips about when and how to use this language and the ways of thinking about the world that come with this language.

So, how do you think like a social science researcher?

- Social science researchers are interested in how to study human behaviour, its causes and consequences.
- They look at factors within society and try to find ways to understand and explain human actions and the results of these.
- They are aware that they, as humans, inevitably play a role within the research process that must be taken into account when coming to conclusions.
- They tend to hold particular beliefs about knowledge and how it can be gained, and select their research approach based on their particular stance within the theoretical framework of social science research.
- They strive to choose a research design that they can argue to be appropriate for the subject of their research.
- They apply particular research methods for collecting and analysing data, chosen from a repertoire of methods devised over many years, on the basis of appropriateness for the particular research problem tackled. If necessary they will adapt existing or even devise new methods to suit.
- They use **argument** in order to build up a case for the validity of their conclusions.
- Social science research is relevant to a wide range of disciplines, so apart from sociology, researchers can be specialists in subjects such as education, healthcare, the built environment, business, welfare, housing and many others.

For the purposes of your course, you will have to talk about research methods in the context of theory, research problems and practical applications for collecting and analysing data in order to come to conclusions.

> **Don't:** Common pitfall! Although research is a very practical subject, don't forget that it is based on theoretical ideas that influence every stage of the process. Be aware of the thinking behind the various research methods.

INTRODUCING THE SUBJECT

Social science research is a 'catch-all' term that includes research into any facet of life in society. Wherever there are people, there is society. 'No man is an island' states the well-known maxim. Social interrelationships, opinions, customs, habits, lifestyles, conditions of life, communities and so many other subjects can be the focus of study. But remember, what courses in social science research methods focus on is not so much what is studied but how is it studied.

The history of social science research is closely bound up with the theoretical developments that were promoted by philosophers and key thinkers and practitioners in the social sciences. The debate about knowledge of human beings and their society is rooted in philosophical thought. Some key figures who have influenced thinking about social research are:

On research in general:

Plato and Aristotle - these represent the two contrasting approaches to acquiring knowledge and understanding the world (epistemology). Plato argued for deductive thinking (starting with theory to make sense of what we observe), and Aristotle for the opposite, inductive thinking (starting with observations in order to build theories).

Hume - recognized the importance of inductive thinking in the advancement of scientific knowledge, but highlighted its restrictions in finding the truth.

Popper - formulated a combination of deductive and inductive thinking in the hypothetico-deductive method, commonly known as scientific method.

Kuhn - revealed that scientific research cannot be separated from human influences and is subject to social norms.

On social research:

Compte - maintained that society could be analysed empirically just like any other subjects of scientific enquiry, and social laws and theories could be established on the basis of psychology and biology.

Marx - defined the moral and social aspects of humanity in terms of material forces.

Durkheim - argued that society develops its own system of phenomena that produce collectively shared norms and beliefs, so-called 'social facts'.

Weber - maintained that in order to describe social practices adequately we must understand what meanings the practices have for the participants themselves. This requires an understanding of the values involved, but without taking sides or making value judgements (often referred to as Verstehen).

Foucault - argued that there was no progress in science, only changing perspectives, as the practice of science is shown to control what is permitted to count as knowledge. He demonstrated how discourse is used to make social regulation and control appear natural.

Being a researcher is as much about doing a practical job as being academically competent. Identifying a subject to research, finding and collecting information and analysing it, presents you with a range of practical problems that need to be solved. Over hundreds of years, techniques, or methods, have been evolved to provide solutions to these problems, and it is these methods that your course is about.

Most courses in research methods are a preparation for actually doing some research. It would be rather a dry subject if learned for its own sake, like memorizing a manual for repairing cars and never looking under a bonnet, let alone attempting a repair. So, instead of exams, most courses in research methods test you by getting you to do an extended essay or dissertation based on some research activities. See this course as a way of gaining useful skills that you will be able to apply when doing research, selecting whichever methods are appropriate for the problems you want to solve. Make sure that you are aware of the curriculum of your course to ensure that you are familiar with everything that is required for your assignments.

Here is a short summary of the range of issues that are likely to appear in a social science research methods course, possibly in the same sort of order:

Theory of research – epistemology and ontology. Conflicting ideas about what knowledge is, our relationship with nature, ways of thinking, etc. all form the basis upon which research is carried out. Social research is open to a lot of debate as the focus of the investigations is humanity – a slippery subject if there ever was one! The problems are compounded by the researchers being human too.

Quality and planning of research – what makes research good and how it can be organized. As a practical subject, there are standards that should be achieved in order to gain credibility, and procedures that make for efficient use of time and resources. There is often a section here on how to choose a suitable research problem for your own research exercise, e.g. dissertation or assignment.

Review of literature – new research is based on a huge legacy of previous work. How to relate your own work to that which has gone before is a skill that needs to be learned.

The nature of data – information is the raw material of research, so a good understanding of the nature of data is required in order to be able to collect it and analyse it efficiently.

Sampling or case selection – it is rarely possible to include everybody or everything in your research. How you select the small number of cases to study is crucial to the credibility of your conclusions to the research.

Collecting data – a wide choice of collection methods have been devised over the years. You will need to know how the methods work and which ones are appropriate for particular types of investigation.

Analysing data – what you do with the data after you have collected them, or even while you are collecting them, depends on the analytical methods you adopt. A knowledge of the possibilities is required in order to make an informed choice.

Ethics – all research with living things, and particularly humans, raises ethical issues about privacy, cruelty, honesty, fairness, etc. When doing social science research you need to take into account all these issues to make sure that you do no harm.

Writing up – how to present your research and findings in a way that convinces.

> **Do:** Carefully read your course or module handbook in order to find out exactly what is the scope and purpose of the course. It is more efficient if you concentrate on the necessary topics, however interesting all the others are!

No matter what type of research methods you are using or writing about, it is probably not too difficult to predict that the subject in question will be marked out by the same running themes that recur throughout social science research.

- Theory of research – what relationship there is between the researcher and his or her knowledge of the world, what constitutes good research, inductive/deductive thinking, how conclusions can be reached and how reliable they are. Theoretical factors form the basis on which any research is carried out, and greatly influence the conduct of the researcher and the research methods chosen.
- Research design – the framework into which the research fits depending on the theory and nature of the research problem.
- The existence and meanings of **concepts** – the building blocks of thinking. Abstract concepts are devised that label social phenomena or qualities. They need to be made tangible in order to explore them and their relationship with each other. How this is done, using indicators and variables, is always a source of discussion.
- The qualitative/quantitative issue – relating to research design, data, methods of data collection and analysis. A combination of both is often employed.
- Argument – how logical argument within the research design can be made to convince the reader of the validity and soundness of the conclusions.
- Selection and application of research methods – the appropriateness and correct use of methods for collecting and analysing data in relation to the research problem.

Take it further

Reading some history of the development of the social sciences will afford you a perspective of why and how the subject has developed to its present state. It will also highlight the different and often opposing positions of different strands of the discipline. Even if your main subject is not sociology as such, but another discipline with a social aspect, read your subject textbooks with a critical eye in relation to the research work of the past and present. Ask how the knowledge presented as fact was acquired in the first place, and how it has been challenged or debated since. Are there different schools of thought, and on what argument are they based?

Although you are unlikely at undergraduate level to be required to debate these issues in detail in an exam, they may make a good introduction to your dissertation or extended essay if you are required to write one. At Master's level you will undoubtedly have to critically discuss theoretical issues in relation to the practice of research.

Social science research is a huge field of work so study at undergraduate level can only provide an introduction to the main issues and methods involved. The 'Taking it further' section adds some additional material that might be beyond the normal scope of the course but is relevant to the subject of the chapter. It provides you with supplementary information or themes that you can usefully use in exams or assignments to impress your examiner or tutor with your grasp of the subject. Beyond what is provided in this companion there are sources of further information that you can usefully look up.

Each research project is different and uses selected research methods in a particular context. Reports on the research always have a section on the methods used for data collection and analysis. These can provide useful examples to illustrate particular points in your written work (exams, assignments or dissertation). Textbooks tend to use these examples liberally, so it should be easy to quote some to make a point or support an argument.

Ask yourself

Although your course may not culminate in an exam, it is always useful to ponder on a few questions that make you think about the material you have been revising. I will help you to make the information you have read active in your mind, something you can use and explain – this is necessary if you are going to do a research project. If you do have to sit for an exam, then being prepared for likely exam questions is obviously beneficial.

The questions I pose at the end of the chapters will provoke you to think about the issues discussed in the previous pages. Although I give some brief guidance to how you could approach the answer, you should go further and try to fill in the detail and think of how you could set up a bit of a discussion of the matters raised. This will help you to move one step forward from just being able to recite the lists of features, etc. provided in the text.

Further reading

Your first port of call for learning should be the textbook(s) that have been recommended on your course. If you are fortunate, one or two core textbooks will have been stipulated, making it easy for you to focus on what is written there. Unfortunately, some courses provide a long list of recommended reading that can leave you completely overwhelmed. What you then have to rely on for guidance on what to read is your course handbook and the subjects covered in your lectures and seminars. And then of course, the publications recommended at the end of each chapter of this book. The references that I list are not just from established research methods textbooks, but are more often from books that concentrate on the issues discussed in the chapter. They should be seen as a way to deepen your understanding.

Your lectures and seminars will be reliable indicators of the material you should learn. Use these not only to guide you to further reading, but also to limit the scope of your enquiries. You could go on for years exploring all there is to know about social research methods – leave that until later if you are really fascinated by the subject!

How much you need to know about each issue depends on the type of course you are doing and the orientation of your subject. Social science research methods are used in a multitude of subject areas, hence their comprehensive character and complexity. If you are required to do a research project, write a dissertation or do an assignment, find out if you can access the best examples of completed work by students from former years. This will give you a good indication of what is required and some examples to emulate.

PART I

PLANNING AND DESIGNING YOUR RESEARCH

ONE
Theoretical Background

WHAT IS RESEARCH?

In everyday speech 'research' is a term loosely used to describe a multitude of activities, such as collecting masses of information, delving into esoteric theories and producing wonderful new products. So how can true 'scientific' research be defined?

The *Oxford Encyclopedic English Dictionary* defines it as:

the systematic investigation into the study of materials, sources etc. in order to establish facts and reach new conclusions; an endeavour to discover new or collate old facts etc. by the scientific study of a subject or by a course of critical investigation.

Leedy and Ormrod (2012) define it from a more utilitarian point of view:

Research is a procedure by which we attempt to find systematically, and with the support of demonstrable fact, the answer to a question or the resolution of a problem.

Kerlinger (1970, p. 8) uses more technical language to define it as:

the systematic, controlled, empirical and critical investigation of hypothetical propositions about presumed relations among natural phenomena.

But is social science research 'scientific' research? Some sociologists would not maintain this. In fact, they would say that there is a distinct difference between research into the natural world and research into the habits, traditions, beliefs, organizations, etc. of human beings. Being human ourselves, we cannot take an impartial view of others, and we cannot establish 'facts' as fixed eternal truths. We can only aim for interpretation and understanding of the social world.

> **Do:** Remember that the debate about the nature of social research is a lively one and is based around the philosophical aspects of epistemology and ontology.

EPISTEMOLOGY AND ONTOLOGY

Epistemology is concerned with how we know things and what we can regard as acceptable knowledge in a discipline. In the study of social (and any other) sciences there is a choice between two ways of acquiring knowledge:

- **Empiricism** - knowledge gained by sensory **experience** (using inductive reasoning).
- **Rationalism** - knowledge gained by reasoning (using deductive reasoning).

The relative merits of these approaches have been argued ever since the time of the Ancient Greeks – Aristotle advocating the first and Plato the second.

Another polarization in the pursuit of knowledge has appeared more recently, and relates to the status of scientific methods and human subjectivity:

- **Positivism** - the application of the natural sciences to the study of social reality. An objective approach that can test theories and establish scientific laws. It aims to establish causes and effects.
- **Interpretivism** - the recognition that subjective meanings play a crucial role in social actions. It aims to reveal interpretations and meanings.
- **Realism** - (particularly social realism) - this maintains that structures do underpin social events and discourses, but as these are only indirectly observable they must be expressed in theoretical terms and are thus likely to be provisional in nature. This does not prevent them being used in action to change society.

All philosophical positions and their attendant methodologies, explicitly or implicitly, hold a view about social reality. This view, in turn, will determine what can be regarded as legitimate knowledge. Thus, the ontological shapes the epistemological (Williams and May, 1996, p. 69).

Ontology is about the theory of social entities and is concerned with what exists to be investigated. Bryman (2012, pp. 32–3) identifies two opposing theoretical attitudes to the nature of social entities:

- **Objectivism** - the belief that social phenomena and their meanings have an existence that is not dependent on social actors. They are facts that have an independent existence.
- **Constructionism** - the belief that social phenomena are in a constant state of change because they are totally reliant on social interactions as they take place. Even the account of researchers is subject to these interactions; therefore social knowledge can only be interdeterminate.

> **Don't:** Forget that the way that social research questions are formulated and the way the research is carried out is based on the ontological viewpoint of the researcher.

The objectivist approach will stress the importance of the formal properties of organizations and cultural systems, while the constructionist approach will concentrate more on the way that people themselves formulate structures of reality, and how this relates to the researcher him- or herself.

WAYS OF REASONING

The ways of reasoning behind the empirical and rationalist approaches to gaining information start from opposite ends of a spectrum. It is not possible practically to apply either extreme in a pure fashion, but the distinct differences in the two opposing approaches are easily outlined. The shortcomings of each can be mitigated by using a combination that is formulated as the hypothetico-deductive method.

INDUCTIVE REASONING - THE EMPIRICIST'S APPROACH

Inductive reasoning starts from specific observations and derives general conclusions from them. A simple example will demonstrate the line of reasoning:

> All swans which have been observed are white in colour.
>
> Therefore one can conclude that all swans are white.

Induction was the earliest and, even now, the commonest popular form of scientific activity. Every day, our experiences lead us to make conclusions, from which we tend to generalize. The development of this approach in the seventeenth century by such scientists as Galileo and Newton heralded the scientific revolution. The philosopher Francis Bacon summed this up by maintaining that in order to understand nature, one should consult nature, and not the writings of ancient philosophers such as Aristotle, or the Bible. Darwin's theory of evolution and Mendel's discovery of genetics are perhaps the most famous theories claimed (even by their authors) to be derived from inductive reasoning.

Three conditions must be satisfied for such generalizations to be considered legitimate by inductivists:

1 There must be a large number of observation statements.
2 The observations must be repeated under a large range of circumstances and conditions.
3 No observation statement must contradict the derived generalization.

Induction's merit was disputed as long ago as the mid-eighteenth century by Hume. He demonstrated that the argument used to justify induction was circular, using induction to defend induction. This has traditionally been called the 'problem of induction'. Two further serious problems for the naive inductivist remain. The first is how large the number of observation statements must be; and the second is how large a range of circumstances and conditions must they be repeated under in order that true conclusions can be reached?

> **Do:** Despite its shortcomings, you use inductive reasoning every day quite successfully without even thinking about it. But be aware that what at first seems obvious may not be so with further systematic research.

DEDUCTIVE REASONING - THE RATIONALIST'S APPROACH

Deductive reasoning was first developed by the Ancient Greeks. An argument based on **deduction** begins with general statements and, through logical argument, comes to a specific conclusion. A syllogism is the simplest form of this kind of argument and consists of a major general premise (**statement**), followed by a minor, more specific premise, and a conclusion that follows logically. Here is a simple example:

> All live mammals breathe.
>
> This cow is a live mammal.
>
> Therefore, this cow breathes.

Research is guided in this case by the theory that precedes it. Theories are speculative answers to perceived problems, and are tested by observation and experiment. While it is possible to confirm the possible truth of a theory through observations that support it, theory can be falsified and totally rejected by making observations that are inconsistent with its statement. In this way, science is seen to proceed by trial and error: when one theory is rejected, another is proposed and tested, and thus the fittest theory survives.

In order for a theory to be tested, it must be expressed as a statement called a **hypothesis**. The essential nature of a hypothesis is that it must be falsifiable. This means that it must be logically possible to make true observational statements that conflict with the hypothesis, and thus can falsify it. However, the process of **falsification** leads to a devastating result of the rejection of a theory, requiring a completely new start.

> **Don't:** Forget that it is not practically possible to be either a pure inductivist or deductivist as you either need some theoretical ideas in order to know what information to look for, or some knowledge in order to devise theories.

HYPOTHETICO-DEDUCTIVE REASONING OR SCIENTIFIC METHOD

The **hypothetico-deductive method** combines inductive and deductive reasoning, resulting in the to-and-fro process of developing hypotheses (testable theories) inductively from observations, charting their implications by deduction and testing them to refine or reject them in the light of the results. It is this combination of experience with deductive and inductive reasoning that is the foundation of modern scientific research, and is commonly referred to as **scientific method**.

A simple summary of the steps in scientific method could go like this:

- Identification or clarification of problems.
- Formulation of tentative solutions or hypotheses.
- Practical or theoretical testing of solutions or hypotheses.
- Elimination or adjustment of unsuccessful solutions.

Problems are posed by the complexity of testing theories in real life. Realistic scientific theories consist of a complex of statements, each of which relies on assumptions based on previous theories. The methods of testing are likewise based on assumptions and influenced by surrounding conditions. If the predictions of the theory are not borne out in the results of the tests, it could be the underlying premises which are at fault rather than the theory itself.

Do: Take note that it was only by the beginning of the 1960s that Popper (1902-92) formulated the idea of the hypothetico-deductive method, even though it must have been used in practice for decades before.

There are certain assumptions that underlie scientific method, some of which are regarded by interpretivists as unacceptable when doing social research:

- Order
- External reality
- Reliability
- Parsimony
- **Generality**.

THE POSITIVIST/INTERPRETIVIST DIVIDE

There is an important issue that confronts the study of the social sciences which is not so pertinent in the natural sciences. This is the question of the position of the human subject and researcher, and the status of social phenomena. Is human society subjected to laws that exist independent of the human actors that make up society, or do individuals and groups create their own versions of social forces? The two extremes of approach are termed **positivism** and **interpretivism**. Again, as in the case of ways of reasoning, a middle way has also been formulated that draws on the useful characteristics of both approaches.

Positivism

According to Hacking (1981, pp. 1–2), the positivist approach to scientific investigation is based on realism, an attempt to find out about the one real world. There is a sharp distinction between scientific theories and other kinds of belief, and there is a unique best description of any chosen aspect of the world that is true regardless of what people think. Science is cumulative, despite the false starts that are common enough. Science by and large builds on what is already known. Even Einstein's theories are a development from Newton's.

There should be just one science about the one real world. Less measurable sciences are reducible to more measurable ones. Sociology is reducible to psychology, psychology to biology, biology to chemistry and chemistry to physics.

Interpretivism

Although scientific method is widely used in many forms of research, it does not, and never has, enjoyed total hegemony in all subjects. Some of the world's greatest thinkers have disagreed with the tenets of positivism contained in scientific method. The alternative approach to research is based on the philosophical doctrines of idealism and humanism. It maintains that the view of the world that we see around us is the creation of the mind.

This does not mean that the world is not real, but rather that we can only experience it personally through our perceptions, which are influenced by our preconceptions and beliefs; we are not neutral, disembodied observers. Unlike the natural sciences, the researcher is not observing phenomena from outside the system, but is inextricably bound into the human situation which he or she is studying. In addition, by concentrating on the search for constants in human behaviour, the researcher highlights the repetitive, predictable and invariant aspect of society and ignores what is subjective, individual and creative.

In order to compare the alternative bases for interpreting social reality, Cohen and Manion (2011, pp. 8–9) produced a useful table that they had adapted from Blaxterfield (1975) as shown in Table 1.1.

Don't: Just because the differences in perspective between positivist and interpretivist approaches are so radical, don't think that you need to espouse purely one or the other approach. Different aspects of life lend themselves to different methods of interpretation.

Table 1.1 Comparison between positivist and interpretivist approaches

Dimensions of comparisons	Positivist	Interpretivist
Philosophical basis	Realism: the world exists and is knowable as it really is. Organizations are real entities with a life of their own.	Idealism: the world exists but different people construe it in very different ways. Organizations are invented social reality.
The role of social science	Discovering the universal laws of society and human conduct within it.	Discovering how different people interpret the world in which they live.
Basic units of social reality	The collectivity: society or organizations.	Individuals acting singly or together.
Methods of understanding	Identifying conditions or relationships which permit the collectivity to exist. Conceiving what these conditions and relationships are.	Interpretation of the subjective meanings which individuals place upon their action. Discovering the subjective rules for such action.
Theory	A rational edifice built by scientists to explain human behaviour.	Sets of meanings which people use to make sense of their world and human behaviour within it.
Research	Experimental or quasi-experimental validation of theory.	The search for meaningful relationships and the discovery of their consequences for action.
Methodology	Abstraction of reality, especially through mathematical models and quantitative analysis.	The representation of reality for purposes of comparison. Analysis of language and meaning.
Society	Ordered. Governed by a uniform set of values and made possible only by these values.	Conflicted. Governed by the values of people with access to power.
Organizations	Goal-oriented. Independent of people. Instruments of order in society serving both the society and the individual.	Dependent upon people and their goals. Instruments of power which some people control and can use to attain ends which seem good to them.
Organizational pathologies	Organizations get out of kilter with social values and individual needs.	Given diverse human ends, there is always conflict among people acting to pursue them.
Prescriptions for change	Change the structure of the organization to meet social values and individual needs.	Find out what values are embodied in organizational action and whose they are. Change the people or change their values if you can.

Source: Cohen and Manion, 2011, pp. 10–11

Critical realism

Critical reasoning can be seen as a reconciliatory approach, which recognizes, like the positivists, the existence of a natural order in social events and **discourse**, but claims that this order cannot be detected by merely observing a pattern of events. The underlying order must be discovered through the process of **interpretation** while doing theoretical and practical work in the social sciences. Unlike the positivists, critical realists do not claim that there is a direct link between the concepts they develop and the observable phenomena. Concepts and theories about social events are developed on the basis of their observable effects, and interpreted in such a way that they can be understood and acted upon, even if the interpretation is open to revision as understanding grows.

The belief that there are underlying structures at work that generate social events, and which can be formulated in concepts and theory, distinguishes critical realists from interpretivists, who deny the existence of such general structures divorced from the specific event or situation and the context of the research and researcher.

Take it further

Social science, a brief theoretical history

As with any subject, some knowledge of its history provides a deeper perspective of why things are how they are at present, and how they come to be so. As you are not actually studying social science as such in this course, the history of the subject is not of central importance, but does show how research methods developed and were used in different contexts.

Social science, the study of human thought and behaviour in society, is a very large area of study that is divided into a range of interrelated disciplines. According to Bernard (2012), the main branches are anthropology, economics, history, political science, psychology and social psychology, each with their own subfields. Other disciplines also involve social research, such as communications, criminology, demography, education, journalism, leisure studies, nursing, social work, architecture and design and many others. A wide range of research methods have been developed and refined by the different disciplines, though these are not specific only to them.

Positivist beginnings

Social science, understood here as the study of human society in the widest sense, is a rich source of research problems. This important, and sometimes controversial, branch of science was first defined and named by Auguste Comte (1798-1857), the nineteenth-century French philosopher. Comte maintained that society could be analysed empirically, just like other subjects of scientific enquiry, and social laws and theories could be established on the basis of psychology and biology. He based his approach on the belief that all genuine knowledge is based on information gained by experience through the senses, and can only be developed through further observation and experiment.

The foundations of modern sociology were built during the end of the nineteenth century and beginning of the twentieth century. Prominent thinkers were Marx (1818-83), Durkheim (1858-1917), Dilthey (1833-1911) and Weber (1864-1920). Marx developed a theory that described the inevitable social progress from primitive communism, through feudalism and capitalism to a state of post-revolutionary communism. Durkheim is famous for his enquiries into the division of labour, suicide, religion and education, as well as for his philosophical discussions on the nature of sociology.

Unlike Marx, who tended to define the moral and social aspects of humanity in terms of material forces, Durkheim argued that society develops its own system of phenomena that produce collectively shared norms and beliefs. These 'social facts', as he called them, for example, economic organizations, laws, customs, criminality etc., exist in their own right, are external to us and are resistant to our will and constrain our behaviour. Having 'discovered' and defined social facts using scientific observation techniques, the social scientist should seek their causes among other social facts rather than in other scientific domains such as biology or psychology. By thus maintaining sociology as an autonomous discipline, the social scientist may use the knowledge gained to understand the origins of, and possibly suggest the cures for, various forms of social ills.

In summary, this approach looks at society as the focus for research, and through understanding its internal laws and establishing relevant facts, we can in turn understand how and why individuals behave as they do. However, not all philosophers agreed that human society was amenable to such a disembodied analysis.

The rise of interpretivism

Another German philosopher, Wilhelm Dilthey, agreed that although in the physical world we can only study the appearance of a thing rather than the thing itself, we are, because of our own humanity, in a position to know about human consciousness and its roles in society. The purpose here is not to search for causal explanations, but to find understanding. As a method, this presupposes that to gain understanding there must be at least some common ground between the researcher and the people who are being studied. He went on to make a distinction between two kinds of sciences: *Geisteswissenschaften* (the human sciences) and *Naturwissenschaften* (the natural sciences).

Max Weber, developing and refining Dilthey's ideas, believed that empathy is not necessary or even possible in some cases, and that it was feasible to understand the intentionality of conduct and to pursue objectivity in terms of cause and effect. He wished to bridge the divide between the traditions of positivism and interpretivism by being concerned to investigate both the meanings and the material conditions of action.

Three main schools of thought can be seen to represent opposition to positivism in the social sciences: **phenomenology**, as developed by Husserl (1859–1938) and Schutz (1899–1959); **ethnography**, developed by Malinowski (1884–1942), Evans-Pritchard (1902–73) and Margaret Mead (1901–78); **ethnomethodology**, pioneered by Garfinkel (1917–87); and **symbolic interactionism**, practised by members of the Chicago School such as George Herbert Mead (1863–1931) and Blumer. They all rejected the assertion that human behaviour can be codified in laws by identifying underlying regularities, and that society can be studied from a detached, objective and impartial viewpoint by the researcher.

Husserl argued that consciousness is not determined by the natural processes of human neurophysiology, but that our understanding of the world is constructed by our human perceptions about our surroundings – we construct our own reality. In order to cope with this, Schutz believed that in social intercourse, each person needs to perceive the different perspectives that others have due to their unique biographies and experiences in order to transcend individual subjectivity. This constructed intersubjective world produces 'common sense'. He saw everyday language as a perfect example of socially

(Continued)

(Continued)

derived preconstituted types and characteristics that enabled individuals to formulate their own subjectivity in terms understandable by others.

The work of anthropologists in the ethnic tribes of the Pacific (Malinowski, M. Mead) and Africa (Evans-Pritchard) developed the ethnographic techniques of studying society. By employing the method of participant observation, knowledge can be gained of the complexities of cultures and social groups within their settings. The central concern is to produce a description that faithfully reflects the worldview of the participants in their social context. Theories and explanations can then emerge from the growing understanding gained by the researcher thus immersed in the context of the society.

Garfinkel developed a method of studying individual subjectivity by observing interaction on a small scale, between individuals or in a small group. He maintained that people were not strictly regulated by the collective values and norms sanctioned by society, but that they made individual choices on the basis of their own experiences and understanding. It was they that produced the social institutions and everyday practices, developing society as a social construction. The analysis of conversation is used as the main method of investigation.

Language was seen by G.H. Mead to be central to human interaction. Human beings are able to understand each other's perspectives, gestures and responses due to the shared **symbols** contained in a common language. It is this symbolic interaction that not only defines the individual as the instigator of ideas and opinions, but also as a reflection of the reactions and perceptions of others. To be able to understand this constantly shifting situation, the researcher must comprehend the meanings that guide it, and this is only possible in the natural surroundings where it occurs. This approach was developed in the University of Chicago from the 1920s and was used in a large programme of field research focusing mostly on urban society in Chicago itself, using interviews, life histories and other ethnographical methods.

The reconciliatory approach

Weber disagreed with the pure interpretivists, maintaining that it is necessary to verify the results of subjective interpretative investigation by comparing them with the concrete course of events. He makes a distinction between what one can perceive as facts (i.e. those things that are) and what one can perceive as values (i.e. those things that may, or may not, be desirable). A differentiation must be maintained between facts and values because they are distinct kinds of phenomenon. However, in order to understand society, we have to take account of both of these elements.

Weber maintained that in order to describe social practices adequately we must understand what meanings the practices have for the participants themselves. This requires an understanding of the values involved, but without taking sides or making value judgements. This understanding (often referred to as *Verstehen*) is the subject matter of social science. It is then possible to investigate the social practices rationally through an assessment of the internal logic of the situation. In this way, one can make a meaningful formulation of the elements, causes and effects within complex social situations, taking into account the values inherent in it.

It is argued that it is impossible for the social scientist to take this detached view of values, as he or she is a member of society and culture, motivated by personal presuppositions and beliefs. Accordingly, any analysis of social phenomena is based on a 'view from somewhere'. This is inescapable and even to be desired.

The philosopher Roy Baskhar has provided an alternative to the dichotomous argument of positivism versus interpretivism by taking a more inclusive and systematic view of the relationships between the natural and social sciences. His approach, known as critical realism, sees nature as stratified, with each layer using the previous one as a foundation and a basis for greater complexity. Thus physics is more basic than chemistry, which in its turn is more basic than biology, which is more basic than the human sciences. The relationships between these domains, from the more basic to the more complex, are inclusive one-way relationships – the more complex emerging from the more basic. While a human being is not able to go against the chemical, physical and biological laws, he or she can do all sorts of things that the chemicals of which he or she is made cannot do if they are following only their specific chemical laws rather than biological laws that govern organisms, or social 'laws' which govern society.

Bhaskar also has a profoundly integrationist view of the relationship between the individual and society, called by him the transformation model of social activity. Rather than, on the one hand, studying society to understand individual actions or, on the other hand, studying individuals to understand the structures of society or, somewhere in between, checking the results of one study against that of the other, Baskhar argues that the reciprocal interaction between individuals and society effects a transformation in both.

Structuralism, post-structuralism and postmodernism

Based primarily on the view that all cultural phenomena are primarily linguistic in character, **structuralism** gained its label because of its assertion that subjectivity is formed by deep 'structures' that lie beneath the surface of social reality. Lévi-Strauss used a geological metaphor, stating that the overt aspects of cultural phenomena are formed by the complex layering and folding of underlying strata. These can be revealed by semiotic analysis. 'Cultural symbols and representations are the surface structure and acquire the appearance of "reality"' (Seale, 1998, p. 34).

Post-structuralism was developed by French philosophers such as Derrida and Foucault in the latter part of the twentieth century. Through the method of 'deconstruction', the claims to authority made in texts and discourses were undermined. According to Seale (1998, p. 34), **postmodernism** subsequently developed and became more widely accepted through the appeal of its three basic principles:

1 **The decentered self** – the belief that there are no human universals that determine identity, but that the self is a creation of society.
2 **The rejection of claims to authority** – the idea of progress through scientific objectivity and value neutrality is a fallacy and has resulted in a moral vacuum. Discourse must be subjected to critical analysis and traditions and values should be constantly attacked.
3 **The commitment to instability in our practices of understanding** – as everything is put to question there can be no established way of thinking. Our understanding of the world is subject to constant flux, all voices within a culture have an equal right to be heard.

In view of the diverse range of theoretical perspectives, it is probably inappropriate to search for and impossible to find a single model of social and cultural life.

Ask yourself

What role do epistemology and ontology play in understanding social research?

They form the theoretical basis of how the world can be experienced, what constitutes knowledge, and what can be done with that knowledge. Social research has been carried out subject to varied epistemological and ontological stances, so it is important to know what assumptions have been made at the outset of the research. You can explain this by outlining the main approaches and describing how these affect the outcomes of the research.

What is the difference between inductive and deductive thinking? Why is this distinction important in the practical aspects of doing a research project and in theory development?

Inductive thinking – going from the specific to the general. Deductive thinking – going from the general to the specific. You can explain this in greater detail. This distinction is important because it determines what data you collect and how you collect them. You can give examples of these. An inductive approach is used to generate theory, whereas a deductive approach is used to test theory.

In what ways does the interpretivist approach particularly suit the study of human beings in their social settings?

Because humans are reflective beings, they are not simply determined by their surroundings. Cause-and-effect relationships are complex and difficult to determine, so a less deterministic approach can provide useful understanding about society, without the need for the kind of verifiable facts aimed for in the natural sciences. It is also impossible for a researcher to take a completely detached view of society, so investigation is necessarily dependent on interpretation.

Further reading

You can go into much greater detail about the philosophy of knowledge and the history of social research if you want to, but I suspect that you will not have enough time to delve too deeply.

For the theoretical background to social research, it might be worth having a look at these for more detail:

Hughes, J. (1997) *The Philosophy of Social Research* (3rd edn). Harlow: Longman.
Seale, C. (ed.) (2012) *Researching Society and Culture* (3rd edn). London: Sage.
Chapter 2 by Miran Epstein deals with the philosophy of science and can be accessed free online at www.uk.sagepub.com/upm-data/45990_Seale.pdf.

Jarvie, I. and Zamora-Bonill, J. (2011) *The SAGE Handbook of the Philosophy of Social Sciences*. London: Sage.
For topics that are more into scientific method see:

Chalmers, A. (2013) *What Is This Thing Called Science?* (4th edn). Indianapolis, IN: Hackett Publishing.
Medawar, P. (1984) *The Limits of Science*. Oxford: Oxford University Press.
For a simple general introduction to philosophy, seek this one out. This approachable book explains the main terminology and outlines the principal streams of thought:

Thompson, M. (1995) *Philosophy. Teach Yourself Books*. London: Hodder and Stoughton.
And here are books that deal in more detail with some aspects of philosophy – for the real enthusiast!

Husserl, E. (1964) *The Idea of Phenomenology*. Trans. W. Alston and G. Nakhnikian. The Hague: Martinus Nijhoff.
Collier, A. (1994) *Critical Realism: An Introduction to Roy Baskhar's Philosophy*. London: Verso.
If you are doing a course in one of the disciplines associated with social research (e.g. healthcare, marketing, etc.), delve into the specific history that has led up to the present state-of-the-art thinking. You will have to make a library search using key words to find what is easily available to you.

TWO

Research Basics

Research methods are the practical means to carry out research. In order to give them a meaning and purpose, you should be clear about the basics of research and the process of carrying out a project. The central generating point of a research project is the research problem. All the activities are developed for the purpose of solving or investigating this problem. Hence the need for total clarity in defining the problem and limiting its scope in order to enable a practical research project with defined outcomes to be devised.

Mostly, social science research methods courses at undergraduate level culminate not in an exam, but in a small research project or dissertation where you can demonstrate how you have understood the process of research and how various research methods are applied. Hence the need to be clear about the process as a whole so that the methods can be seen within the context of a project.

OVERVIEW OF THE RESEARCH PROCESS

A research project, whatever its size and complexity, consists of defining some kind of a research problem, working out how this problem can be investigated, doing the investigation work, coming to conclusions on the basis of what one has found out and then reporting the outcome in some form or other to inform others of the work done. The differences between research projects are due to their different scales of time, resources and extent, pioneering qualities and rigour.

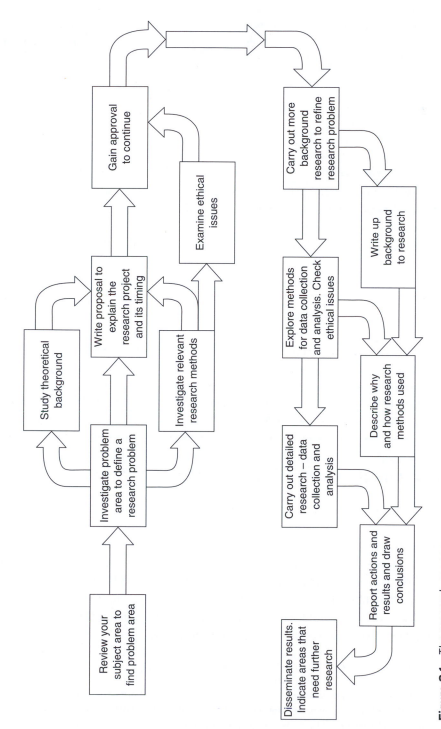

Figure 2.1 The research process

Whatever the research approach, it is worth considering generally what the research process consists of and what are the crucial decision stages and choices that need to be made. The answers to four important questions underpin the framework of any research project:

- What are you going to do?
- Why are you going to do it?
- How are you going to do it?
- When are you going to do it?

The actual doing of the research is subject to the nature of these answers and involves the most crucial decision making. Obviously the answers are not simple – this book has been written to help you formulate your own answers in relation to your own research project.

Figure 2.1 shows a rather linear sequence of tasks, far tidier than anything in reality, which is subject to constant reiteration as the knowledge and understanding increases. However, a diagram like this can be used as a basis for a programme of work in the form of a timetable, and the progress of the project can be gauged by comparing the current stage of work with the steps in the process.

> **Do:** Notice how, in the latter stages, the requirement for writing up the work becomes important. There is no point in doing research if the results are not recorded, even if only for your own use, though usually many more people will be interested to read about the outcomes, not least your examiner.

THE RESEARCH PROBLEM

One of the first tasks on the way to deciding on the detailed topic of research is to find a question, an unresolved controversy, a gap in knowledge or an unrequited need within the chosen subject. This search requires an awareness of current issues in the subject and an inquisitive and questioning mind. Although you will find that the world is teeming with questions and unresolved problems, not every one of these is a suitable subject for research. So what features should you look for which could lead you to a suitable research problem? Here is a list of the most important.

Checklist: features of a suitable research problem.

- You should be able to state the problem clearly and concisely.
- It should be of great interest to you.
- The problem should be significant (i.e. not trivial or a repeat of previous work).
- It should be delineated. You will not have much time, so restrict the aims of the research.
- You should be able to obtain the required information.
- You should be able to draw conclusions related to the problem. The point of research is to find some answers.

The problem can be generated either by an initiating idea, or by a perceived **problem area**. For example, investigation of 'rhythmic patterns in conflict settlement' is the product of an idea that there are such things as rhythmic patterns in conflict settlement, even if no one had detected them before. This kind of idea will then need to be formulated more precisely in order to develop it into a researchable problem.

Do: You will find it easy to discover problem areas. Your difficulty will lie in choosing an area that contains possible specific research problems suitable for the type and scope of your assignment.

We are surrounded by problems connected with society, healthcare, education, etc., many of which can readily be perceived. Take, for example, social problems such as poverty, crime, unsuitable housing, problematic labour relationships and bureaucratic bungles. There are many subjects where there may be a lack of knowledge that prevents improvements being made; for example, the influence of parents on a child's progress at school or the relationship between designers and clients.

Don't: When choosing a research problem don't:

- Make the choice of a problem an excuse to fill in gaps in your own knowledge.
- Formulate a problem which involves merely a comparison of two or more sets of data.
- Set a problem in terms of finding the degree of correlation between two sets of data.
- Devise a problem to which the answer can be only yes or no.

AIDS TO LOCATING AND ANALYSING PROBLEMS

Booth et al. (2008) suggest that the process for focusing on the formulation of your research problem looks like this:

- Find an interest in a broad subject area (problem area).
- Narrow the interest to a plausible topic.
- Question the topic from several points of view.
- Define a rationale for your project.

Do: Initially, it is useful to define no more than a problem area, rather than a specific research problem, within the general body of knowledge.

Research problem definition

From the interest in the wider issues of the chosen subject, and after the selection of a problem area, the next step is to define the research problem more closely so that it becomes a specific research problem, with all the characteristics already discussed. This stage requires an enquiring mind, an eye for inconsistencies and inadequacies in current theory and a measure of imagination. The **research problem** is often formulated in the form of a theoretical research question that indicates a clear direction and scope for the research project.

> **Do:** It is often useful in identifying a specific problem to pose a simple question. Such a question can provide a starting point for the formulation of a specific research problem, whose conclusion should aim to answer the question.

The sub-problems

Most research problems are difficult, or even impossible, to solve without breaking them down into smaller problems. The short sentences devised during the problem formulation period can give a clue to the presence of sub-problems. **Sub-problems** should delineate the scope of the work and, taken together, should define the entire problem to be tackled as summarized in the main problem.

Questions used to define sub-problems include:

- Can the problem be split down into different aspects that can be investigated separately (e.g. political, economic, cultural, technical)?
- Are there different personal or group perspectives that need to be explored (e.g. employers, employees)?
- Are different concepts used that need to be separately investigated (e.g. health, fitness, well-being, confidence)?
- Does the problem need to be considered at different scales (e.g. the individual, group, organization)?

SECOND REVIEW OF LITERATURE

A more focused review of literature follows the formulation of the research problem. The purpose of this review is to learn about research already carried out into one or more of the aspects of the research problem.

The purposes of a literature review are to:

- Summarize the results of previous research to form a foundation on which to build your own research.
- Collect ideas on how to gather data.
- Investigate methods of data analysis.
- Study instrumentation that has been used.
- Assess the success of the various research designs of the studies already undertaken.

For more detail on doing literature reviews, see Chapter 5.

Take it further

Evaluation of social research

How can you tell whether a piece of research is any good? When doing your background reading, you should be able to assess the quality of the research projects you read about, as described by the research reports. Taking a critical look at completed research is a good preparation for doing some research yourself. You may later also have to defend the quality of some research that you have done.

It is not unusual that you will have to make comments on a particular research report as part of an assignment. If you can scrutinize it in a critical way, rather than just providing a description, you will impress your tutor with your expertise.

Below is one approach of how to do an evaluation of a social research study. It is only a short summary of the things to evaluate. You will have to refer to your textbooks for examples and a more detailed explanation of the process.

Consider these four major factors:

- Validity
- Reliability
- Replicability
- Generalizability.

Validity of research is about the degree to which the research findings are true. Seale and Filmer (1998, p. 134) usefully list three different types of validity:

- **Measurement validity** – the degree to which measures (e.g. questions on a questionnaire) successfully indicate concepts.
- **Internal validity** – the extent to which causal statements are supported by the study.
- **External validity** – the extent to which findings can be generalized to populations or to other settings.

Bryman (2012, p. 48) adds one more:

- **Ecological validity** – the extent to which the findings are applicable to people's everyday, natural social settings.

Reliability is about the degree to which the results of the research are repeatable. Bryman (2012, p. 168) lists three prominent factors that are involved:

- **Stability** – the degree to which a measure is stable over time.
- **Internal reliability** – the degree to which the indicators that make up the scale or index are consistent.
- **Inter-observer consistency** – the degree to which there is consistency in the decisions of several 'observers' in their recording of observations or translation of data into categories.

Replicability is about whether the research can be repeated and whether similar results are obtained. This is a check on the objectivity and lack of **bias** of the research findings.

(Continued)

(Continued)

It requires a detailed account of the concepts used in the research, the measurements applied and methods employed.

Generalizability refers to the results of the research and how far they are applicable to locations and situations beyond the scope of the study. There is little point in doing research if it cannot be applied in a wider context. On the other hand, especially in qualitative research, there may well be limits to the generalizability of the findings, and these should be pointed out.

Read news reports about research projects (education, old age, criminality, etc.) critically. Look for 'spin', vested interests, choice of evidence and use/misuse of statistics.

Ask yourself

What are the desirable qualities of a research problem?

You can provide a simple list. Here are some suggestions. It should be:

- Limited – to the scope of the research project.
- Significant – no point doing trivial research.
- Novel – ideally some new knowledge or greater understanding should be uncovered.
- Clearly defined – so that the purpose of the research is obvious.
- Interesting – in order to motivate you while doing the work.

What relationship do sub-problems have to a research problem, and what function do they carry out?

The sub-problems break the main problem down into researchable components. The main problem is usually couched in rather abstract concepts. The sub-problems help to make the concepts more concrete by suggesting several indicators and even variables that can be investigated and together they may provide answers to the main problem. You could give examples to illustrate the points.

Why review the literature again once you have decided on your research problem?

Once you have decided on your research problem, you can narrow down your review of the literature to concentrate on the specific topics raised by it. It is always possible to go into greater depth when you are clear about the subject you are investigating. You will need to find out about similar research and the 'state of the art' in the subject, and you can check on the methods that were used in projects with similar aims.

Further reading

At an undergraduate level, most advice on locating and assessing research problems appears in books on how to write dissertations. Specific guidance on topics in a particular subject can be gained from books dedicated to one particular discipline. Explore your own **library catalogue** for both general and subject-related guides to dissertation writing. But do be careful not to get bogged down in technicalities – peck like a bird at the juicy pieces useful to you now and leave the rest. The list below is in order of detail and complexity – the simplest first. Here is a selection:

Mounsey, C. (2013) *How to Write: Successful Essays, Dissertations, and Exams* (2nd edn). Oxford: Oxford University Press.
Chapter 2 looks at ways to develop research questions.

Swetnam, D. (2000) *Writing Your Dissertation: How to Plan, Prepare and Present Successful Work*. Oxford: How To books.
See chapter 1 for simple guidance on how to get started.

Naoum, S.G. (2013) *Dissertation Research and Writing for Construction Students* (3rd edn). Abingdon: Routledge.
Chapter 2 gives advice on choosing a topic (not just for construction students).

Blaxter, L., Hughes, C. and Tight, M. (2010) *How to Research* (4th edn). Buckingham: Open University Press.
A much bigger book, but see chapter 2 on how to get started.

THREE

Research Strategies and Design

RESEARCH STRATEGIES - QUANTITATIVE AND QUALITATIVE RESEARCH

A common distinction is made between two different strategies in research, one using quantitative methodology and the other using qualitative methodology. Apart from the simple distinction of the use of measurement or description as the main approach to collecting and analysing data, there is seen to be an underlying epistemological difference in the two approaches.

Bryman (2012, p. 36) lists three characteristics in each that make the point:

Quantitative research

- Orientation - uses a deductive approach to test theories.
- Epistemology - is based on a positivist approach inherent in the natural sciences.
- Ontology - objectivist in that social reality is regarded as objective fact.

Qualitative research

- Orientation - uses an inductive approach to generate theories.
- Epistemology - it rejects positivism by relying on individual interpretation of social reality.
- Ontology - constructionist, in that social reality is seen as a constantly shifting product of perception.

These distinctions are useful in describing and understanding social research, but are not to be seen as mutually exclusive, but rather as polarizations. There are many examples of social research that do not conform to all of the conditions listed above. There are also examples of research that combine the two approaches, usually to examine different aspects of the research problem.

The two different methodologies imply the use of different methods of data collection and analysis. Quantitative techniques rely on collecting data that are numerically based and amenable to such analytical methods as statistical correlations, often in relation to hypothesis testing. Qualitative techniques rely more on language and the interpretation of its meaning, so data collection methods tend to involve close human involvement and a creative process of theory development rather than testing.

However, Bryman (2012, p. 613) warns against too dogmatic a distinction between the two types of methodology. He concludes that research methods are not determined by epistemology or ontology and that the contrast between natural and artificial settings for qualitative and quantitative research is frequently exaggerated. Furthermore, quantitative research can be carried out from an interpretivist perspective, as can qualitative research from one of natural science. Quantitative methods have been used in some qualitative research, and analyses of quantitative and qualitative studies can be carried out using the opposite approaches.

MIXED METHODS

There is no reason why you should rigidly stick to either quantitative or qualitative methods of data collection and analysis; in fact, there are some real advantages in doing both. For a start, you can compare your results from different approaches – called **triangulation**. It will strengthen your conclusions if the results point in the same direction. Sometimes, your different research questions can better be answered using different methods; for example, to find out the extent of a problem it would be better to collect quantitative data, but to examine the nature of the problem, qualitative data would be more appropriate. The weaknesses and strengths of each approach can be exploited. Quantitative methods can cope with large amounts of narrowly specified data and use statistical analysis to quickly produce results of measured accuracy, but lack the subtlety and nuanced elucidation possible with qualitative methods. On the other hand, the richness and variety of data collected through qualitative approaches can be difficult to distil into verifiable conclusions.

Because of the different nature of quantitative and qualitative data collection and analysis, they may involve different timings during the project and interact in different ways. Here are some options:

- Sequential. The work is carried out in two distinct phases. It is usually quicker to carry out a quantitative study. This can be an advantage if you want to use the qualitative methods to elaborate or extend the quantitative findings.
- Concurrent. The quantitative and qualitative data collection and analysis are carried out at the same time but independently and the amount of convergence of the outcomes is investigated to strengthen the conclusions.
- Nested. A primary method (either quantitative or qualitative) is used and the other is embedded within it to provide supplementary data on a particular aspect.

If the results from the two strands of the mixed methods agree with each other, this helps to reinforce the strength of the conclusions. But what happens if the results disagree? You could argue that the methods are completely different and the results should be seen as complementary rather than duplication. Alternatively, it might be revealed that certain important and influential factors were revealed by one method and not by the other. This can be useful information for further research.

RESEARCH OBJECTIVES

The objectives of a particular research project delineate the intentions of the researchers and the nature and purpose of the investigations. The range of possible objectives can be listed as to:

- Describe
- Explain and evaluate
- Compare
- Correlate
- Act, intervene and change.

Description

Descriptive research relies on observation as a means of collecting data. It attempts to examine situations in order to establish what is the norm; that is, what can be predicted to happen again under the same circumstances.

'Observation' can take many forms. Depending on the type of information sought, people can be interviewed, questionnaires distributed, visual records made, even sounds and smells recorded. The important point is that the observations are written down or recorded in some way, in order that they can be subsequently analysed. It is important that the data so collected are organized and presented in a clear and systematic way, so that the analysis can result in valid and accurate conclusions.

The scale of the research is influenced by two major factors:

- The level of complexity of the survey.
- The scope of the survey.

For example, seeking relationships between specific events inevitably requires a more complex survey technique than aiming merely to describe the nature of existing conditions. Likewise, surveying a large number of cases over a wide area will require greater resources than a small, local survey.

⊗

> **Don't:** As descriptive research depends on human observations and responses, don't allow distortion of the data to occur. This can be caused, among other ways, by inadvertently including biased questions in questionnaires or interviews, or through the selective observation of events. Although bias cannot be wholly eliminated, an awareness of its existence and likely extent is essential.

Explanation and evaluation

This is a descriptive type of research specifically designed to deal with complex social issues. It aims to move beyond 'just getting the facts' in order to make sense of the myriad human, political, social, cultural and contextual elements involved. The latest form of this type of research, named by Guba and Lincoln as fourth-generation evaluation, has, according to them, six properties (Guba and Lincoln, 1989, pp. 8–11):

1   The evaluation outcomes are not intended to represent 'the way things really are, or how they work', but present the meaningful constructions which the individual actors or groups of actors create in order to make sense of the situations in which they find themselves.
2   In representing these constructions, it is recognized that they are shaped to a large extent by the values held by the constructors. This is a very important consideration in a value-pluralistic society, where groups rarely share a common value system.
3   These constructions are seen to be inextricably linked to the particular physical, psychological, social and cultural context within which they are formed and to which they refer. These surrounding conditions, however, are themselves dependent on the constructions of the actors, which endow them with parameters, features and limits.
4   It is recognized that the evaluation of these constructions is highly dependent on the involvement and viewpoint of the evaluators in the situation studied.
5   This type of research stresses that evaluation should be action-oriented, define a course that can be practically followed and stimulate the carrying out of its recommendations. This usually requires a stage of negotiation with all the interested parties.
6   Due regard should be given to the dignity, integrity and privacy of those involved at any level, and those who are drawn into the evaluation should be welcomed as equal partners in every aspect of design, implementation, interpretation and resulting action.

A common purpose of **evaluation research** is to examine programmes or the working of projects from the point of view of levels of awareness, costs and benefits, cost-effectiveness, attainment of objectives and quality assurance. The results are generally used to prescribe changes to improve and develop the situation, but in some cases might be limited to descriptions giving a better understanding of the programme (Robson, 2011, pp. 176–88).

Comparison

The examination of two or more contrasting cases can be used to highlight differences and similarities between them, leading to a better understanding of social phenomena. Suitable for both qualitative and quantitative methodologies, **comparative research** is commonly applied in cross-cultural and cross-national contexts. It is also applicable to different organizations or contexts (e.g. firms, labour markets, etc.).

Problems in cross-cultural research stem from the difficulties in ensuring comparability in the data collected and the situations investigated. Different languages and cultural contexts can create problems of comparability. It is also criticized for neglecting the specific context of the case in the search for contrasts, and that this search implies the adoption of a specific focus at the expense of a more open-ended approach.

The strength of the comparative approach using multiple case studies is that it may reveal concepts that can be used for theory building, and that theory building can be improved in that the research is more able to establish the extent to which the theory will or will not hold. Comparative design is akin to the simultaneous scrutiny of two or more cross-sectional studies, sharing the same issues of reliability, validity, replicability and generalizability.

Correlation

The information sought in **correlation research** is expressed not in the form of artefacts, words or observations, but in numbers. While historical and descriptive approaches are predominantly forms of qualitative research, analytical survey or correlation research is principally quantitative. 'Correlation' is another word to describe the measure of association or the relationships between two phenomena. In order to find meaning in the numerical data, the techniques of statistics are used. What kinds of statistical tests are used to analyse the data depends very much on the nature of the data.

This form of quantitative research can be broadly classified into two types of study:

* Relational studies
* Prediction studies.

Relational studies investigate possible relationships between phenomena to establish if a correlation exists and, if so, its extent. This exploratory form of research is carried out particularly where little or no previous work has been done, and its outcomes can form the basis for further investigations.

Prediction studies tend to be carried out in research areas where correlations are already known. This knowledge is used to predict possible future behaviour or events, on the basis that if there has been a strong relationship between two or more characteristics or events in the past, then these should exist in similar circumstances in the future, leading to predictable outcomes.

Do: In order to produce statistically significant results, quantitative research demands data from a large number of cases. Greater numbers of cases tend to produce more reliable results; 20-30 is considered to be about the minimum, though this depends on the type of statistical test applied. You must convert the data, whatever their original character, into numbers.

One of the advantages of correlation research is that it allows for the measurement of a number of characteristics (technically called variables, see Chapter 4 for detailed explanation) and their relationships simultaneously. Particularly in social science, many variables contribute to a particular outcome (e.g. satisfaction with housing depends on many factors). Another advantage is that, unlike other research approaches, it produces a measure of the amount of relationship between the variables being studied. It also, when used in prediction studies, gives an estimation of the probable accuracy of the predictions made. One limitation to what can be learned from correlation research is that, while the association of variables can be established, the cause-and-effect relationships are not revealed.

Action, intervention and change

This is related to **experimental research**, although it is carried out in the real world rather than in the context of a closed experimental system. A basic definition of this type of research is: 'a small-scale intervention in the functioning of the real world and a close examination of the effects of such an intervention' (Cohen and Manion, 2011, p. 345).

Its main characteristic is that it is essentially an 'on the spot' procedure, principally designed to deal with a specific problem evident in a particular situation. No attempt is made to separate a particular feature of the problem from its context in order to study it in isolation. Constant monitoring and evaluation are carried out, and the conclusions from the findings are applied immediately, and monitored further.

Action research depends mainly on observation and behavioural data. As a practical form of research, aimed at a specific problem and situation, and with little or no **control** over independent variables, it cannot fulfil the scientific requirement for generalizability. In this sense, despite its exploratory nature, it is the antithesis of experimental research.

RESEARCH DESIGN

Once the objectives of a research project have been established, the issue of how these objectives can be met leads to a consideration of which research design will be appropriate. Research design provides a framework for the collection and analysis of data and subsequently indicates which research methods are appropriate.

Fixed and flexible design strategies

Robson (2011, pp. 83–90) makes a useful distinction between fixed and flexible design strategies.

Fixed designs call for a tight pre-specification at the outset, and are commonly equated with a quantitative approach. The designs employ experimental and non-experimental research methods.

Flexible designs evolve during data collection and are associated with a qualitative approach, although some quantitative data may be collected. The designs employ, among other things, case study, ethnographic and grounded theory methods.

Short descriptions of the main designs follow, starting with fixed designs.

Cross-sectional design

Cross-sectional design often uses survey methods, and surveys are often equated with cross-sectional studies. However, this kind of study can use other methods of data collection, such as observation, content analysis and official records. Bryman (2012, p. 59) summarizes the characteristics of this kind of design in the following way:

- It entails the collection of data on more than one case (usually many more than one), generally using a sampling method to select cases in order to be representative of a population. Random methods of sampling lead to good external validity.
- The data are collected at a single point in time, that is, they provide a snapshot of ideas, opinions, information, etc. Because the data collection methods tend to be intrusive, ecological validity may be put at risk. When the methods and procedures of data collection and analysis are specified in detail, replicability is enhanced.
- Quantitative or quantifiable data are sought in order that variations in the variables can be systematically gauged according to specific and reliable standards. The variables are non-manipulable; that is, the researcher cannot change their values in order to gauge the effects of the change.
- Patterns of association between variables are examined in order to detect associations. Causal influences might be inferred, but this form of design cannot match experiments in this respect due to weak internal validity.

Longitudinal design

Longitudinal design consists of repeated cross-sectional surveys to ascertain how time influences the results. Because this design can trace what happens over time, it may be possible to establish causation among variables if the cases remain the same in successive surveys. Because of the repeated nature of this research design, it tends to be expensive and time consuming, unless it relies on information that has already been collected as a matter of course within an organization (e.g. initial interview assessments and final exam results of students in different years at a university). Some large national surveys are based on longitudinal design, such as the British Household Panel Survey, National Child Development Study, Millennium Cohort Study.

Two types of study are commonly identified:

Panel studies – these consist of a sample of people, often randomly selected, who are questioned on two or more occasions.

Cohort studies – these concentrate on a group that shares similar characteristics, such as students from a particular year of matriculation or people on strike at a certain time.

Experimental

Experimental research differs from the other research approaches noted above through its greater control over the objects of its study. The researcher strives to isolate and control every relevant condition that determines the events investigated, so as to observe the effects when the conditions are manipulated. Chemical experiments in a laboratory represent one of the purest forms of this type of research. But experiments can also be carried out in more natural settings with people as subjects, it is just more difficult to isolate and control the relevant variables. The most important characteristic of the experimental approach is that it deals with the phenomenon of 'cause and effect'.

> **Do:** Remember that at its simplest, an experiment involves making a change in the value of one variable – called the independent variable – and observing the effect of that change on another variable – called the dependent variable.

However, the actual experiment is only a part of the research process. There are several planned stages in experimental research. When the researcher has established that the study is amenable to experimental methods, a prediction (technically called a hypothesis) of the likely cause-and-effect patterns of the phenomenon has to be made. This allows decisions to be made as to what variables are to be tested and how they are to be controlled and measured. This stage, called the design of the experiment, must also include the choice of relevant types of test and methods of analysing the results of the experiments (usually by statistical analysis). Pre-tests are then usually carried out to detect any problems in the experimental procedure.

Only after this is the experiment proper carried out. The procedures decided upon must be rigorously adhered to and the observations meticulously recorded and checked. Following the successful completion of the experiment, the important task – the whole point of the research exercise – is to process and analyse the data and to formulate an interpretation of the experimental findings.

> **Don't:** Believe that all experimental research has to, or even can, take place in a laboratory. What experimental methods do stress is how much it is possible to control the variables, in whatever setting.

Writers of textbooks on research have classified experimental designs in different ways. They tend to make their categorization into four classes:

1 Pre-experimental
2 True experimental
3 Quasi-experimental
4 Correlation and ex post facto.

Pre-experimental designs are unreliable and primitive experimental methods in which assumptions are made despite the lack of essential control of variables. An example of this is the supposition that, faced with the same stimulus, all samples will behave identically to the one tested, despite possible differences between the samples.

True experimental designs are those that rigorously check the identical nature of the groups before testing the influence of a variable on a sample of them in controlled circumstances. Parallel tests are made on identical samples (control samples) that are not subjected to the variable.

In **quasi-experimental designs**, not all the conditions of true experimental design can be fulfilled. However, the nature of the shortcomings is recognized, and steps are taken to minimize them or predict a level of reliability of the results. The most common case is when a group is tested for the influence of a variable and compared with a non-identical group with known differences (control group) that has not been subjected to the variable. Another, in the absence of a control group, is repeated testing over time of one group, with and without the variable (i.e. the same group acts as its own control at different times).

Correlation design looks for cause-and-effect relationships between two sets of data, while **ex post facto designs** turn experimentation into reverse, and attempt to interpret the nature of the cause of a phenomenon with the observed effects. Both of these forms of research result in conclusions that are difficult to prove and they rely heavily on logic and inference.

Case study design

Sometimes you may want to study a social group, community, system, organization, institution, event, or even a person or type of personality. It can be convenient to pick one example or a small number of examples from this list to study in detail within their own context, and make assessments and comparisons. These are called case studies.

Commonly, in **case study design**, no claim is made for generalizability. It is rather about the quality of theoretical analysis that is allowed by intensive investigation into one or a few cases, and how well theory can be generated and tested, using both inductive and deductive reasoning.

However, if the research is based on the argument that the case studies investigated are a sample of some or many such systems, organizations, etc., and what you can find out in the particular cases could be applicable to all of them, you need to make the same kind of sampling choice as described above in order to reassure yourself, and the reader, that the cases are representative.

If there are large variations between such systems/organizations, etc., it may not be possible to find 'average' or representative cases. What you can do is to take a comparative approach by selecting several very different ones, for example, those showing extreme characteristics, those at each end of the spectrum and perhaps one that is somewhere in the middle, and compare their characteristics. Alternatively, choose an 'exemplifying' or 'critical' case, one that will provide a good setting for answering the research question.

Both quantitative and qualitative methods are appropriate for case study designs, and multiple methods of data collection are often applied.

Do: Case study design tends to be a flexible design, especially if the research is exploratory. Despite this, devise an explicit plan before starting the research, even if you expect that aspects of the plan may change during the course of the project.

Take it further

Ethnographic and grounded theory approaches

There are other theoretical approaches that are not really a research design in the sense of the above, but do present a specific way of working that greatly influences the research efforts of the researcher. The two that are commonly mentioned in relation to social science research are ethnographic approach and the grounded theory approach. Look in your course description and lecture notes to see if these are included in your course. If they are, then what follows is necessary reading. If not, some knowledge about these will stand you in good stead when answering exam questions or writing an essay or dissertation. They are probably too sophisticated for you to use as a research method if you have to do a research project.

Ethnographic approach

This approach is based on the techniques devised by anthropologists to study social life and cultural practices of communities by immersing themselves in the day-to-day life of their subjects. Robson (2011, p. 145) describes **ethnography** as follows:

- The purpose is to uncover the shared cultural meanings of the behaviour, actions, events and contexts of a group of people.
- This requires an insider's perspective.
- The group must be observed and studied in its natural setting.
- No method of data collection is ruled out, although participant observation in the field is usually considered essential.
- The focus of the research and detailed research questions will emerge and evolve in the course of the involvement. Theoretical orientations and preliminary research questions are subject to revision.

(Continued)

(Continued)

- Data collection is usually in phases over an extended time. Frequent behaviours, events, etc. tend to be focused on to permit the development of an understanding of their significance.

This is a difficult design for beginners as it requires specialist knowledge of socio-cultural concepts, and also tends to take a very long time. Writing up succinctly is problematic due to the complexity of the observations and it is easy to lose one's independent view because of the close involvement in the group.

Don't: Forget that ethnographic studies concentrate on depth rather than breadth of enquiry.

Grounded theory

Glaser and Strauss (1967) developed grounded theory as a reaction to the then current stress on the need to base social research on pre-defined theory. Grounded theory takes the opposite approach – it does the research in order to evolve the theory. This gives rise to a specific style of procedure and use of research methods.

The main emphasis is on continuous data collection process interlaced with periodic pauses for analysis. The analysis is used to tease out categories in the data on which the subsequent data collection can be based. This process is called 'coding'. This reciprocal procedure continues until these categories are 'saturated'; that is, the new data no longer provide new evidence. From these results, concepts and theoretical frameworks can be developed. This gradual emergence and refinement of theory based on observations is the basis for the 'grounded' label of this approach.

Although mostly associated with qualitative approaches, there is no reason why quantitative data are not relevant. A grounded theory design is particularly suitable for researching unfamiliar situations where there has been little previous research on which to base theory.

Do: Note that because of its flexible design, grounded theory is not an easy option for novice researchers, despite a wide range of examples of this kind of research in many different settings.

Ask yourself

What are the distinctions between quantitative and qualitative research. How do these relate to epistemological and ontological considerations?

Quantitative research tends to measure, qualitative research tends to describe. You can go into more detail than this by describing how. The nature of data is defined by different epistemological viewpoints, and what you can do with it is defined by ontological considerations.

You can go on to explain how. These raise the issue of the appropriateness of quantitative or qualitative approaches, and the type of information that can usefully be gained by the methods associated with each approach.

> Describe four possible objectives of research, and describe each using a simple example.

Here are three examples:

- To explain – e.g. the motives of disruptive teenagers on a housing estate. This may help to find a solution to vandalism in a particular area.
- To predict – e.g. how different options in the introduction of a new claim scheme for pensioners will affect take-up.
- To compare – e.g. how different climates tend to affect people's leisure activities.

You could be more expansive in describing the examples by elaborating on what you might do to reach the objectives.

> You want to investigate the important factors that should be taken into account when designing a children's play area. What factors could you explore by using different research designs? Outline how you would do it?

First think of a range of possible factors that could influence the design of a play area. Do this by looking at technical issues (e.g. design of play equipment, maintenance), community issues (e.g. surrounding housing, siting, access, surveillance, meeting place), age-related issues (e.g. supervision, different areas and facilities for different ages), play and movement questions (e.g. what is 'play', exercise, safety), family matters (e.g. who would come, parent's requirements and activities, older children, picnics and refreshment). This could be a good candidate for a mixed method approach, either used to cover a range of different perspectives (concurrent study) or to delve deeper into aspects revealed by the one or other method (sequential study).

Then take some or all of the issues and select a research design that would be used to investigate it. For example, you could do experiments to test the strength of the equipment, do a case study on play activities in an existing play area, do a cross-sectional study of parents' and children's wishes, etc.

Further reading

All standard textbooks on social science research methods will have a section on research design. I found the following books to be particularly useful. Look in the contents and index to track down the relevant sections. There is usually a summary of designs near the beginning of the book, and greater detail about each one later.

Bryman, A. (2012) *Social Research Methods* (4th edn). Oxford: Oxford University Press. See Part 1.

(Continued)

(Continued)

Bernard, H.R. (2012) *Social Research Methods: Qualitative and Quantitative Approaches* (2nd edn). Thousand Oaks, CA: Sage.
No short summary here. You will have to look up each design.

Seale, C. (ed.) (2004) *Researching Society and Culture* (2nd edn). London: Sage.
See chapter 11.

Robson, C. (2011) *Real World Research*: *A Resource for Social Scientists and Practitioner Researchers* (3rd edn). Oxford: Blackwell.
See part II, chapters 4–7 for great detail.

FOUR

The Nature of Data

Data means information or, according to the *Oxford English Dictionary*, 'known facts or things used as basis for inference or reckoning'. Strictly speaking, data is the plural of datum, so is always treated as plural. When you do any sort of enquiry or research, you will collect data of different kinds. In fact, data can be seen as the essential raw material of any kind of research. They are the means by which we can understand events and conditions in the world around us.

Data, when seen as facts, acquire an air of solidity and permanence, representing the truth. This is, unfortunately, misleading. Data are not only elusive, but also ephemeral. They may be a true representation of a situation in one place, at a particular time, under specific circumstances, as seen by a particular observer. The next day, all might be different. For example, a daily survey of people's voting intentions in a forthcoming general election will produce different results daily, even if exactly the same people are asked, because some change their minds because of what they have heard or seen in the interim period. If the same number of people are asked in a similar sample, a different result can also be expected. Anyway, how can you tell whether they are even telling the truth about their intentions? Data can therefore only provide a fleeting and partial glimpse of events, opinions, beliefs or conditions.

Data are not only ephemeral, but also corruptible. Inappropriate claims are often made on the basis of data that are not sufficient or close enough to the event. Hearsay is stated to be fact, second-hand reports are regarded as being totally reliable and biased views are seized on as evidence. The further away you get from the event the more likely it is that inconsistencies and inaccuracies creep in. Memory fades, details are lost, recording methods do not allow a full picture to be given and distortions of interpretations occur.

⊗ | **Don't:** Be a rash researcher who insists on the infallibility of your data, and of the findings derived from them.

A measure of humility in the belief of the accuracy of knowledge, and also practical considerations that surround the research process, dictate that the outcomes of research tend to be couched in 'soft' statements, such as 'it seems that', 'it is likely that', 'one is led to believe that', etc. This does not mean, however, that progress towards useful 'truths' cannot be achieved.

PRIMARY AND SECONDARY DATA

It is important to be able to distinguish between different kinds of data because their nature has important implications for their reliability and for the sort of analysis to which they can be subjected. Data that have been observed, experienced or recorded close to the event are the nearest one can get to the truth, and are called **primary data**. Written sources that interpret or record primary data are called **secondary data**. For example, you have a more approximate and less complete knowledge of a political demonstration if you read the newspaper report the following day than if you were at the demonstration and had seen it yourself. Not only is the information less abundant, but it is coloured by the commentator's interpretation of the facts.

Primary data

Primary data are present all around us. Our senses deal with them all our waking lives – sounds, visual stimuli, tastes, tactile stimuli, etc. Instruments also help us to keep a track of factors that we cannot so accurately judge through our senses – thermometers record the exact temperature, clocks tell us the exact time and our bank statements tell us how much money we have. Primary data are as near to the truth as we can get about things and events. Seeing a football match with your own eyes will certainly get you nearer to what happened than reading a newspaper report about it later. Even so, the truth is still somewhat elusive – 'was the referee really right to award that penalty? It didn't look like a handball to me!'

There are many ways of collecting and recording primary data. Some are more reliable than others. It can be argued that as soon as data are recorded, they become secondary data due to the fact that someone or something had to observe and interpret the situation or event and set it down in a form of a record; that is, the data have become second hand. But this is not the case. The primary data are not the actual situation or event, but a record of it, from as close to it as possible – that is, the first and most immediate recording. 'A researcher assumes a personal responsibility for the reliability and authenticity of his or her information and must be prepared to answer for it' (Preece, 1994, p. 80). Without this kind of recorded data it would be difficult to make sense of anything but the simplest phenomenon and be able to communicate the facts to others.

There are four basic types of primary data:

Observation - records, usually of events, situations or things, of what you have experienced with your own senses, perhaps with the help of an instrument (e.g. camera, tape recorder, microscope, etc.).

Participation - data gained by experiences that can perhaps be seen as an intensified form of observation (e.g. the experience of learning to drive a car tells you different things about cars and traffic than just watching).

Measurement - records of amounts or numbers (e.g. population statistics, instrumental measurements of distance, temperature, mass etc.).

Interrogation - data gained by asking and probing (e.g. information about people's beliefs, motivations, etc.).

These can be collected, singly or together, to provide information about virtually any facet of our life and surroundings. So, why do we not rely on primary data for all our research? After all, it gets as close as possible to the truth. There are several reasons, the main ones being time, cost and access. Collecting primary data is a time-consuming business. As more data usually means more reliability, the efforts of just one person will be of limited value. Organizing a huge survey undertaken by large teams would overcome this limitation, but at what cost?

> **Do:** Note that it is not always possible to get direct access to the subject of research. For example, many historical events have left no direct evidence.

Secondary data

Secondary data are data that have been interpreted and recorded. We could drown under the flood of secondary data that assails us every day. News broadcasts, magazines, newspapers, documentaries, advertising, the internet, etc. all bombard us with information wrapped, packed and spun into digestible soundbites or pithy articles. We are so used to this that we have learned to swim, to float above it all and only really pay attention to the bits that interest us. This technique, learned through sheer necessity and quite automatically put into practice every day, is a useful skill that can be applied to speed up your data collection for your research.

Books, journal papers, magazine articles and newspapers present information in published, written form. The quality of the data depends on the source and the methods of presentation. For detailed and authoritative information on almost any subject, go to refereed journals – all the papers will have been vetted by leading experts in the subject. Other serious journals, such as some professional and trade journals, will also have authoritative articles by leading figures, despite the tendency of some to emphasize one side of the issue. For example, a steel federation journal will support arguments for the use of steel rather than other building materials. There are magazines for every taste, some entirely flippant, others with useful and reliable information. The same goes for books – millions of them! They range from the most erudite and deeply researched volumes, such as specialist encyclopedias and academic tomes, to ranting polemics and commercial pap.

It is therefore always important to make an assessment of the quality of the information or opinions provided. You actually do this all the time without even noticing it. We have all learned not to be so gullible as to believe everything that we read. A more conscious approach entails reviewing the evidence that has been presented in the arguments. When no evidence is provided, on what authority does the writer base his or her statements? It is best to find out who are the leading exponents of the subject you are studying.

Television broadcasts, films, radio programmes, recordings of all sorts provide information in an audio-visual non-written form. The assertion that the camera cannot lie is now totally discredited, so the same precautions need to be taken in assessing the quality of the data presented. There is a tendency, especially in programmes aimed at a wide public, to oversimplify issues.

⊗ **Don't:** Be seduced by the powerful nature of films and television into a less critical mood. Emotions can be aroused that cloud your better judgement. Repeated viewings help to counter this.

The internet and DVDs combine written and audio-visual techniques to impart information.

You cannot always be present at an event, but other people might have experienced it. Their accounts may be the nearest you can get to an event. Getting information from several witnesses will help to pin down the actual facts of the event.

⊘ **Do:** Compare the data from different sources. It is good practice, and is especially necessary with secondary data. This will help you to identify bias, inaccuracies and pure imagination. It will also show up different interpretations that have been made of the event or phenomenon.

QUANTITATIVE AND QUALITATIVE

The other main categories applied to data refer not to their source but to their nature. Can the data be reduced to numbers or can they be presented only in words? It is important to make a distinction between these two types of data because it affects the way that they are collected, recorded and analysed. Numbers can provide a very useful way of compressing large amounts of data, but if used inappropriately, lead to spurious results.

Much information about science and society is recorded in the form of numbers (e.g. temperatures, bending forces, population densities, cost indices, etc.). The nature of numbers allows them to be manipulated by the techniques of statistical analysis. This type of data is called **quantitative data**. In contrast, there is a lot of useful information that cannot be reduced to numbers. People's opinions, feelings, ideas and traditions need to be described in words. Words cannot be reduced to averages, maximum and minimum values or percentages. They record not quantities, but qualities. Hence they are called **qualitative data**. Given their distinct characteristics, it is evident that when it comes to analysing these two forms of data, quite different techniques are required.

Quantitative data

Quantitative data have features that can be measured, more or less exactly. Measurement implies some form of magnitude, usually expressed in numbers. As soon as you can deal with numbers, then you can apply mathematical procedures to analyse the data. These might be extremely simple, such as counts or percentages, or more sophisticated, such as statistical tests or mathematical models.

Some forms of quantitative data are obviously based on numbers: population counts, economic data, scientific measurements, to mention just a few. There are, however, other types of data that initially seem remote from quantitative measures but that can be converted to numbers. For example, people's opinions about fox hunting might be difficult to quantify, but if, in a questionnaire, you give a set choice of answers to the questions on this subject, then you can count the various responses and the data can then be treated as quantitative.

Typical examples of quantitative data are census figures (population, income, living density, etc.), economic data (share prices, gross national product, tax regimes, etc.), performance data (e.g. sport statistics, medical measurements, engineering calculations, etc.) and all measurements in scientific endeavour.

Qualitative data

Qualitative data cannot be accurately measured and counted, and are generally expressed in words rather than numbers. The study of human beings and their societies and cultures requires many observations to be made that are to do with identifying, understanding and interpreting ideas, customs, mores, beliefs and other essentially human activities and attributes. These cannot be pinned down and measured in any exact way. These kinds of data are therefore descriptive in character, and rarely go beyond the nominal and ordinal levels of measurement. This does not mean that they are any less valuable than quantitative data; in fact their richness and subtlety lead to great insights into human society.

Words, and the relationships between them, are far less precise than numbers. This makes qualitative research more dependent on careful definition of the meaning of words, the development of concepts and the plotting of interrelationships between variables. Concepts such as poverty, comfort, friendship, etc., while elusive to measure, are nonetheless real and detectable.

Typical examples of qualitative data are literary texts, minutes of meetings, observation notes, interview transcripts, documentary films, historical records, memos and recollections, etc. Some of these are records that are taken very close to the events or phenomena, whereas others may be remote and highly edited interpretations. As with any data, judgements must be made about their reliability. Qualitative data, because they cannot be dispassionately measured in a standard way, are more susceptible to varied interpretations and valuation. In some cases even, it is more interesting to see what has been omitted from a report than what has been included.

> **Do:** Check the reliability and completeness of qualitative data about an event by obtaining a variety of sources of data relating to the same event. This is called triangulation.

The distinction between qualitative and quantitative data is one of a continuum between extremes. You do not have to choose to collect only one or the other. In fact, there are many types of data that can be seen from both perspectives. For example, a questionnaire exploring people's political attitudes may provide a rich source of qualitative data about their aspirations and beliefs, but might also provide useful quantitative data about levels of support for different political parties. What is important is that you are aware of the types of data that you are dealing with, either during collection or analysis, and that you use the appropriate levels of measurement.

MEASUREMENT OF DATA

There are different ways of measuring data, depending on the nature of the data. These are commonly referred to as **levels of measurement – nominal**, **ordinal**, **interval** and **ratio**.

Nominal level

The word 'nominal' is derived from the Latin word *nomen*, meaning 'name'. Nominal measurement is very basic and unrefined. Its simple function is to divide the data into separate categories that can then be compared with each other. By first giving names to or labelling the parts or states of a concept, or by naming discrete units of data, we are then able to measure the concept or data at the simplest level. For example, many theoretical concepts are conceived on a nominal **level of quantification**. 'Status structure', as a theoretical concept, may have only two states: either a group of individuals have one or they do not (such as a collection of people waiting for a bus). Buildings may be classified into many types, for example, commercial, industrial, educational, religious, etc.

Many **operational definitions** are on a nominal level, for example, sex (male or female), marital status (single, married, separated, divorced or widowed). This applies in the same way for some types of data, for example, dividing a group of children into boys and girls, or into fair-haired, brown-haired or black-haired children, and so on.

Don't: Ignore the fact that different states of a concept or different categories of data which are quantified at a nominal level can only be labelled, and it is not possible to make statements about the differences between the states or categories, except to say that they are recognized as being different.

We can represent nominal data by certain graphic and statistical devices. Bar graphs, for example, can be appropriately used to represent the comparative measurement of nominal data. By measuring this type of data, using statistical techniques, it is possible to locate the mode, find a percentage relationship of one subgroup to another or of one subgroup to the total group, and compute the chi-square. We will discuss the mode and chi-square (in Chapter 10); they are mentioned here merely to indicate that nominal data may be processed statistically.

Ordinal level

If a concept is considered to have a number of states, or the data have a number of values that can be rank-ordered, it is assumed that some meaning is conveyed by the relative order of the states. The ordinal level of measurement implies that an entity being measured is quantified in terms of being more than or less than, or of a greater or lesser order than. It is a comparative entity and is often expressed by the symbols < or >.

For anyone studying at school or at university, the most familiar ordinal measures are the grades that are used to rate academic performance. An A always means more than a B, and a B always means more than a C, but the difference between A and B may not always be the same as the difference between B and C in terms of academic achievement. Similarly, we measure level of education grossly on an ordinal scale by saying individuals are unschooled, or have an elementary school, a secondary school, a college or a university education. Likewise, we measure members of the workforce on an ordinal scale by calling them unskilled, semi-skilled or skilled.

> **Do:** Note that most of the theoretical concepts in the social sciences seem to be at an ordinal level of measurement.

In summary, 'ordinal level of measurement' applies to concepts that vary in such a way that different states of the concept can be rank-ordered with respect to some characteristic. The ordinal scale of measurement expands the range of statistical techniques that can be applied to data. Using the ordinal scale, we can find the mode and the median, determine the percentage or percentile rank, and test by the chi-square. We can also indicate relationships by means of rank correlation.

Interval level

The interval level of measurement has two essential characteristics: it has equal units of measurement and its zero point, if present, is arbitrary. Temperature scales are one of the most familiar types of interval scale. In each of the Fahrenheit and Celsius scales, the gradation between each degree is equal to all the others, and the zero point has been established arbitrarily. The Fahrenheit scale clearly shows how arbitrary is the setting of the zero point. At first, the zero point was taken by Gabriel Fahrenheit to be the coldest temperature observed in Iceland. Later he made the lowest temperature obtainable with a mixture of salt and ice, and took this to be 0 degrees. Among the measurements of the whole range of possible temperatures, taking this point was evidently a purely arbitrary decision. It placed the freezing point of water at 32 degrees, and the boiling point at 212 degrees above zero.

> **Do:** Notice that although equal-interval theoretical concepts like temperature abound in the physical sciences, they are harder to find in the social sciences.

Though abstract concepts are rarely inherently interval-based, operational measures employed to quantify them often use quantification at an interval level. For example, attitudes are frequently measured on a scale like this:

Unfavourable -4 -3 -2 -1 0 $+1$ $+2$ $+3$ $+4$ Favourable

If it is assumed that the difference between +2 and +4 is the same as the difference between say 0 and −2, then this can be seen as an attempt to apply an interval level of quantification to this measurement procedure. This is quite a big assumption to make! The tendency for some social scientists to assume the affirmative is probably because some of the most useful summary measures and statistical tests require quantification on an interval level (e.g. for determining the mode, mean, standard deviation, *t*-test, *F*-test and product moment correlation).

> **Don't:** Ignore doubts frequently raised about the precision of responses to question-naires. Are the meanings intended by your questions equivalent to those understood by the respondent? Is the formulaic choice of answers you provide compatible with what the respondent wishes to reply?

I am sure you remember your reaction to attitude quizzes, where the answer 'it all depends' seems more appropriate to a question than any of the multiple choice answers offered.

Ratio level

The ratio level of measurement has a true zero; that is, the point where the measurement is truly equal to nought – the total absence of the quantity being measured. We are all familiar with concepts in physical science that are both theoretically and operationally conceptualized at a ratio level of measurement. Time, distance, velocity (a combination of time and distance), mass and weight are all concepts that have a zero state in an interval scale, both theoretically and operationally. So, there is no ambiguity in the statements 'twice as far', 'twice as fast' and 'twice as heavy'. Compared with this, other statements that use this level of measurement inappropriately are meaningless (e.g. 'twice as clever', 'twice as prejudiced' or 'twice the prestige'), since there is no way of knowing where zero clever, zero prejudice or zero prestige are.

A characteristic difference between the ratio scale and all other scales is that the ratio scale can express values in terms of multiples of fractional parts, and the ratios are true ratios. A metre rule can do that: a metre is a multiple (by 100) of a centimetre distance, a millimetre is a tenth (a fractional part) of a centimetre. The ratios are 1:100 and 1:10. Of all levels of measurement, the ratio scale is amenable to the greatest range of statistical tests. It can be used for determining the geometric mean, the harmonic mean, the percentage variation and all other statistical determinations.

In summary, one can encapsulate this discussion in the following simple test for various kinds of concept and data measurement:

If you can say that:

One object is different from another, you have a **nominal** scale.

One object is bigger, better or more of anything than another, you have an **ordinal** scale.

One object is so many units (degrees, inches) more than another, you have an **interval** scale.

One object is so many times as big or bright or tall or heavy as another, you have a **ratio** scale.

HOW DATA RELATE TO THEORY

There is a hierarchy of expressions, going from the general to the particular, from abstract to concrete, that makes it possible to investigate research problems couched in theoretical language. The briefest statement of the research problem will be the most general and abstract, while the detailed analysis of components of the research will be particular and concrete.

Theory - the abstract statements that make claims about the world and how it works. Research problems are usually stated at a theoretical level.

Concepts - the building blocks of the theory, which are usually abstract and cannot be directly measured.

Indicators - the phenomena that point to the existence of the concepts.

Variables - the components of the indicators that can be measured.

Values - the actual units or methods of measurement of the variables. These are data in their most concrete form.

Note that each theory may have several concepts, each concept several indicators, each indicator several variables and each variable several values. To clarify these terms, consider this example, which gives only one example of each expression.

Theory - poverty leads to poor health

Concept - poverty

Indicator - poor living conditions

Variable - provision of sanitary facilities

Value - numbers of people per WC.

> **Do:** Be aware of levels of expression as they will help you to break down your investigations into manageable tasks. This will enable you to come to overall conclusions about the abstract concepts in your research problem based on evidence rooted in detailed data at a more concrete level.

Theory

Although the word 'theory' is rather imprecise in its meaning, in research it refers to a statement that expresses what is going on in the situation, phenomenon or whatever is being researched. Theories can range from complex large-scale systems developed in academic research, to informal guesses or hunches about specific situations. In research it is common to refer to existing theories, either to challenge them or to develop them by refining them or applying them to new situations. Novel theories are only developed successfully after much research and testing. A theory is expressed in theoretical statements, for example, 'taking examinations leads to stress'.

Research activities can be divided into two categories:

1   Those that verify theory.
2   Those that generate theory.

In both cases it is necessary to break down the theoretical statements in such a way as to make them researchable and testable. As mentioned above, several steps are required to achieve this.

Concepts

A concept is a general expression of a particular phenomenon (e.g. cat, human, anger, speed, alienation, socialism, etc.). Each one of these represents an idea, and the word is a label for this idea.

We use concepts all the time as they are an essential part of understanding the world and communicating with other people. Many common concepts are shared by everyone in a society, although there are variations in meaning between different cultures and languages. For example, the concept 'respect' will mean something different to a streetwise rapper than to a noble lord. There are other concepts that are only understood by certain people, such as experts, professionals and specialists, for example, dermatoglyphics, milfoil, parachronism, anticipatory socialization, etc.

> **Don't:** Label concepts in an exotic fashion, perhaps in order to impress or confuse, for example, a 'domestic feline mammal' instead of a 'cat'. This is called jargon, and should be avoided.

It is important to define concepts in such a way that everyone reading the work has got the same idea of what is meant. This is relatively easy in the natural sciences where precise definition is usually possible (e.g. acceleration, radio waves, elements). In the social sciences this may be much more difficult. Human concepts such as fidelity, dishonesty, enthusiasm, and even more technical concepts such as affluence, vagrancy and dominance, are difficult to pin down accurately, as their meanings are often based on opinions, emotions, values, traditions, etc.

> **Do:** Carefully formulate definitions when using concepts that are not precise in normal usage. You will be able to find definitions of the concepts that you are planning to use in your investigations from your background reading.

Because definitions for non-scientific and non-technical concepts can vary in different contexts, you may have to decide on which meaning you want to give to those concepts. Rarely, you might even have to devise your own definition for a particular word.

Indicators

Many concepts are rather abstract in nature, and difficult or even impossible to evaluate or measure. Take 'anger' as an example. How will you detect anger in a person? The answer is to look for indicators – those perceivable phenomena that give an indication that the concept is present. What, in this case might these be? Think of the signs that might indicate anger – clenched fists, agitated demeanour, spluttering, shouting, wide-open eyes, stamping, reddened face, increased heart-beat, increased adrenaline production, and many others. Again, you can see what indicators were used in previous studies – this is much easier and more reliable than trying to work them out for yourself. For more technical subjects, indicators are usually well defined and universally accepted, for example, changes of state like condensation, freezing, magnetism.

Variables

If you want to gauge the extent or degree of an indicator, you will need to find a measurable component. In the case of anger above, it would be very difficult to measure the redness of a face or the degree of stamping, but you could easily measure a person's heartbeat. You could even ask the subject how angry he or she feels.

In the natural sciences, the identification of variables is usually more simple. Temperature, density, speed and velocity are examples. Some of these may be appropriate to social science, particularly in quantitative studies, for example, number of people in crowds, frequency and type of activities, etc.

Values

The values used are the units of measurement. In the case of heartbeat, it would be beats per minute, and the level of anger felt could be declared on a scale of 1–10. Obviously the precision that is possible will be different depending on the nature of the variable and the type of values that can be used. Certain scientific experiments require incredibly accurate measurement, while some social phenomena (e.g. opinions) might only be gauged on a three-point scale such as 'agree', 'neutral', 'disagree'.

Ask yourself

What are the essential differences between primary and secondary data, and how does this relate to where and how you would find them?

Primary data are first-hand data, observed or collected directly from the field. Secondary data are interpreted primary data. You can elaborate on this by giving examples. There is plenty of scope to describe where and how you would find the different types of data, for example by doing experiments, surveys, etc. for primary data, and archive searches, official statistics, etc. for secondary data. Keep making the distinction between the immediacy of primary data and the second-hand nature of secondary data.

Can all data be measured in the same way? If not, describe the different ways. Can both quantitative and qualitative data be measured in all these ways? If not, explain why not and what consequences this has.

This obviously relates to the levels of measurement (nominal, ordinal, etc.), which you can describe and give examples of. The main point to be made is that qualitative data are limited in how they can be measured (i.e. only nominal and ordinal levels of measurement), which limits the types of statistical test that can be carried out on them.

Describe how values relate to theoretical statements.

They are at the opposite ends of the scale of abstraction. Values are the most concrete notions (e.g. metres, seconds, etc.). You will have to explain the sequence of values, indicators, concepts and theoretical statements, and how they relate in **levels of abstraction**. Give examples to make your points clear (e.g. using the example of the theory given above, 'taking exams leads to stress', one concept is 'stress') An indicator of stress might be 'raised heartbeat', for which a value could be 'beats per minute'. You can then point out the relationship between the values and the theory.

Take it further

More about theory

Theory underlies all of our understanding of the world. Animals cannot theorize, which sets them apart from humans. From an early age we use observations of the world around us to make sense of what we experience and to predict what will happen and what the results of our actions might be. Scientific research is all about theories and their ability to explain phenomena and reveal the 'truth'.

(Continued)

(Continued)

Consider the following list of criteria for judging the quality of theory:

- A theoretical system must permit deductions that can be tested empirically; that is, it must provide the means for its confirmation or rejection. One can test the validity of a theory only through the validity of the propositions (hypotheses) that can be derived from it. If repeated attempts to disconfirm its various hypotheses fail, then greater confidence can be placed in its validity. This can go on indefinitely, until possibly some hypothesis proves untenable. This would constitute indirect evidence of the inadequacy of the theory and could lead to its rejection (or, more commonly, to its replacement by a more adequate theory that can incorporate the exception).
- Theory must be compatible with both the observation and previously validated theories. It must be grounded in empirical data that have been verified and must rest on sound postulates and hypotheses. The better the theory, the more adequately it can explain the phenomenon under consideration, and the more fact it can incorporate into a meaningful structure of ever-greater generalizability.
- Theories must be stated in simple terms; that is, theory is best that explains the most in the simplest way. This is the law of parsimony. A theory must explain the data adequately and yet must not be so comprehensive as to be unwieldy. On the other hand, it must not overlook the variables simply because they are difficult to explain.

This sounds all very well for the natural sciences, but some of these conditions cannot be achieved in the social sciences. In point 2, it may be impossible to ground the theory on empirical data that have been verified in the sense of measurement and repeated observations. Following this, it may be difficult therefore to test objectively the validity of its various hypotheses as demanded in point 1.

What it is important to stress, though, is the relationship between developing theory and previously validated theory, as mentioned in point 2. The theoretical background to one's enquiries will determine how one looks at the world. As Quine (1969) argued, our experience of the world of facts does not impose any single theory on us. Theories are underdetermined by facts, and our factual knowledge of the external world is capable of supporting many different interpretations of it. The answer to the question 'what exists?' can only receive the answer 'what exists is what theory posits'. Since there are different theories, these will posit different things. There will always be more than one logically equivalent theory consistent with the evidence we have. This is not because the evidence may be insufficient, but because the same facts can be accommodated in different ways by alterations in the configuration of the theory (Hughes and Sharrock, 1997, pp. 88–91).

One philosopher of science expressed it this way: 'it is generally agreed ... that the idea of a descriptive vocabulary which is applicable to observations, but which is entirely innocent of theoretical influences, is unrealizable' (Harré, 1972, p. 25). Therefore, one can argue that phenomena cannot be understood, and research cannot be carried out, without a theoretical underpinning:

> Models, concepts and theories are self-confirming in the sense that they instruct us to look at phenomena in particular ways. This means that they can never be disproved but only found to be more or less useful. (Silverman, 1998, p. 103).

Do: Note that it follows, then, that all theories must, by their very nature, be provisional. However sophisticated and elegant a theory is, it cannot be all-encompassing or final. The fact that it is a theory, an abstraction from real life, means that it must always be subject to possible change or development and, in extreme cases, even replacement.

Further reading

What counts as data, and what to do with it, is a big subject in research and gets dealt with exhaustively in most books about academic writing, which can be overwhelming at this stage of your studies.

Below are some useful other ways of looking at this aspect, without getting too deeply into technicalities. If you have other books about research to hand, check the index to see what they have to say about data.

Seale, C. (ed.) (2004) *Researching Society and Culture* (2nd edn). London: Sage.
A well-explained section on theories, models and hypotheses appears in chapter 5.

Leedy, Paul D. and Ormrod, J. (2012) *Practical Research: Planning and Design* (10th edn). New Jersey: Pearson.
Chapter 2 provides thoughts on data and how to deal with them.

Blaxter, L., Hughes, C. and Tight, M. (2010) *How to Research* (4th edn). Buckingham: Open University Press.
The first part of chapter 8 provides another angle on data and their forms.

FIVE

Doing a Literature Review

Whatever topic you wish to study for your dissertation or project, you will certainly not be the first person to investigate that topic area. There will be a wealth of writings describing previous work that has been done, latest findings and conclusions from research projects, commentaries from experts, and other literature. Therefore, the first thing you should do after you have selected your topic for study is to read what other people have written and make some kind of an assessment of the present 'state of the art' and where your research will fit into that body of work. Swales and Feak explain that literature reviews fall into two basic types: a survey article (a general review of current literature on a particular topic), and a review that forms part of a research paper, proposal, thesis or dissertation (2000, p. 115).

Writing a survey article (or it could be an assignment essay) is useful if you want to find out about the latest thinking on a particular topic. By interrogating the literature you will discover who the important experts are, the nature of the problems confronted, the solutions found, and the methods used to gain and analyse the necessary data. You might also detect that there are competing approaches to the topic that are based on different interpretations of the issues, possibly derived from political or philosophical stances. You should do this type of review if you want to know more about a particular subject with a view to informing your professional work or to explore what topics might be interesting for you to research into more deeply.

The second type of review, which we will consider in more detail, forms an important introduction to a research project and underpins the argument about why the project is worth doing. In order to construct this argument, you need to identify what work has been done in the area of interest, and where there is a gap in knowledge that is worth investigating. This involves searching the literature in the form of research papers, reports, books, etc. that deal with your topic of interest to find out what the latest thinking is, what differences of approach are and conclusions they breach, and what suggestions there are for further research. This will help to define your research aims and focus them on a defined issue. The literature review therefore forms a distinctly recognizable section near the beginning of a research proposal and leads on to the statement of the problems to be tackled and a more specific and practical description of the research activities that will be undertaken.

Not all of the material you will read will be relevant to your interests and, where it is relevant, not all of the ideas put forward will be agreeable to you. Doing this kind of a literature review means not only tracking down all the relevant information, but also taking a critical position on the ideas contained therein, and producing an argument that leads to the exposition of the research problem.

HOW TO GET STARTED

The first step in doing a literature review is to identify and get hold of the relevant literature. This will be in the form of books, articles, papers and reports that can be accessed by various means. Your first port of call should be your library, which is dedicated to sourcing and providing you with the necessary information. Find out how to do searches through both the library catalogue and the wide range of electronic sources that are available. Most university and college libraries organize training sessions for students on the use of the facilities provided.

The internet, if used in the right way, is also a convenient way to source information. However, be aware that amongst the jewels of information there is a wealth of rubbish!

> **Do:** Carefully check on the sources and authors of the writings to ensure that they are sufficiently well informed and authoritative.

The best way to check is to find out whether the writings have either been peer reviewed; that is, checked over by fellow experts in the subject, or are written by an acknowledged author on the subject.

> **Do:** Use the quick route to academic literature through Google Scholar, which is a search engine that concentrates on scholarly literature - particularly papers in peer-reviewed journals. To ensure that you can get access to the full papers rather than just the abstracts, log into your university library account before searching - there will be a note on the list of references to indicate full access.

SEARCHING FOR SOURCES

The quickest way to direct your searches using any electronic guide (e.g. library catalogue, internet search, database, citation index, etc.) is to use key words, so it is worth identifying the relevant ones for your area of research at an early stage. Where do you find the key words? Start with the obvious terms and concepts used in your course. As you delve deeper into the literature, you will come across more specialist words that will enable you to focus more narrowly on the specific aspects of your subject that particularly interest you.

Once you have sourced some literature, additional leads to further information can be found in the list of references located at the end of the book, chapter or paper. These of course refer back in time to previous writings. If the book or paper is rather old, the sources referred to might be rather out of date. To project your search forward in time, look for the title of the literature you have found (particularly relevant for papers and articles) in citation indexes. These list where the selected literature has been added to the list of references in later publications. This way can bring you bang up to date with the latest writings.

To locate the sections of interest in a book, look for key words in the index at the end of the book. This will lead you to the exact pages where the works appear. Look at the chapter headings in the list of contents too to help you identify the sections that are of interest.

⊗ | **Don't:** Ever read a book from beginning to end in order to identify the useful bits - life is too short for this!

ASSESSING THE TEXT

Doing a literature review means not only tracking down all the relevant information, but also taking a critical position on the ideas contained therein.

⊘ | **Do:** Remember that critical reading is a skill that you will need to develop.

Perhaps a better word in this context would be analytical reading, because the point of the exercise is not just to denigrate or find fault with the style of writing or ideas, but to present a critique, a scrutiny, an analysis or an examination of them.

⊗ | **Don't:** Think that providing a description of the literature is enough; your task is to give your own personal and professional appraisal of the content and quality of the text in question.

In order to be able to do this, you will have to look at the text from different perspectives to reveal a multi-dimensional view of the work. So, what are these perspectives?

The structure of the argument

You can analyse this by first detecting the conclusion-type words, or so-called conclusion indicators (e.g. therefore, it follows that, etc.), in order to pinpoint the conclusion(s). The main conclusions should normally appear towards the end of the work, though there may be intermediate conclusions scattered throughout. There are then three aspects that need to be examined:

1   What evidence is given to support the conclusions?
2   Is the evidence credible, that is, does it come from reliable sources?
3   Is the logic of the argument sound, that is, what are the steps in the argument that lead from the evidence to the conclusions?

> **Do:** This kind of analysis coolly, like a judge appraising the argument of a lawyer making a case.

The assumptions upon which the writings and arguments are based

All writing is rooted in theory and based on values, and must be appraised in relation to these. Sometimes these are quite clearly stated at the beginning of the text, sometimes they are obscured or not mentioned. You will need to have some knowledge of the different theoretical positions in your subject in order to be able to detect them and know what they imply. Some common examples of these are: a feminist approach in social science, a Keynesian approach in economics, a Modernist approach in architecture and a Freudian approach in psychology. In each subject there are competing theoretical standpoints with their own values. Only by being aware of these can you make your own considered evaluation of the literature.

The wider context of the work

Intellectual work is carried out in a complex arena where power, politics, fashion, economics, competing orthodoxies and many other factors play influential roles. These can be determining factors in the formulation of views and need to be exposed in order to understand the forces behind them. For example, the forces behind the Industrial Revolution were formative in the thinking of the day, just as those of the electronic revolution are today.

Comparison with other work

There are no absolute values to which you can appeal in order to make assessments. There are no clear rules about what is right and wrong.

> Research writing is a contested terrain, within which alternative views and positions may be taken up. (Blaxter et al., 2010, p. 101).

Critical reading can, however, be used to make comparisons between texts in order to highlight the different approaches, levels of thoroughness, contradictions, strength of arguments, implications of theoretical stances and accepted values and types of conclusion. This will enable you to group together or divide the various strands in the literature to help you map out the larger picture that forms the background to your project.

BACKGROUND REVIEW FOR A RESEARCH PROJECT

The review will need to be carried out in four major directions, not just narrowly confined to your specific subject area. Here they are, arranged from the general to the particular, their relative importance depending on the nature of your subject:

1 Research theory and philosophy - to establish the intellectual context(s) of research related to your subject.
2 History of developments in your subject - to trace the background to present thinking.
3 Latest research and developments in your subject - to inform about the current issues being investigated and the latest thinking and practice, to discuss the conflicting arguments, and to detect a gap in knowledge.
4 Research methods - to explore practical techniques that have been used, particularly those that might be relevant to your project.

> **Do:** Literature reviews do not all follow the same structure, so it is difficult to be prescriptive as to the form it should take. Look at similar reviews to the one you have to do to see the options.

Research projects usually begin with a review of the background to the research and use this to develop the research problem of the project. Research proposals should also contain a short review of previous research. The review should begin with a general outline of the features of the relevant literature. This gives you a good excuse to introduce literature that supports your introductory statements. Here is a checklist of useful points for you to review the content and form of your literature review, based on a compilation of comments from professors, listed by Swales and Feak (2000, p. 149):

- Make sure that your review is not just a list of previous research papers or other literature, devoid of any assessment of their relative importance and their interconnections. Make an overview of the literature to produce a guide to the rich interplay and major steps in the development of research in your subject.
- Check that the important issues of your research problem are introduced through the analysis of the literature. A simple chronological account of previous research will not give a sufficient thrust to the argument of why your research problem is significant and how it continues the research effort.
- Ensure that the general theoretical background is intimately connected to your examination of the more detailed writings about ideas and specific research that lead up to your own research project. The theory should help the reader understand the attitudes behind the reviewed literature and your own philosophical stance.
- Make links across discipline boundaries when doing an interdisciplinary review, rather than keeping each separate and examined in turn. Many research subjects cannot be hermetically sealed within one discipline, so the connections are there to be exposed. You might even be able to suggest some new links that need to be investigated.
- Ensure that you have included some account of how the previous research was done, so that you have a precedent for your own approach to methodology.

WHEN TO STOP

Reading the literature can be a fascinating activity, which leads along one interesting avenue to another.

Don't: It is easy to get carried away, especially now that access to a huge range of sources is so easy using the internet and library electronic resources. The danger is that you get carried away and spend too much time browsing.

You will need to judge how much is enough, based on the scale of your assignment or thesis, the complexity of the subject and simply the time you have available to you. Keep your reading and note-taking focused on relevant issues – acknowledging though that exploring the literature is a learning process, so you cannot plan everything out in advance, and hence the necessity to stand back occasionally to take stock.

How many references should you have? This depends on the subject and extent of the review. As the literature review part of a research proposal has to be very short and compact due to space limitations, you are unlikely to be able to cite more than 15–20 authors, 5–10 might even be sufficient in a narrowly defined field. For a literature review chapter of a dissertation or research project, 20–35 references are more likely. The important thing is to select those that are really significant for your work.

Do: It is a good idea to look at previous proposals or dissertations in your subject area to see what has been successful before.

A useful technique is to extract the evidence and conclusions in the form of short phrases, and arrange them in the sequence of the argument. This lets you examine the logic form without being distracted by the surrounding text. This process sounds a lot simpler than it often is, arguments can be quite convoluted or incomplete, but just like a judge, you should make a note of your summing up of this aspect of your critique.

Example of a literature review

Forced migration: An understanding of the coping strategies of the Hazara communities in Oxfordshire

Fatima Hashmi, MA - Development and Emergency Practice, Oxford Brookes University, 2015

Literature review

It is necessary to understand Britain's housing and employment immigration policy restrictions in order to comprehend the need for and type of coping mechanisms of the immigrant Hazara communities in Oxfordshire (Zetter and Pearl, 2000; UNHCR, 2013).

Considering the UK immigration discourse, Article 1 (A) (2) of the United Nations Convention Relating to the Status of Refugees defines a refugee as, 'someone with a well-founded fear of being persecuted for reasons of race, religion, and nationality, membership of a particular social group or political opinion'. In the light of this research, the terms 'asylum seeker' and 'refugee' will be aggregated together as 'forced migrants' (FMO, 2015), to examine the coping strategies in both phases of their lives.

Looking at the Hazaras history, the largest Hazara migration and displacement (Ibrahimi, 2012), which included the author's great grandfather, originated from the 'Hazarajat'. It began between 1880 and 1899, to Meshed-Iran, Russian Turkestan and Quetta-Pakistan (Gharjistani, 1986). It was as a result of persecution due to ethnicity and Shi'a sect (Bacon, 1958). The second wave of migration was attributable to the resistance to the Soviet war (Ibrahimi, 2012). And finally, the Taliban/Lashkare-Jhangvi era led to another wave of migration from Quetta (HRW, 2014) and Afghanistan to Australia and Europe (Koser, 2013).

Glancing at the main theme of 'coping', Baerenholdt and Aarsaether (1998: 30) describe it as 'how people engage in strategies which make sense to themselves'. Putman's (1995; Zetter et al., 2006: 9) pioneering typology of 'social capital', bonding (intra-community), bridging (inter-community) and linking (community–public agency) can be used to understand the coping mechanisms of communities. However, 'bonding capital' may be necessary for refugees to 'get by' (Begum, 2003), can arguably cause social fragmentation (Haezewindt, 2003). A qualitative study by Begum (2003) and Korac's (2005) ethnographic fieldwork found that 'bridging social capital' allowed successful integration with the host community. Mindful of this research, it will be worth investigating this aspect amongst the Hazara communities in Oxfordshire.

Williams' (2006) participatory observation study on the concept of 'coping strategy' found that 'transnationalism' helped refugees stay connected to their cultural identity. Likewise, Monsutti (2004) agrees that the Hazaras in Afghanistan have developed strong translational migratory networks. This translational experience of refugees provides the basis for the concept of 'networks' as suggested by Marx (1990) in a conceptual framework. More so, based on ethnographic evidences Monsutti (2008) asserts that Hazara refugees use 'tactics' such as transnational networks to manage within limited means while still making use of their social and cultural skills. It will be interesting to compare how the diasporic discourse has helped the Hazara 'communities'.

Equally important, Ibrahimi (2012) emphasizes that, historically the international Shi'a religious institutions that are central to the Hazara ideology, laid the foundations of trans-nationalism. Such as, acknowledged by Creasy (2009: 49) in her ethnographic study on the Hazaras in Quetta, 'physical space plays an integral role within religion'. Moreover, using the RCOPE measure of religious coping, Pargament et al. (2000) found 'religious capital' (Baker and Miles-Watson, 2010) plays a multifunctional role by offering a variety of ways to manage in difficult situations. Therefore, it will be important to understand how religion and religious institutions in Oxfordshire have helped the Hazara communities develop efficient coping mechanisms, in addition to how their ideology has evolved.

Another important aspect is the work of Refugee Community Organizations (RCOs), which offer invaluable cultural, emotional and economic support. In Britain, destitution amongst refugees is the result of the dispersal policy and inappropriate structure of social support (Morrell and Wainwright, 2006). Remarkably, Crawley et al. (2011) in using the Participatory Ethnographic Evaluation and Research (PEER) method discovered that refugees rely heavily on their communities and their RCOs due to housing, employment and cultural barriers. However, this creates negative consequences of dependency on informal contacts (Bloch, 2004) with low-paid exploitative work (Community Links and Refugee Council, 2011). It will be of interest to understand in what capacity the informal networks and organizations have helped the Hazaras.

Research questions

The author's interest in the understanding of the problems faced by the Hazara community in Oxfordshire stems from her upbringing by her Hazara grandparents in Quetta. This experience forms the foundation of the research question:

What are the coping strategies of the Hazara communities in Oxfordshire who have been subjected to forced migration?

Moreover, several important questions were raised, such as:

- How has 'transnationalism' helped the Hazara community cope and has it played the main role in regaining the sense of belonging?
- What coping strategies have the Hazara adopted in the process of dealing with the UK's asylum procedures?
- In the light of 'bridging social capital' how well is the community integrating within Oxfordshire?

(Continued)

(Continued)

List of references

Bacon, E. (1958) *OBOK: A Study of Social Structure in Eurasia*. New York: Wenner-Gren Foundation for Anthropological Research.

Baerenholdt, J.O. and Aarsaether, N. (1998) 'Coping strategies in the north', in N. Aarsaether and J.O. Baerenholdt (eds), *Coping Strategies in the North – Local Practices in the Context of Global Restructuring*. Copenhagen: MOST and Nordic Council of Ministers, pp. 15–44.

Baker, C. and Miles-Watson, J. (2010) 'Faith and traditional capitals: defining the public scope of religious capital', *Implicit Religion*, 13(2): 17–69.

Begum, H. (2003) *Social Capital in Action: Adding Up Local Connections and Networks, a Pilot Study in London*. Centre for Civil Society. London: NCVO Publications.

Bloch, A. (2004) *Making it Work: Refugee Employment in the UK*. Asylum and Migration Working Paper 2. London: Institute for Public Policy Research.

Community Links and Refugee Council (2011) *Understanding Informal Economic Activity of Refugees in London*. London: Community Links and Refugee Council.

Crawley, H., Hemmings, J. and Price, N. (2011) *Coping with Destitution Survival and Livelihood Strategies of Refused Asylum Seekers living in the UK*. Centre for Migration Policy Research (CMPR), Swansea University. Oxford: Oxfam.

Creasy, J. (2009) *The Religious Identity of the Hazaras of Afghanistan and Modern-Day Pakistan*. MA Thesis, University of Glasgow. Available at: http://theses.gla.ac.uk/1277/1/2009CreasyMTh.pdf (accessed 2 July 2015).

Forced Migration Online (FMO) (2015) 'What is forced migration?' Available at: www.forcedmigration.org/about/whatisfm (accessed 2 July 2015).

Gharjistani, M.E. (1986) 'Brief history of Afghanistan in general', Paper presented at the 1987 Conference. Oxford: Oxford University, Refugee Studies Centre (paper held at the RSP Documentation Centre).

Haezewindt, P. (2003) 'Investing in each other and the community: the role of social capital', *Social Trends*, 33: 19–26.

Human Rights Watch (HRW) (2014) *We are the Walking Dead: Killings of the Shia Hazara in Balochistan, Pakistan*. Human Rights Watch.

Ibrahimi, N. (2012) 'Shift and drift in Hazara ethnic consciousness: the impact of conflict and migration', Crossroads Asia Working Paper Series, No. 5. Bonn: Center for Development Research/ZEF, Department of Political and Cultural Change, University of Bonn.

Korac, M. (2005) 'The role of bridging social networks in refugee settlement: the case of exile communities from the former Yugoslavia in Italy and the Netherlands', in P. Waxman and V. Colic-Peisker, (eds), *Homeland Wanted*. New York: Nova Science Publishers, Inc., pp. 87–107.

Koser, K. (2013) 'Migration and displacement impacts of Afghan transitions in 2014: implications for Australia', Irregular Migration Research Program Occasional Paper Series, no. 03/2013. Australian Department of Immigration and Citizenship.

Marx, E. (1990) 'The Social World of Refugees: A Conceptual Framework', *Journal of Refugee Studies*, 3: 189–203.

Monsutti, A. (2004) 'Cooperation, remittances, and kinship among the Hazaras', *Iranian Studies*, 37(2): 219–40.

Monsutti, A. (2008) 'Afghan migratory strategies and the three solutions to the refugee problem', *Refugee Survey Quarterly*, 27(1): 58–73.

Morrell, G. and Wainwright, S. (2006) *Destitution amongst Refugees and Asylum Seekers in the UK, Briefing*. London: Information Centre about Asylum and Refugees (ICAR).

Pargament, K., Koenig, H. and Perez, L. (2000) 'The Many methods of religious coping: development and initial validation of RCOPE', *Journal of Clinical Psychology*, 56(4): 519–43.

Putnam, R.D. (1995) 'Tuning in, tuning out: The strange disappearance of social capital in America', *Political Science & Politics*, 28(4): 664–83.

UNHCR (2013) *Immigration Bill 2013: Parliamentary Briefing*. House of Commons Committee Stage. London: UNHCR.

Williams, L. (2006) 'Social networks of refugees in the United Kingdom: tradition, tactics and new community spaces', *Journal of Ethnic and Migration Studies*, 32(5): 865–79.

Zetter, R. and Pearl, M. (2000) 'The minority within the minority: refugee community-based organisations in the UK and the impact of restrictionism on asylum-seekers', *Journal of Ethnic and Migration Studies*, 26(4): 675–97.

Zetter, R., Griffiths, D., Sigona, N., Flynn, F., Pasha, P. and Beynon, R. (2006) *Immigration, Social Cohesion and Social Capital: What are the Links?* York: Joseph Rowntree Foundation.

PLAGIARISM AND REFERENCING

There is no shame in referring to other writers, in fact that is what a literature review is all about.

> **Do:** Use a sound system of citation and referencing as the best way to avoid any suspicion of plagiarism.

Apart from blatantly copying chunks of someone else's work or cutting and pasting from the internet, there are degrees of using the writings of others for your own text where you will have to employ your judgement. Paraphrasing or condensing existing work is OK if referenced, but don't be tempted to pass this off as your own ideas. What you do need to express in your own words is your interpretation of the literature, the comparisons between positions, the problems revealed, the issues raised, etc. You will undoubtedly be able to find specific guidance on the issue of avoiding plagiarism from your library, as well as instructions about the system of citation and referencing you should use. You may also be able to use the program Turnitin to check how well you have done. This program is increasingly available in colleges and universities and, apart from helping you to write well, is used to reveal cases of plagiarism in submitted work.

Take it further

Instead of just searching for published sources, why not try people? There may be experts in your chosen field of study right next to you in your college or university. They will have not only their own publications, but first-hand knowledge of the latest thinking in their specialization. They are there to help students widen their horizons.

You can spread your networking wider by attending conferences and workshops where the leading experts gather to exchange news about their latest research projects and results. Although large international conferences tend to be held in rather nice city locations throughout the world, and are expensive to attend, there are sure to be more local national gatherings, run by institutions, universities and professional organizations, many offering free attendance. Check on the internet using suitable key words or find out from your university research office what conferences and workshops are coming up.

Joining online discussion forums is another way to get in contact with other like-minded researchers. You will need to do a bit of searching with key words including your research topic title, particular concepts or technical terms that interest you in order to find suitable groups. Often, very eminent experts are willing to take part in these discussions and hand out free advice to those who pose questions.

Another source of internet information is Wikis, which are resources open to everyone to contribute to. The most familiar is of course Wikipedia, but you will find many others that are more specialist in their content. Your college or university might even run their own Wikis, based on specific subject areas. You do need to be careful though how you use the information on these sites – if anyone can post up material it could be of very dubious quality. Most Wikis have some form of monitoring, but check out the quality of referencing and sources quoted to make checks yourself.

Ask yourself

How have you connected the literature review to your research problem?

The question can also be reversed – how has the research problem and resultant questions/hypotheses emerged from the discussion of the literature? The content of the literature review needs to be focused towards revealing the problem, going from a more general overview of the context to homing in on the specific issue to be researched. This will help to define what literature is relevant to include in the review. Of course, you may not be aware of the problem until you have researched the literature, so you will need to carry out a certain amount of iteration before you can judge the relevance of all that you have read to the focus of your research project.

Can you find all the notes you have previously made on a particular topic or key word?

This is a good way to test the effectiveness of your note taking and storage/retrieval system. Best to do this exercise soon after you have started using your system, so that you can improve it if finding the notes proves to be time consuming and incomplete. If you have used a paper system, you might have to make duplicates of your notes to put into different categories (e.g. subject, author, time, etc.) so that you can search by different criteria. If you are using a computer-based system, check that you can easily paste all the relevant notes into a first draft of your text. Check also that all the bibliographic details are connected to the notes, so that you can cite the contents as necessary.

> As another person who is reading your review, can you easily trace the source of the topics raised in the review by using the supplied bibliographic information?

You can test this by making a search using only the information of sources you have given. You will notice that if you have quoted from the source, you will have to give the page number in order to find the exact text and also the correct date and edition of the book or journal, or else you will be flicking through endless pages trying to locate the quoted text. Expect the readers to want to refer back to the original sources of your review if they want more information about the literature.

Further reading

Here are some books that have more detail about finding out the latest information on your subject and writing a literature review.

Oliver, P. (2012) *Succeeding with your Literature Review*. Maidenhead: Open University Press.
A comprehensive handbook for students covering all aspects of this subject.

Ridley, D. (2012) *The Literature Review: A Step-by-Step Guide for Students (SAGE Study Skills Series)*. London: Sage.
Practical strategies for conducting a systematic search of the available literature, reading and note taking and writing up your literature review as part of an undergraduate research project, Master's dissertation or PhD thesis.

Machi, L.A. and McEvoy, B.T. (2012) *The Literature Review: Six Steps to Success* (2nd edn). London: Sage.
Offers graduate students in education and the social sciences a road map to developing and writing an effective literature review for a research project, thesis or dissertation.

Hart, C. (2001) *Doing a Literature Search*. London: Sage.
A whole book providing a guide on how to search the literature in the social sciences.

Hart, C. (1998) *Doing a Literature Review: Releasing the Social Science Research Imagination*. London: Sage.
A guide through the multi-dimensional sea of academic literature with techniques on how to deal with the information when you have found it – an enduring classic!

In the Oxford Brookes University library catalogue there were 2,350 references to information guides! Many of these were bibliographies devoted to a particular subject; you could search on your university or college catalogue for one relevant to your topic. Here are a few examples of books on specific subject areas.

(Continued)

(Continued)

O'Brian, N. (2000) *Education: A Guide to Reference and Information Sources (Reference Sources in the Social Sciences)* (2nd edn). Englewood, CO: Libraries Unlimited.
This guide identifies and describes key reference and information sources in the field of education today and also major social science reference sources that have a direct or overlapping relationship to education.

Amico, E.B. (ed.) (1998) *Reader's Guide to Women's Studies*. London: Fitzroy Dearborn.
Foreman, L. (2003) *Information Sources in Music*. Munich: K. G. Saur.
And here are some of the multitude of books to help you navigate the internet. Always try to get the latest edition; they get out of date fast! The first one, as the name suggests, is specifically aimed at those carrying out literature reviews from online information.

Man, T. (2015) *The Oxford Guide to Library Research: How to Find Reliable Information Online and Offline*. Oxford: Oxford University Press.
This book will answer two basic questions: first, what is the extent of the significant research resources that will you miss if you confine your research entirely, or even primarily, to sources available on the open internet? Second, if you are trying to get a reasonably good overview of the literature on a particular topic, rather than just 'something quickly' on it, what are the several alternative methods of subject searching – which are not available on the Web – that are usually much more efficient for that purpose than typing key words into a blank search box, with the results displayed by relevance-ranking computer algorithms?

Fink, A. (2013) *Conducting Research Literature Reviews: From the Internet to Paper*. 4th edition. London: Sage.
Nearly 100 online examples and references from the social, behavioural and health sciences with clarification of some of the basic concepts of research essential in making judgements about the quality of research methods, and examples of how to write up reviews and how others have done it.

O'Dochartaigh, N. (2012) *Internet Research Skills* (3rd edn). London: Sage.
A clear, concise guide to effective online research for social science and humanities students.

SIX
Defining the Research Problem

In all research projects, on whatever subject, you need to define and delineate the research problem clearly. The **research problem** is a general statement of an issue meriting research. Its nature will suggest appropriate forms for its investigation. Here are several forms in which the research problem can be expressed to indicate the method of investigation.

The research problem in some social science research projects using the **hypothetico-deductive method** is expressed in terms of the testing of a particular hypothesis. It is therefore important to know what make good hypotheses and how they can be formulated. However, it is not appropriate to use the hypothetico-deductive method, or even scientific method, in every research study. Much research into society, design, history, philosophy and many other subjects cannot provide the full criteria for the formulation of hypotheses and their testing, and it is inappropriate to try to fit such research into this method. What are the alternative ways of stating the research problem in a researchable form?

HYPOTHESES AND THEIR FORMULATION

Hypotheses are nothing unusual; we make them all the time. They are hunches or reasonable guesses made in the form of statements about a situation or a cause, the latter referred to as **causal statements**. If something happens in our everyday life, we tend to suggest a reason for its occurrence by making rational guesses. When a particular hypothesis is found to be supported, we have a good chance of understanding the situation and taking the right action, if needed, to remedy it, or if rejected, know that the hunch was wrong in some way. Many of the greatest discoveries in science were based on hypotheses: Newton's theory of gravity, Einstein's general theory of relativity and a host of others.

You will encounter hypotheses in your background reading, sometimes overt and clearly stated, and at other times, in less scholarly documents, hidden in the text or only hinted at. If you use one in your own research study, a hypothesis should arise naturally from the literature review and the resulting research problem, and should appear to the reader to be reasonable and sound.

There are two grounds on which a hypothesis may be justified: logical and empirical. Logical justification is developed from arguments based on concepts and theories and premises relating directly to the research problem; empirical justification is based on reference to other research found in the literature.

There are important qualities of hypotheses that distinguish them from other forms of statement. According to Kerlinger (1970), hypotheses are:

- Assertions (not suggestions)
- Limited in scope
- Statements about the relationships between certain variables
- Clear in their implications for testing the relationships
- Compatible with current knowledge
- Expressed as economically as possible using correct terminology.

> **Do:** Develop a good hypothesis as a very useful aid to organizing your research effort. It specifically limits your enquiry to the interaction of certain variables; it suggests the methods appropriate for collecting, analysing and interpreting the data; and the resultant confirmation or rejection of the hypothesis through empirical or experimental testing gives a clear indication of the extent of knowledge gained.

While a hypothesis, as described above, is tested in order to provide evidence to support, or to reject the existence of the stated relationships between the variables, another related type of hypothesis, called a **null hypothesis**, starts with an assumption that those relationships do not exist, and maintains that the assumptions are correct if the null hypothesis is not refuted by the results of the tests. It is often appropriate to balance an alternative hypothesis against a null hypothesis. If the null hypothesis is rejected, then the logical alternative is the alternative hypothesis. The alternative hypothesis is not specific and is not directly tested. An example will illustrate this:

Null hypothesis - people with more than the national average annual personal income do not have more than the national average annual personal spending.

Alternative hypothesis - people with more than the national average annual personal income have more than the national average personal spending.

Formulating hypotheses

Hypotheses can be very varied in nature, ranging from concrete to abstract and from narrow to wide in scope, range and inclusiveness. In order to formulate a useful researchable hypothesis, you need to have a thorough knowledge of the background to the subject and the nature of the problem or issue that is being addressed. The hypothesis is developed from the result of a successive division and delineation of the problem, and provides a focus around which the research will be carried out.

Researchers work on two levels of reality, the operational level and the conceptual level. On the operational level, they work with events in observable terms, involving the reality necessary to carry out the research. On a conceptual level, events are defined in terms of underlying communality with other events on a more abstract level. Researchers move from single specific instances to general ones and thereby gain an understanding of how phenomena operate and variables interrelate, and vice versa to test whether the conceptual generalizations can be supported in fact.

> **Don't:** Overlook the fact that the formulation of the hypothesis is usually made on a conceptual level, in order to enable the results of the research to be generalized beyond the specific conditions of the particular study. This widens the applicability of the research.

Operationalizing hypotheses

It is one of the fundamental criteria of a hypothesis that it is testable. However, a hypothesis formulated on a conceptual level cannot be directly tested; it is too abstract. It is therefore necessary to convert it to an operational level. This is called **operationalization**. It consists of reversing the conceptionalization process described above.

Often, the first step is to break down the main hypothesis into two or more sub-hypotheses. These represent components or aspects of the main hypothesis and together should add up to its totality. Each sub-hypothesis will intimate a different method of testing and therefore implies different research methods that might be appropriate.

The operationalization of the sub-hypotheses follows four steps in the progression from the most abstract to the most concrete expressions by defining concepts, indicators, variables and values, as described in Chapter 5.

> **Do:** Although the term 'hypothesis' is used with many different meanings in everyday and even academic situations, use it in your research only in its strictest scientific sense. This will avoid you being criticized of sloppy, imprecise use of terminology.

ALTERNATIVES TO HYPOTHESES

Question or questions

You can express the method of investigating the problem through asking a question or a series of questions, the answers to which require scrutiny of the problem from one or more directions. I must admit that this is an easy option because it comes so naturally to us to ask questions when we see a problem. This makes the posing of questions a very intuitive and effective way to initiate a research project. Here is an example:

> Four broad, interrelated research questions are raised about the problem-posed main question regarding the representation of contemporary art in the media and the agenda for public debate that this implies. These questions are:
>
> 1   What are the characteristics of the overall representation of contemporary art issues in the media?
> 2   What agenda for contemporary art does this imply, and how does this relate to broad values of contemporary art and media?
> 3   How does this representation differ in coverage presented in different types of media (e.g. television, press, online)?
> 4   What role is played by specialist journalists, and specifically art correspondents, in shaping this representation?

Obviously, the question or questions should be derived directly from the research problem, and give a clear indication of the subject to be investigated and imply the methods that will be used. Often the relationships of the questions can be similar to those of hypotheses: a main question is divided into sub-questions that explore aspects of the main question.

Propositions

Focusing a research study on a **proposition** (a theoretical statement that indicates the clear direction and scope of a research project), rather than on a hypothesis, allows the study to concentrate on particular relationships between events, without having to comply with the rigorous characteristics required of hypotheses. Consider this example.

The main research problem was formulated in the form of three interrelated propositions:

> 1   Specifically designed public sector housing provided for young single people to rent has been, and continues to be, designed according to the recommendations and standards in the design guidance for young persons' housing.
> 2   The relevant design guidance is not based on accurate perceptions of the characteristics of young single people.
> 3   From these two propositions the third one should follow: there is a mismatch between the specifically designed public sector housing provided for single young people and their accommodation requirements.

Statement of intent to investigate and evaluate critically

Not all research needs to answer a question or to test a hypothesis. Especially at Master's degree level or in smaller studies, you can use a more exploratory approach. You can express the subject and scope of the exploration in a statement of intent. Again, this must be derived from the research problem, imply a method of approach and indicate the outcome. An example of this form of research definition is:

> This study examines the problems in career development of women lawyers in the British legal establishment. It focuses on the identification of specific barriers (established conventions, prejudices, procedures, career paths) and explores the effectiveness of specific initiatives that have been aimed at breaking down these barriers.

Definition of research objectives

When you have identified a research problem, in order to indicate what measures will be taken to investigate the problem or provide means of overcoming it, you must formulate a definition of the research objectives. You should accompany this by some indication of how the research objectives will be achieved.

The following example indicates how it is proposed to provide an adequate assessment of the relationship between the design of security systems in public buildings and the resulting restrictions to the accessibility of these buildings to the general public. The research problem previously highlighted a lack of such methods of assessment.

To overcome this problem it is necessary to do the following:

- Propose a method of measurement by which the extent of incorporation of security systems can be assessed. This will enable an objective comparison to be made between alternative design proposals in terms of the extent of incorporation of security features. There is a need to identify and categorize the main security systems advocated in past studies of publicly accessible buildings in order to establish the general applicability of the methods of measurement proposed.
- Propose a method of measurement by which the extent of public accessibility to buildings can be assessed. This will enable an objective comparison to be made between different buildings in terms of the extent of their accessibility in use. In order to arrive at a method of measurement, a more comprehensive interpretation of accessibility needs to be developed so that the measures proposed will not be confined to any one particular type of public building.
- Assess the extent of accessibility achieved after the incorporation of security systems, by a study of public buildings in use. To achieve this, a number of publicly accessible buildings need to be examined.

The objectives of the research

How you define the research problem is a crucial part of the design of a research project. A good way to help you to decide what the nature of the problem will be and therefore what the nature of the research will be, is to decide on the

objectives of the research. When reading about research already completed, look
to see where the objectives of the research are explained, as these will give you a
strong indication of the nature of the research efforts.

Reynolds (1977, pp. 4–11) listed five things that he believed most people
expected scientific knowledge to provide. These, together with one that I have
added myself, can conveniently be used as the basis for a list of the possible
objectives of research:

- Categorization
- Explanation
- Prediction
- Creating understanding
- Providing potential for control
- Evaluation.

Categorization involves forming a typology of objects, events or concepts. This
can be useful in explaining what 'things' belong together and how. One of the
main problems is to decide which is, or are, the most useful methods of categorization, depending on the reasons for attempting the categorization in the first place.
Following from this is the problem of determining what criteria to use to judge the
usefulness of the categorization. Two obvious criteria are mentioned by Reynolds
(1977): that of exhaustiveness, by which all items should be able to be placed
into a category, without any being left out; and that of mutual exclusiveness, by
which each item should, without question, be appropriately placed into only one
category. Finally, it should be noted that the typologies must be consistent with
the concepts used in the theoretical background to the study.

Take it further

There are many events and issues that we do not fully, or even partly, understand. The
objective of providing an explanation of particular phenomena has been a common one in
many forms of research. An explanation is an attempt to describe how and why things work.

On the basis of an explanation of a phenomenon it is often possible to make a prediction
of future events related to it. In the natural sciences these predictions are often made in
the form of abstract statements, for example, given C1, C2, ,..., Cn: if X, then Y. More readily understood are predictions made in text form. For example, if a person disagrees with a
friend about his attitude towards an object, then a state of psychological tension is produced.

While explanation and prediction can reveal the inner workings of phenomena – what
happens and when – they do not always provide a sense of understanding of phenomena – how
or why they happen. A complete explanation of a phenomenon will require a wider study of
the processes that surround the phenomenon and influence it or cause it to happen.

A good level of understanding of a phenomenon might lead to the possibility of finding
a way to control it. Obviously, not all phenomena lend themselves to this. For example, it is
difficult to imagine how the disciplines of astronomy or geology could include an element

of control. However, all of technology is dependent on the ability to control the behaviour, movement or stability of things. Even in society there are many attempts, often based on scientific principles, to control events such as crime, poverty, the economy, etc., though the record of success is more limited than in the natural sciences, and perhaps there are cases of attempting the impossible. The problem is that such attempts cannot be truly scientific as the variables cannot all be controlled, nor can one be certain that all relevant variables have been considered. The crucial issue in control is to understand how certain variables affect one another, and then be able to change the variables in such a way as to produce predictable results.

Evaluation is making judgements about the quality of objects or events. Quality can be measured either in an absolute sense or on a comparative basis. To be useful, the methods of evaluation must be relevant to the context and intentions of the research. For example, level of income is a relevant variable in the evaluation of wealth, while degree of marital fidelity is not. Evaluation goes beyond measurement, as it implies allotting values to objects or events. It is the context of the research which will help to establish the types of value that should be used.

Do: Remember that research can have several legitimate objectives, either singly or in combination. The main, overriding objective must be that of gaining useful or interesting knowledge.

Ask yourself

What are hypotheses and why and how are they used in research?

Describe how they are specific statements that are open to testing. You can list the necessary qualities of a good hypothesis. They are obviously used as a focus for research efforts and to test theory – you can expand on this by giving examples. How they are used is a good lead-in to explaining scientific method – there is plenty to write about that.

When is the use of a hypothesis to formulate the research not appropriate?

As you will have explained in the previous answer, scientific method comes with a list of assumptions about the nature of facts and theory. Much research in social science does not conform to the strictures of natural science, being more qualitative in nature and dedicated to gaining an understanding of events, often from a specific viewpoint. You can give several examples where the alternatives to hypotheses would be more appropriate (e.g. when examining the mores of a pop idol's fan club).

Discuss the relative merits of the alternatives to the use of a hypothesis.

Developing from the points made in the previous answer, you should go through the range of alternative choices outlined in this chapter, and by using simple examples, explain how research can be carried out in different ways in response to its formulation. For example, a research question with its sub-questions can focus the research to a narrowly defined topic and clearly identifies the aims (i.e. finding answers to the questions).

Further reading

Hypotheses and alternative ways of setting out the research problem form the foundation of research projects. The clarity with which they are formulated greatly influence the quality of the research.

Seale, C. (ed.) (2004) *Researching Society and Culture* (2nd edn). London: Sage.
Chapter 6 is devoted to what is a social problem.

Look also at the following for more debate about the workings of hypotheses:

Preece, R. (1994) *Starting Research: An Introduction to Academic Research and Dissertation Writing.* London: Pinter.
A bit old but still relevant. See pp. 60–70.

Robson, C. (2011) *Real World Research*: *A Resource for Social Scientists and Practitioner-Researchers* (3rd edn). Oxford: Blackwell.
See chapter 3 for alternative ways to present your research problem.

For some really sophisticated reading about hypotheses and the logic behind testing them, see:

Trusted, J. (1979) *The Logic of Scientific Inference.* London: Methuen.
King, G., Keohane, R.O. and Verba, S. (1994) *Designing Social Inquiry: Scientific Inference in Qualitative Research.* Princeton, NJ: Princeton University Press.

SEVEN

Ethics

The value of research depends as much on its ethical veracity as on the novelty of its discoveries. How can we believe in the results of a research project if we doubt the honesty of the researchers and the integrity of the research methods used? It is easy to cheat and take short cuts, but is it worth it? The penalties resulting from discovery are stiff and humiliating. It is also easy to follow the simple guidelines of citation that avoid violations of intellectual property, and which also enhance your status as being well-read and informed about the most important thinkers in your subject.

To treat participants in your research with respect and due consideration is a basic tenet of civilized behaviour. Official concern about the ethical issues in research at any level that involves human subjects is growing. This means that there is a greater need to analyse the methods used in research in detail and to account for the decisions made when seeking official approval. Admittedly, the issues can become quite complicated, with no clear-cut solutions. It is therefore important that you consult with others, especially advisors appointed for that purpose.

Miller and Bell (2002, p. 67) suggest that keeping a constant record of decisions made is a good safeguard against sloppy thinking and inadvertent overlooking of ethical issues.

Using a research diary to document access routes and decisions made throughout the research process is one practical way of developing an ethics checklist. This practice of regular reflection helps ensure that ethical and methodological considerations are continually reassessed.

Ethics are the rules of conduct in research. You must know about ethics if you are required to do some research as part of your assessment. If you have to do an exam, it is likely that you will have a question about research ethics, as this is a really important issue that affects every aspect of research about people.

There are two perspectives from which you can view the ethical issues in research:

- The values of honesty and frankness and personal integrity.
- Ethical responsibilities to the subjects of research, such as consent, confidentiality and courtesy.

If you are working with human participants, it is likely that you will have to obtain some kind of ethical approval from your university or organization. It is necessary for you to find out what conditions apply in your situation.

Do: Note that while the principles underpinning ethical practice are fairly straightforward and easy to understand, their application can be quite difficult in certain situations. Not all decisions can be clear-cut in the realm of human relations.

HONESTY IN YOUR WORK

First consider those issues which are concerned with research activities generally, and the conduct of researchers in particular. Honesty is essential, not only to enable straightforward, above-board communication, but to engender a level of trust and credibility that promotes debate and the development of knowledge. This applies to all researchers, no matter what the subject. Although honesty must be maintained in all aspects of the research work, it is worth focusing here on several of the most important issues.

Intellectual ownership and plagiarism

Unless otherwise stated, what you write will be regarded as your own work; the ideas will be considered your own unless you say to the contrary. The worst offence against honesty in this respect is called plagiarism – directly copying someone else's work into your report, thesis, etc. and letting it be assumed that it is your own.

Don't: Use the thoughts, ideas and work of others without acknowledging the source, even if you have paraphrased them into your own words. This is unethical. Equally serious is claiming sole authorship of work that is in fact the result of collaboration or amanuensis ('ghosting').

Citation and acknowledgement

Obviously, in no field of research can you rely entirely on your own ideas, concepts and theories. Therefore standard practices have been developed to permit the originators of the work and ideas to be acknowledged within your own text. This is called **citation**. These methods of reference provide for direct quotations from the work of others and references from a wide variety of sources (such as books, journals, conferences, talks, interviews, television programmes, etc.), and should be meticulously used. You should also acknowledge the assistance of others and any collaboration with others.

Responsibility and accountability of the researcher

You do have responsibilities to fellow researchers, respondents, the public and the academic community. Apart from correct attribution, honesty is essential in the substance of what you write. Accurate descriptions are required of what you have done, how you have done it, the information you obtained, the techniques you used, the analysis you carried out and the results of experiments – a myriad of details concerning every part of your work.

Data and interpretations

There is often a temptation to be too selective in the data used and in presenting the results of the analysis carried out. Silently rejecting or ignoring evidence that happens to be contrary to one's beliefs constitutes a breach of integrity. What could be of vital importance in developing a theory could be lost. For example, the hypo-thetico-deductive method depends on finding faults in theoretical statements in order not only to reject them but to refine them and bring them nearer to the truth.

> **Don't:** It is difficult, and some maintain that it is impossible, to be free from bias. However, don't distort your data or results knowingly as this is a serious lapse of honesty.

Scientific objectivity should be maintained (or attained as closely as is practical). If you can see any reason for a possibility of bias in any aspect of the research, it should be acknowledged and explained. If the study involves personal judgements and assessments, the basis for these should be given. The sources of financial support for the research activities should be mentioned, and pressure and sponsor-ship from sources that might influence the impartiality of the research outcomes should be avoided.

> **Do:** It is good practice to admit to limitations of competence and resources. Promising more than you can deliver can be seen as not only foolhardy but also dishonest.

WHERE DO YOU STAND? - EPISTEMOLOGY

There are often lively debates about how research should be carried out, and the value and validity of the results derived from different approaches. The theoretical perspective, or **epistemology**, of the researcher should be made clear at the outset of the research so that the 'ground rules' or assumptions that underpin the research can be understood by the readers and, in some instances, the subjects of the research.

Do: Although others might disagree with your epistemology, you should at least make it clear to all what it is.

In many subjects it will initially be a challenging task to become aware of, and understand, all the current and past theoretical underpinnings to relevant research. One of the principal functions of doing background research is to explore just this aspect, and to come to decisions on theory that will form the basis of your research approach. You will have the opportunity to make this clear in your research proposal.

Don't: Ignore the fact that data analysis is an ethical issue and data analysis methods are not ethically neutral. They are founded on both ontological and epistemological assumptions.

SITUATIONS THAT RAISE ETHICAL ISSUES

Now let us consider ethics in terms of the personal relationships often involved in research projects. Social research, and other forms of research that study people and their relationships to each other and to the world, needs to be particularly sensitive about issues of ethical behaviour. As this kind of research often impinges on the sensibilities and rights of other people, researchers must be aware of necessary ethical standards that should be observed to avoid any harm which might be caused by carrying out or publishing the results of the research project.

Research aims

The aims of the research can be analysed from an ethical viewpoint. Is the research aimed merely at gaining greater knowledge and understanding of a phenomenon? If so, this kind of quest, seen in isolation, has little or no ethical consequences – the expansion of scientific knowledge is generally regarded as a good thing.

The aims of applied research are more easily subjected to ethical investigation. A series of questions can be posed to tease out the ethical issues:

- Are the aims clearly stated?
- Are the aims likely to be achieved by the outcomes of the research?
- Will the results of the research benefit society, or at least not harm it?
- Will there be losers as well as those who gain from the research?
- Are the aims of your research in accordance with the ethical standards proscribed by your university or organization?

Do: Aims that are too ambitious and that cannot be achieved by the planned research can be seen as a form of deception, or at least, self-delusion. It is necessary to be realistic.

Means and ends

How the aims, however laudable, are achieved should also be examined from an ethical viewpoint. 'No pain, no gain' is a popular expression, but can this approach be justified in a research project? There are many famous controversies that surround this issue, for example, the experiments on animals for developing and testing medicines, or the growing of test areas of genetically modified crops on open farmland.

Do: There might be several ways that the research aims can be achieved. You should look at the alternatives to see if there are any ethical implications in the choice.

ETHICS IN RELATION TO OTHER PEOPLE

Quite obviously, research ethics are principally concerned with the effects of research on people, and, importantly, on those people who get involved in the research process in one way or another. It is the researcher who plans the project who has the responsibility to predict what the effect will be on those people that he or she will approach and involve in the research, as subject, participant, respondent, interviewee, etc.

Use of language

Before going into details about the process of the research, it is worth discussing briefly the important influences of terminology used during the research. Let us look at the use of language first. According to an Open University guide to language and image (1993), there are five aspects to be aware of when writing:

Age – avoid being patronizing or disparaging.

Cultural diversity – avoid bias, stereotyping, omission, discrimination.

Disability – avoid marginalizing, patronizing.

Gender – avoid male centricity, gender stereotyping.

Sexual orientation – avoid prejudice, intolerance, discrimination.

The aim is to be as neutral as possible in the use of terminology involving people – who and what they are, and what they do.

> **Don't:** Use any of the many words and phrases in common usage that make unwarranted assumptions and assertions about people, or are at least imprecise and possibly insulting. Acceptable terminology changes with time, so you should be aware that what is used in some older literature is not suitable for use now. It requires you to be constantly aware of the real meaning of terms, and their use within the particular context.

Presentation

How will you present yourself in the role of the researcher? As a student-researcher, you can present yourself as just that, giving the correct impression that you are doing the research as an academic exercise that may reveal useful information or understanding, but do not have the institutional or political backing to cause immediate action. If you are a practitioner embarking on research (e.g. a teacher-researcher, nurse-researcher or social worker-researcher), then you have a professional status that lends you more authority and possibly power to instigate change. This may influence the attitude and expectations of the people you involve in your project.

> **Do:** Be aware – how one behaves with people during the research sends out strong signals and might raise unforeseen expectations.

Stopping people in the street and asking them a set of standardized questions is unlikely to elicit much engagement by the subjects. However, if you spend a lot of time with a, perhaps lonely, old person delving into her personal history, the more intimate situation might give rise to a more personal relationship that could go beyond the simple research context. How 'friendly' should you become? Even more expectations can be raised if you are working in a context of deprivation or inequality – will the subjects begin to expect you to do something to improve their situation?

Participants

Participants, subjects, respondents or whatever term you wish to use for the people you will approach for information to help your research, need to be treated with due ethical consideration, both on their own part and on the part of the information they provide. There are several issues that need to be considered when you use human participants. Here are some comments on a range of these to take into consideration.

Choosing participants

In some cases, participants themselves choose whether to take part in a survey. If you simply drop off a questionnaire at their house, they are quite free to fill it in or not, assuming that there is nothing in the questionnaire that threatens or otherwise affects a free choice. There are situations, however, where pressure, inadvertent or not, might be exerted on participants.

> **Don't:** Enlist friends or relatives, people who feel they have an obligation to help you despite reservations they may have and which could result in a restriction of their freedom to refuse. Leaving too little time for due consideration might also result in participants regretting their decision to take part.

Freedom from coercion. Reward or not?

Obviously, dishonest means of persuasion, for example, posing as an official, making unrealistic and untrue promises, allowing the belief that you have come to help, being unduly persistent and targeting people in vulnerable situations, must be avoided. Although it is easy to detect crass instances of these, you can sometimes find yourself employing them almost inadvertently if you are not alert to people's situations and reactions.

The question of whether, what and how much to reward the participants is one that is not often posed in research student projects, as the financial means are rarely sufficient to cover such incentives beyond perhaps the inclusion of reply-paid envelopes. However, in funded research this can be a real issue. Some commensurate recompense for time and inconvenience can usually be justified.

Gaining consent

An important aspect about participants' decisions to take part or not is the quality of the information they receive about the research, enabling them to make a fair assessment of the project so that they can give **informed consent**. The form that this information takes depends on the type of respondent, the nature of the research process and the context.

There may be several layers of consent required. When working within an organization, the managers or other people with overall responsibilities may need to be consulted before the individual participants.

> **Do:** Research can sometimes result in a conflict of interest, say between management and employees or unions. Do make clear and be agreed at all levels how the investigation will be conducted, how confidentiality will be maintained and what issues are to be discussed.

This is a particularly sensitive matter in cases where criticism may be made of persons, organizations or systems of work or conditions. There must be some obvious form of protection for those making criticisms and those at the receiving end.

> **Do:** Remember that clarity, brevity and frankness are key attributes in providing information on which consent is based.

Verbal explanations may suffice in informal situations, although a written résumé on a flyer could be useful. Questionnaires should always provide the necessary written information as an introduction. Gaining consent from vulnerable people (this includes children, some old people, the illiterate, foreign language speakers, those who are ill and even the deceased) requires particular consideration, depending on the circumstances.

> **Do:** Notwithstanding any agreement to take part in a research project, you must ensure that participants have the right to terminate their participation at any time.

The ethical issues raised by a research project have been vividly described by Emma Williams. The study was called 'Analysing public disposal behaviour: observational research' (Williams, 2015).

Of all the projects I have been involved with, the one that most clearly showed the range of issues that can confront an observational researcher was a study of littering behaviour in Australian cities, conducted some years ago. It led to follow-up studies and evaluations, a research method still in use and a series of publications – one of which received an award – while the issues that it raised, including ethical issues, still influence much of my research work today.

This case presented a number of ethical issues.

Informed consent

Generally, all research requires participants' informed consent. However, asking people whether they were willing to be research subjects would affect the 'naturalness' of the site and their behaviour, even if it was logistically possible in a site with hundreds of people moving in and out rapidly. Research institutions typically review research designs to see whether they comply with ethical guidelines before giving permission to proceed. They allow consent to be waived in certain conditions, such as where it would make the research impossible – as in the case of observing 'natural' behaviour in public places – and risks are minimal. (Examples of guidelines used in Australia and in Canada are in the reference list.)

Covert versus overt observation

Ethics guidelines also consider whether the research is overt or covert (i.e. whether participants are aware of the researcher); in some cases, researchers actively conceal themselves, and these cases require special justification. Generally in our observation sites – beaches, outdoor markets, parks and so on – we were not hidden from view, and people watched us while we were watching them. Observers placed themselves in a spot where they had a good vantage point of many potential disposal incidents and generally, to maintain the 'naturalness' of the site, tried to observe and record inconspicuously. However, there were times when some of those observed could see the researcher, but others would have had their view impeded. This was particularly the case when the observer was in a spot higher than some of those observed, such as watching from a restaurant balcony.

Ethics of matching data

Another potential ethical issue arose from matching observational and questionnaire data. By comparing people's responses about their behaviour to the actual observations of their behaviour, it would be possible to identify occasions when people littering misrepresented their behaviour to the interviewer and said that they had never littered or had not littered for years. However, the study met formal ethical guidelines as all information was provided anonymously, including the questionnaire responses. Even if an external party were to hack the data, all they could find would be that an elderly woman dressed in yellow had been seen littering in Adelaide but told an interviewer that she had never littered.

Balancing harm versus benefit

Finally, where there are ethical concerns relating to harm, these are balanced against the potential benefits of the research in order to determine whether it is to go ahead. This research project produced minimal risk, while benefits included the potential to develop better strategies to prevent future littering, therefore reducing pollution, and even the potential of the research to expose and correct stereotypes about who litters.

A European ethicist offered an interesting perspective when we were on a panel discussing the ethical issues posed by this project and others. The ethicist challenged those in the audience disapproving of observational research to consider more than human concerns in their thinking. As littering, particularly of plastic objects, is a known danger to marine life in particular, the interests of birds, fish and sea mammals should be included in the ethical decisions. This resulted in lively discussion, with many disagreeing.

CARRYING OUT THE RESEARCH

Potential harm and gain

Ethical research is aimed at causing no harm and, if possible, producing some gain, not only in the wider field, but for the participants in the project. A prediction must be made by the researcher about the potential of the chosen research methods and their outcomes for causing harm or gain.

> **Do:** The implications of involving people in your research are not always obvious, so if there are issues about which you are uncertain, you should consult with experts in the field who have had more experience.

What sorts of precaution should be taken? Find out how you can avoid risk to participants by recognizing what the risks might be, and choosing methods that minimize these risks.

Other types of harm to avoid are those that may result from the outcomes of the investigation. For example, can the results of the research be harmful in any way to the reputation, dignity or privacy of the subjects? Can it in any way alter the status quo to the disadvantage of the participants, for example, by unjustifiably raising their expectations or by souring their relationships with other people?

> **Do:** Take particular care when you are working in an unfamiliar social situation, for example, in an institution or among people of a different cultural or ethnic background. Being aware of the problems is halfway to solving them!

Interviews and questionnaires

When recording data, particularly from interviews and open questions, there is a danger of simplifying transcripts, and in the process losing some of the meaning. By cleaning up, organizing, ignoring vocal inflections, repetitions and asides, etc. you start to impose your own view or **interpretation**. This is difficult to avoid as the grammar and punctuation of written text impose their own rules that are different from those of verbal forms. Losing subtleties of humour can misrepresent emotional tone and meaning. Alldred and Gillies (2002, pp. 159–61) point out that speech is a 'messy' form of communication, and by writing it down we tend to make an account 'readable' and interpret 'what was meant'.

> **Don't:** Impose your own particular assumptions (e.g. in interviews), especially when questioning people of different backgrounds, culture or social status. Is the content of your interview based, perhaps, on white, western assumptions, or other assumptions inherent in your own cultural milieu?

Participant involvement – experiments, observations, groups

If your research entails close communication between you, the researcher and the participants, the issues of 'getting involved' and the question of rapport are raised. How will those involved understand your actions and are these in balance with your judgement about your own practice? Your intentions for your research might be to gain as much revealing information as possible, and by 'doing rapport' or faking friendship you might encourage the interviewee to open up. The intimacy between researcher and respondent can resemble friendship. This raises the question: is it taken so far as to deceive in order 'to encourage or persuade interviewees to explore and disclose experiences and emotions which – on reflection – they may have preferred to keep to themselves or even "not-to-know"' (Duncombe and Jessop, 2002, p. 120)?

Sensitive material

Research into human situations, whether it is in the workplace, in social settings, in care institutions or in education, can throw up information that is of a sensitive nature. This means that if the information is revealed, it could do damage to the participants or to other people. Revelations about the treatment of individuals due to the actions of others or due to the workings of an organization may call for action on the part of the researcher that is outside the remit of the project.

Every case must be judged individually, and careful thought must be given to the implications of divulging information to any third party. It may be possible to give advice to the participant about who to contact for help, such as a school tutor, trade union or ombudsman.

> **Don't:** Get personally involved as this can lead to unforeseen and unfortunate consequences that can not only cause harm to the participant and other people, but can also endanger your integrity and that of the research project. Take advice from your supervisor or ethics officer if the decisions are difficult.

Honesty, deception and covert methods

An ethically sound approach to research is based on the principle of honesty. This precludes any type of deception and use of covert methods. However, it may be argued that some kinds of information, which can be of benefit to society, can only be gained by these methods, because of obstruction by people or organizations that are not willing to risk being subjected to scrutiny. Injustices might be brought to light that are otherwise obscured by lack of information, such as discrimination, unfair working practices or the neglect of duties.

If the argument is based on the principle of doing good without doing harm, it must be recognized that the prediction of the outcomes of the research are speculative. How can one be sure of the benign consequences of the actions?

> **Do:** Be aware that the risks involved are such as to make the use of deception and covert methods extremely questionable, and even in some cases dangerous.

Storing and transmitting data

The data that you have collected will be, in many cases, sensitive; that is, they contain confidential details about people and/or organizations. It is therefore important to devise a storage system that is safe and only accessible to you. Paper-based and audio data should be locked away, and computer databases should be protected by a password. If it is necessary to transmit data, make sure that the method of transmission is secure. Emails and file transfers can be open to unauthorized access, so precautions should be taken to use the securest transmission method available.

The Data Protection Act 1998 covers virtually all collections of personal data in whatever form and at whatever scale in the UK. It spells out the rights of the subjects and the responsibilities of the compilers and holders of the data. You can search for a copy of this on the UK government website and for equivalent regulations on sites in other countries.

Checking data and drafts

It is normal practice to produce drafts of your work in order for you and others to check it for spelling and grammatical errors and for structure and content. It is appropriate to pass the drafts on to colleagues or supervisors for comment, with the proviso that the content is kept confidential, as at this stage it is not ready for publication and dissemination. It is generally not appropriate, however, to allow sponsors to make comments on a draft because of the danger that they may demand changes to be made to conclusions that are contrary to their interests. This could undermine the intellectual independence of the findings of the report.

> **Don't:** Let respondents read and edit large amounts of primary data, due to the delays it would cause and as they are unlikely to have the necessary skills to judge its validity and accuracy.

Dissemination

You may wish to disseminate your work by publishing the results in the form of conference or journal papers, a website or other types of publication. As this process inevitably involves reducing the length of the material, and perhaps changing the style of the writing for inclusion into professional journals or newspapers, you must be careful that the publication remains true to the original. Oversimplification, bias towards particular results or even sensationalization may result from targeting a particular readership.

> **Do:** Be aware of the fact that in most cases, the intellectual ownership of sponsored research remains with the researchers.

Disposing of records

When the data have been analysed and are no longer needed, a suitable time and method for disposal should be decided. Ideally, the matter will have been agreed with the participants as a part of their informed consent, so the decision will have been made much earlier.

One basic policy is to ensure that all the data are anonymous and non-attributable. This can be done by removing all labels and titles that can lead to identification.

> **Do:** When destroying data, make sure that they are disposed of in such a way as to be completely indecipherable. This might entail shredding documents, formatting discs and erasing tapes.

Take it further

Ethics policies, permissions and ethics committees

Organizations

All organizations that are involved in research concerning human participants will have set up a code of practice for their researchers. To see typical examples of these types of guidelines, you can refer to the web page produced by the British Educational Research Association (which can be found by searching for BERA guidelines on Google or the British Sociological Association statement of ethical practice). Your university will certainly have set up its own code of practice.

(Continued)

(Continued)

Ethics committees

The role of ethics committees is to oversee the research carried out in their organizations in relation to ethical issues. It is they who formulate the research ethics code of conduct and monitor its application in the research carried out by members of their organizations. Your university or other institution will probably have a system that makes it possible for its research committee to do its job. This, inevitably, involves filling in forms.

Beyond the moral obligations of research, there are forms of behaviour and etiquette desirable in the civilized pursuit of knowledge that should be observed when communicating with people. A considerate and courteous attitude to people will also help to improve their readiness to assist you and provide you with the information you require.

> **Do:** Remember that you are relying on their cooperation and generosity to make your research possible, and this should be acknowledged in your attitude and behaviour.

You should devise a systematic method of making requests for information, interviews, visits, etc., together with one for confirmation of appointments, letters of thanks, and some follow-up and feedback where appropriate.

Ask yourself

Summarize the major areas in which ethics plays an important role in social research.

You could easily write a lot in response to this. Two areas can be highlighted: honesty and integrity in the writing and presentation of the research, and the due consideration for the people involved in the research project. You can then detail the various and numerous aspects within these areas, as is outlined quite briefly in this chapter.

What is the difference between being an observer and a participant in a research project? What different ethical issues are associated with these roles?

Observing without being involved in the process under examination implies a certain detachment from the events. The issue of whether you are seen to be observing by the subjects is also relevant. Invasion of privacy and lack of consent are two possible major ethical issues here. Taking part in the process raises the concern about how to avoid unduly influencing the proceedings, or being carried away by them. Intimate and sensitive material might be revealed. Numerous other ethical issues are likely to be involved, many of which will be shared by other methods of data collection and handling.

What precautions must you take to avoid being accused of plagiarism?

Unlike journalists, it is incumbent on researchers to reveal their sources. It is accepted that all investigation work is at least partly based on previous work, and you must acknowledge the authors of the material you use. As long as you acknowledge your sources, you cannot be accused of plagiarism, although you may be accused of unoriginality! You can run through the different ways in which you can legitimately use other people's writing and thinking, and the accepted forms of citation, reference and acknowledgement.

Further reading

Although ethical behaviour should underlay all academic work, it is in the social sciences (as well as medicine, etc.) that the really difficult issues arise. Researching people and society raises many ethical questions that are discussed in the books below. The first set of books are aimed generally at student and professional researchers, the second set are examples of more specialized books, although the issues remain much the same for whoever is doing research involving human participants.

Oliver, P. (2010) *The Student's Guide to Research Ethics*. Maidenhead: Open University Press.
This is an excellent review of the subject, going into detail on all aspects of ethics in research, and providing useful examples of situations where ethical questions are raised. It demonstrates that there are not always simple answers to these questions, but suggests precautions that can be taken to avoid transgressions.

Laine, M. de (2000) *Fieldwork, Participation and Practice: Ethics and Dilemmas in Qualitative Research*. London: Sage.
The main purposes of this book are to promote an understanding of the harmful possibilities of fieldwork and to provide ways of dealing with ethical problems and dilemmas. Examples of actual fieldwork are provided that address ethical problems and dilemmas, and show ways of dealing with them.

Mauthner, M. (ed.) (2002) *Ethics in Qualitative Research*. London: Sage.
This book explores ethical issues in research from a range of angles, including: access and informed consent, negotiating participation, rapport, the intentions of feminist research, epistemology and data analysis, and the tensions between being a professional researcher and a 'caring' professional. The book includes practical guidelines to aid ethical decision making rooted in feminist ethics of care.

Geraldi, O. (ed.) (2000) *Danger in the Field: Ethics and Risk in Social Research*. London: Routledge.
Read this if you are going into situations that might be ethically hazardous.

Townend, D. (2000) 'Can the law prescribe an ethical framework for social science research?', in D. Burton (ed.), *Research Training for Social Scientists*. London: Sage.
There are also books about ethics that specialize in certain fields. Here are some examples. You can also search out some in your subject.

(Continued)

(Continued)

Whitbeck, C. (2011) *Ethics in Engineering Practice and Research*. Cambridge: Cambridge University Press.

Farrell, A. (2005) *Ethical Research with Children*. Maidenhead: Open University Press.

Alderson, P. and Morrow, V. (2011) *The Ethics of Research with Children and Young People*. London: Sage.

McNamee, M. and Bridges, D. (eds) (2002) *The Ethics of Educational Research*. Oxford: Blackwell Publishers.

For nurses, the best resource is probably the online document from the Royal College of Nursing on Research Ethics: www.rcn.org.uk/__data/assets/pdf_file/0007/388591/003138.pdf

EIGHT

Writing a Research Proposal

Before you have to do an undergraduate dissertation or any other research project, you will normally be asked to produce a proposal of what you are planning to research and write about. This will enable your tutor to make sure that the subject is suitable and that the planned project is 'do-able' within the time and resources available.

We have already discussed the literature review that forms a part of the proposal, but what about the rest? Here is a summary of what you need to write.

A proposal is a careful description of what your dissertation or research project will be about and how you intend to carry out the work involved until its completion. It is a really useful document that challenges you to think very carefully about what you are going to do, how you will do it and why. It will be required in order to inform your supervisor of your intentions so that he or she can judge whether:

- The subject and suggested format conforms to the requirements of the course
- It is a feasible project in respect to scope and practicality
- You have identified some questions or issues that are worth investigating
- Your suggested methods for information collection and analysis are appropriate
- The expected outcomes relate to the aims of the project.

> **Do:** When you write your proposal, it not only gives you an opportunity to crystallize your thoughts before you embark on the project, but it also allows you to consider how much you will actually be able to achieve within the few weeks/months allowed.

You will not be able to sit down and write your proposal without referring to your background research. A good proposal will indicate how your chosen topic emerges from issues that are being debated within your subject field, and how your work will produce a useful contribution to the debate. At this level of research, you do not have to produce any earth-shattering discoveries, but it is necessary to produce some useful insights through the appropriate application of research theory and methods.

Because the proposal must be quite short (usually not more than one or two sides of paper) a lot of thought needs to be put into its production in order to cover all the matter that needs to be conveyed in an elegantly dense manner. Several redrafts will be needed in order to pare it down to the limited length allowed, so don't panic if you cannot get it all together first time. A really informative proposal will not only impress your supervisor, but will also give you a good guide to the work. It will also help you to focus on the important issues if (and probably, when) you get diverted on to branching paths of investigation later on in the project.

There is a fairly standardized format for writing proposals that, if followed, ensures that you cover all the important aspects that must be included. The following advice will help you to focus on the essential matters and help you to make the hard choices required at this early stage in the project.

THE SUBJECT TITLE

The subject title summarizes in a few words the entire project. You will probably not be able to formulate this finally until you have completed the proposal, but you will need something to be going on with in order to focus your thinking.

A title should contain the key words of the dissertation subject, that is, the main subjects, concepts or situations. Added to these are normally a few words that delineate the scope of the study. For example:

> Temporary housing in the suburbs: the expansion of residential caravan sites in British cities in the 1970s.

Start, therefore, by summing up the core of your chosen subject by its principal concepts. To find these, refer to the background reading you have done. What words are mentioned in the book titles, the chapter headings and the contents lists? These may be quite esoteric, but should represent the very heart of your interest. They should also, when linked together, imply an issue or even a question.

This part of the title will, by its nature, be rather general and even abstract. In order to describe the nature of the project itself, more detail will be required to state its limitations, such as the location, time and extent. Locations can be countries or towns, types of place or situations. Time might be historical periods, the present or during specific events.

The previous delineations help to define the extent of the project, but further factors can be added, such as under certain conditions, in particular contexts, etc.

A few examples here will give you the general idea:

In Brazil

In market towns

In one-to-one teaching lessons

In the sixteenth century

Contemporary trends

During the General Strike

After motorway accidents

High-altitude mountaineering

THE AIMS OR OBJECTIVES

The aims or objectives of the project should be summarized in three or four bullet points. This then provides a very succinct summary of the thrust of the research and provides an introduction to the rationale that follows.

> **Don't:** Ignore the importance of your aims. If you find it difficult to write your aims, then you have probably not thought sufficiently about what you are actually going to do.

Some useful indicative words you can use are: to explore, to test, to investigate, to explain, to compare, to predict. Ensure that there is an indication of the limits of the project by mentioning place, time, extent, etc. Here is an example:

Social interaction in children's playgrounds in parks

Aims

- To examine the range of social interactions that occur in children's playgrounds in four different parks.
- To compare the design of the playgrounds and types of park in which they are situated.
- To explore the possible connections between characteristics of the playgrounds and parks, and types of social interactions.

THE BACKGROUND

Anyone reading your proposal for the first time needs to be informed about the context of the project and where it fits in with current thinking. Do not assume that the reader knows anything about the subject, so introduce it in such a way that any intelligent person can understand the main issues surrounding your work. That is the one function of the background section. The other function is to convince your supervisor that you have done the necessary reading into the subject, and that you have reviewed the literature sufficiently. This is why it is necessary to have a good range of references in this section. See Chapter 5 on how to write a literature review.

DEFINING THE RESEARCH PROBLEM

Based on the issues explained and discussed in the background section you should be able to identify the particular part of the subject that you want to investigate.

> **Do:** Every subject could be studied for a lifetime, so it is important that you isolate just one small facet of the subject that you can manageably deal with in the short amount of time that you are given.

Once you have explained the topic of your study, and argued why it is necessary to do work in this area, it is a good idea briefly to state the research problem in one or two clear sentences. This will be a direct reflection of your title, and will sum up the central question or problem that you will be investigating.

> **Do:** Devise a clear definition of the research problem, as this is an essential ingredient of a proposal; after all, the whole project hinges on this.

The nature of the problem also determines the issues that you will explore, the kind of information that you will collect and the types of analysis that you will use. The main research problem should grow naturally and inevitably out of your discussion of the background. You can state it clearly as a question, hypothesis, etc. Then explain briefly how it will be broken down into sub-problems, hypotheses, etc. in order to make it practicable to research. There should be a connection between these and the aims or objectives of the project – everything should link up neatly.

THE MAIN CONCEPTS AND VARIABLES

Every subject has its own way of looking at things, its own terminology and its own ways of measuring. Consider the differences between analysing the text of a Shakespearean play and the data transmitted back from a space probe. You will certainly be familiar with some of the concepts that are important in your subject – just look at the title you have chosen for examples of these. It will probably be necessary to define the main concepts in order to dispel any doubts as to their exact meaning. There might even be some dispute in the literature about terminology. If so, highlight the nature of the discussion.

A mention of the indicators that are used to make the concepts recognizable will be the first step to breaking down the abstract nature of most concepts. Then a description of the variables that are the measurable components of the indicators can be used to demonstrate how you will actually be able to collect and analyse the relevant data to come to conclusions about the concepts and their nature.

You do not need to write much here, just enough to convince the reader that you are clear as to how you can investigate the abstract concepts with which you might be dealing, for example, suitability, success, creativity, quality of life, etc. Even well-known terms might need to be broken down to ensure that the reader understands just how you will study them.

METHODS

What exactly will you do in order to collect and analyse the necessary information? This is the practical part of the proposal where you explain what you will do, how you will do it and why. It is important to demonstrate the way that your research activities relate to the aims or objectives of your project and thus will enable you to come to conclusions relevant to the research problem. Different methods will be required for different parts of the research. At this stage you need not know in detail just how you will implement them, but you should quite easily be able to choose those that seem appropriate for different aspects of your enquiry. Consider the following actions that you might need to take:

- Do a literature search and critical analysis of sources.
- Consult with experts.
- Identify research population(s), situations, possible case studies.
- Select samples - size of sample(s), location of sample(s), number of case studies.
- Collect data (quantitative, qualitative and combination of both) - questionnaires, interviews, study of documents, observations, etc.
- Set up experiments or models and run them.
- Analyse data - statistical tests, enumerating and classifying, data displays for data reduction and analysis.
- Evaluate results of analysis - summarizing and coming to conclusions.

It is best to spell out what you intend to do in relation to each sub-problem or question when they require different methods of data collection and analysis.

Try to be precise and add reasons for what you are planning to do (i.e. add the phrase 'in order to …'). This methods section of the proposal can be in the form of a list of actions.

> **Do:** This whole process will need quite a lot of thought and preparation, especially as you will not be familiar with some of the research methods. But time spent now to make informed decisions is well spent. It will make you much more confident that you can plan your project, that you have not overreached yourself and that you have decided on activities that you will enjoy doing.

EXPECTED OUTCOMES

It is a good idea to spell out to the reader, and to yourself, just what you hope will be achieved by doing all this work. Since the proposal is a type of contract to deliver certain results, it is a mistake to 'promise mountains and deliver molehills'. Although you cannot predict exactly what the outcomes will be (if you could, there would be little point in carrying out the research), you should try to be quite precise as to the nature and scope of the outcomes and as to who might benefit from the information. Obviously you should make sure that the outcomes relate directly to the aims of the research that you described at the beginning of the proposal. The outcomes may be a contribution at a practical and/or theoretical level.

PROGRAMME OF WORK

A simple bar chart showing the available time in weeks and the list of tasks you will need to complete, and their sequence and duration, will be a sufficient programme of work. Don't forget to give yourself plenty of time to write up and present your dissertation. You will quickly spot if you have been too ambitious in your intentions if the tasks just will not fit realistically into time allowed. If you see problems ahead, now is the time to adjust your proposal to make it more feasible. Reduce the scope of the investigations by narrowing the problem still further (you can do this by becoming more specific and by reducing the number of sub-problems or questions), being less ambitious with the amount of data to collect and by simplifying the analytical stages.

Take it further

Start to write your proposal! The biggest danger is that you agonize for ages over what to do before you even write anything down. This is a mistake, for if you try to work out everything in your head you cannot realistically review it. Committing yourself to paper not only relieves your memory from having to retain all your decisions, but also forces you to construct an argument to structure your intentions. Once you have something written down, you can review it, build on it, add detail to it and alter it as required.

The best way to start is by sketching out your ideas, perhaps as a series of headings or points, and you don't have to worry too much what you write down, as it can so easily be altered, moved, expanded or even deleted. You can work like a painter who first sketches out a few indicative lines, then builds on these to produce, stage by stage, a finished picture. Assuming you have a good idea of the sort of problem you wish to address, you don't even have to start at the beginning. You could work back from the desired outcomes and create a rationale on how you would get there. Or you could select the activities that you enjoy doing most and explore how you could exploit these to devise a project. Once you have a framework that looks feasible, you can add the detail – work that will require rather more reflection and reference to further information.

You should set out the final version according to the structure outlined above. You will also need to add a list of references that give the details about the publications cited in your text. Check with any coursework instructions you have been given to make sure that you are fulfilling the requirements. When you have finished, why not give a copy to your supervisor and request his or her comments? Be prepared to alter your proposal in response to any comments you receive, but first think carefully about the implications of these changes. The comments should help to make life easier for you, or clarify the implications of your proposals. It is also in the interest of your supervisor that you do well and enjoy the experience of writing your dissertation.

Once finalized and approved, the proposal will form a firm foundation for your research work. You should refer to it from time to time during the next weeks when you get into the detail of your work, in order to check that you are not going astray, getting too bogged down on one particular aspect or missing out on an essential detail.

Ask yourself

What is the connection between words in the title of your project and the research questions?

The words you use in your title will be the main concepts at the heart of the research, and perhaps something about their relationship. Your main research question should definitely contain all of those concepts, and the sub-questions should be expressed in such a way that in answering them, you will examine those concepts and their relationships. Do make sure that you always use the same terminology – never different words in different parts of the dissertation even if they mean much the same thing.

How can you relate the research methods to the research questions?

You should select the research methods for collecting and analysing data based on their suitability for finding answers to the research questions, not the other way round.

(Continued)

(Continued)

When a student comes to me and says 'I want to do a survey', I always ask 'why?' Actually, it makes it much easier to decide on the methods to use from the huge choice in front of you when you can identify the functions that they will have to fulfil.

What is the sequence of sections of a typical research proposal?

The sections should follow a logical sequence, going from the general to the particular, after the introduction consisting of the title and aims and objectives. The background research and literature review (general) should result in the identification of the problem and identify the research questions (getting more specific). The explanation of selection of research methods details how these research questions will be answered (even more specific). The expected outcomes and programme of work tie the project down to results and timing (bang on specific to this project).

Further reading

There are books that are solely dedicated to writing academic proposals of all kinds. The principles are the same for all of them; it is the extent and detail that vary. All are reasoned arguments to support a plan of action. If you want to read more, or find different approaches to proposal writing, you can explore some of these books. Some will be rather too detailed for your purposes, but you will undoubtedly find something useful. Every book on how to do dissertations will also have a section on writing a proposal. Several have been mentioned in previous chapters.

Denscombe, M. (2012) *Research Proposal: a Practical Guide*. Maidenhead: Open University Press.
This explains the basic principles and gives clear guidance on what to include in your proposal.

Locke, L.F. (2007) *Proposals That Work: a Guide for Planning Dissertations and Grant Proposals* (5th edn). London: Sage.
Another clear guide to all the aspects of proposal writing.

Coley, S.M. and Scheinberg, C.A. (2008) *Proposal Writing* (3rd edn). London: Sage with the University of Michigan.
This book is written for employees in the non-profit sector who are asked to write a proposal and for students who may ultimately have careers that require this skill.

Punch, K. (2006) *Developing Effective Proposals* (2nd edn). London: Sage.
Dealing with both qualitative and quantitative approaches to empirical research across the social sciences, this book comprehensively covers the topics and concerns relevant to the subject and is organized around three central themes: what is a research proposal, who reads proposals and why? How can we go about developing a proposal? What might a finished proposal look like?

Denicolo, P. and Becker, L. (2012) *Developing Research Proposals.* London: Sage.
This will help you to understand the context within which your proposal will be read, what the reviewers are looking for and will be influenced by, while also supporting the development of relevant skills through advice and practical activities.

Vithal, R. and Jansen, J. (2010) *Designing Your First Research Proposal: A Manual for Researchers in Education and the Social Sciences* (2nd edn). Cape Town: Juta.
This manual presents a simple, clear and coherent strategy for preparing research proposals. It is a practical, application-focused guide to writing a proposal for basic and advanced research projects.

PART II

COLLECTING AND ANALYSING YOUR DATA

NINE
Sampling

A census is a survey of all of the cases in a population. An example of this is a National Census, where everyone in the nation is asked to return a questionnaire. A census is a very costly and time-consuming project.

If you want to get information about a large group of people or organizations, it is normally impossible to get all of them to answer your questions – it would take much too long and be far too expensive. The solution is to just ask some of them and hope that the answers they give are representative (or typical) of the ones the rest would give. If their answers really are the same as the others would give, then you need not bother to ask the rest; rather, you can draw conclusions from those answers, which you can then relate to the whole group. This process of selecting just a small group of people from a large group is called sampling. There are several things you must consider in selecting a **sample**, so before discussing the different methods of data collection, let us first deal with the issue of sampling.

A REPRESENTATIVE SAMPLE?

When conducting any kind of survey to collect information, or when choosing some particular cases to study in detail, the question inevitably arises: how representative is the information collected of the whole population? In other words, how similar are the characteristics of the small group of cases that are chosen to those of all the cases in the whole type group.

> **Do:** To be able to make accurate judgements about a population from a sample, you should make sure that the sample is as representative as possible.

When we talk about population in research, it does not necessarily mean a number of people. **Population** is a collective term used to describe the total quantity of things (or cases) of the type that is the subject of your study. So a population can consist of objects, people or even events (e.g. schools, miners, revolutions). A complete list of cases in a population is called a **sampling frame**. This list may be more or less accurate. A sample is a number of cases selected from the sampling frame that you want to subject to closer study.

⊗ | **Don't:** Forget that it is not always possible to obtain a representative sample. You might not know what the characteristics of the population are, or you might not be able to reach sectors of it. Non-representative samples cannot be used to make accurate generalizations about the population.

For example, if you wish to survey the opinions of the members of a small club, there might be no difficulty in getting information from each member, so the results of the survey will represent those of the whole club membership. However, if you wish to assess the opinions of the members of a large trade union, apart from organizing a national ballot, you will have to devise some way of selecting a sample of the members whom you can question, and who are a fair representation of all the members of the union. Sampling must be done whenever you can gather information from only a fraction of the population of a group that you want to study. Ideally, you should try to select a sample that is free from bias. You will see that the type of sample you select will greatly affect the reliability of your subsequent generalizations.

There are basically two types of sampling procedure:

Probability sampling - based on random selection.

Non-probability sampling - based on non-random selection.

Probability sampling techniques give the most reliable representation of the whole population, while non-probability techniques, relying on the judgement of the researcher or by accident, cannot be used to make generalizations about the whole population.

PROBABILITY SAMPLING

This is based on using random methods to select the sample. Populations are not always quite as uniform or one-dimensional as, say, a particular type of component in a production run, so simple random selection methods are not always appropriate. The selection procedure should aim to guarantee that each element (person, group, **class**, type, etc.) has an equal chance of being selected and that every possible combination of the elements also has an equal chance of being selected.

The first question asked should be about the nature of the population: is it homogeneous or are there distinctly different types of case within it? If there are different types within the population, how are they distributed (e.g. are they grouped in different locations, found at different levels in a hierarchy or are all mixed up together)? Different sampling techniques are appropriate for each.

The next question to ask is: which process of randomization will be used? The following gives a guide to which technique is suited to the different population characteristics.

Simple random sampling is used when the population is uniform or has common characteristics in all cases (e.g. medical students, international airports, dairy cows). A simple form of random selection would be to pick names from a hat or, for samples from larger populations, assigning a number to each case on the sampling frame and using random numbers generated by computer or from random number tables to make the selection.

Systematic sampling is an alternative to random sampling and can be used when the population is very large and of no known characteristics (e.g. the population of a town), or when the population is known to be very uniform (e.g. cars of a particular model being produced in a factory). The method of systematic selection involves the selection of units in a series (e.g. on a list or from a production line) according to a predetermined system. There are many possible systems. Perhaps the simplest is to choose every *nth* case on a list, for example, every 10th person in a telephone directory or list of ratepayers, or every 100th model off the production line. In using this system, it is important to pick the first case randomly (i.e. the first case on the list is not necessarily chosen). The type of list is also significant: not everyone in the town owns a telephone or is a ratepayer.

Simple stratified sampling should be used when cases in the population fall into distinctly different categories or strata (e.g. a business whose workforce is divided into the three categories of production, research and management). With the presence of distinctly different strata in a population, in order to achieve simple randomized sampling, an equally sized randomized sample is obtained from each stratum separately to ensure that each is equally represented. The samples are then combined to form the complete sample from the whole population.

Proportional stratified sampling is used when the cases in a population fall into distinctly different categories (strata) of a known proportion of that population (e.g. a university in which the proportions of the students studying arts and sciences is 61 per cent and 39 per cent, respectively). When the proportions of the different strata in a population are known, then each stratum must be represented in the same proportions within the overall sample. In order to achieve proportional randomized sampling, a randomized sample is obtained from each stratum separately, sized according to the known proportion of each stratum in the whole population, and then combined as previously to form the complete sample from the population.

Cluster sampling is used in cases when the population forms clusters by sharing one or some characteristics but are otherwise as heterogeneous as possible, for example, travellers using main railway stations. They are all train travellers, with each cluster experiencing a distinct station, but individuals vary as to age, sex, nationality, wealth, social status, etc. Also known as **area sampling**, cluster sampling is used when the population is large and spread over a large area. Rather than enumerating the whole population, it is divided into segments, and then several segments are chosen at random. Samples are subsequently obtained from each of these segments using one of the above sampling methods.

Multi-stage cluster sampling is an extension of cluster sampling, where clusters of successively smaller size are selected from within each other. For example, you might take a random sample from all UK universities, then a random sample from subjects within those universities, then a random sample of modules taught in those subjects, then a random sample of the students doing those modules.

Sean D. Cleary, Lauren Simmons, Idalina Cubilla, Elizabeth Andrade and Mark Edberg explained in 2014 how they carried out 'Community sampling: sampling in an immigrant community' (Cleary et al., 2014).

They describe how the sample was selected to evaluate the *Adelante* intervention, a community-based participatory research study addressing a complex of contributing factors for substance abuse, violence and sexual risk behaviours in an immigrant Hispanic community.

Boundary study

The first research challenge was to define a community that does not have geopolitical boundaries. Through the *Adelante* intervention, we aimed to provide intervention activities across the entire community. To do so, under the direction of Mark Edberg, a community boundary study was conducted with the goal of defining the geographic boundaries of the target community *from the perspective of community residents*. Using geographic information system software, we mapped utilization of services provided by a partner community organization. We observed that many residents were outside the census tract boundaries used in the *SAFER* study.

To ensure that we covered the entire community in the *Adelante* study, an ethnographic team was created, including public health professionals and anthropology graduate students. The team made multiple visits to the community to collect descriptive data on the 'community' areas and to conduct interviews with residents to assess the geographic 'boundaries' of the community. This information was used to create new community boundaries and to stratify the community into five geographic regions of similar residential characteristics. The new community boundaries were validated by comparing them to maps created by other community groups. These groups had conducted similar studies and used their maps as the basis for both community survey sampling and outreach planning.

Population estimates

The US Census, conducted every 10 years, is a valuable source of information about the size and characteristics of the population as well as subpopulations. In 2005, we conducted an intervention study, *SAFER*, within the same community. As part of that study, we completed three community surveys that covered a smaller geographic region (based on two census tracts). However, when the baseline survey was conducted, we found many more people living in the community than was indicated by census data. There are many factors related to the accuracy of the census that were relevant to the intervention community including the high rates of migration into and out of the community, the large proportion of the population that does not have legal residency status and the high density of renters. Despite the likely underestimate of the population in the intervention community, data from the 2010 US Census were abstracted for population counts by Hispanic ethnicity, gender and age. We used the observed distribution of the surveyed population by gender and age to guide the stratification for the current study.

Stratified two-stage random cluster sampling plan

To evaluate the impact of the *Adelante* intervention, we defined the unit of analysis as youth (aged 12–17 years) and/or young adults (aged 18–24 years) living in an apartment or single-family home. The sampling unit was the apartment or single-family home, and clusters were defined as either apartments within a building or an artificial cluster of single-family homes of approximately equal density and size. The target sample size for the community survey was $n = 1200$. The approximate number of subjects sampled from the eligible population by age and gender was estimated based on available census estimates as well as previous surveys in the community. We utilized a stratified two-stage random cluster sampling approach. Following is a step-by-step description of the process.

Step 1

Population estimates were computed and combined across the five geographic regions (strata) to get an estimate of the total population aged 12–17 and 18–24 years. For an apartment complex, we multiplied the number of buildings by the number of apartments per building to get the total number of apartments. We multiplied the density estimate by the number of apartments to get an approximate total population. We then multiplied the total population by the estimate of the proportion of Hispanics in the complex to get the total Hispanic population size. For single-family homes, we multiplied the number of households by the estimated density, and then by the estimated proportion of Hispanics to get an estimate of the total Hispanic population. Estimates were summed across all apartment complexes and single-family home clusters in each of the five regions and then multiplied by the proportion of youth and young adults observed from our previous study for the age-group-specific target sample size in each region. Totals for the entire community were computed and compared with abstracted census data. On average, our estimates were 48 per cent and 62 per cent higher than the census data for youth and young adults, respectively.

(Continued)

(Continued)

Step 2

Estimating the number of households needed to be visited to achieve the target sample size. Sample size calculations for each age- and gender-specific group in the intervention community were computed based on previously observed prevalence estimates of violent behaviour. For the *Adelante* intervention, we estimated that surveyors would have to approach at least 10 per cent more households to reach an eligible youth and/ or young adult in each household. We divided the total number of households required to achieve the target sample size by 10 per cent to get our target number of households, then divided by 30 to estimate the number of days of work required to complete the survey.

Sampling - stage 1

Step 3

Apartment complexes and single-family homes were divided into approximately equal sized clusters in all five regions. The total number of households (apartments or single-family homes) in each complex or geographic region was divided by 30 to identify a cluster; 30 households is the estimated number of households that could be visited by the data collection team on any given day. The total number of clusters for each apartment complex and section of single-family homes were summed to get an estimate of the number of households. Maps of each apartment complex and single-family homes with addresses in each geographic region were divided into equally sized clusters. These maps were used by surveyors in the field to guide the data collection.

Sampling - stage 2

Step 4

We identified clusters in each region to be sampled. In total, 54 of the 200 clusters needed to be sampled to achieve the target age-specific samples. We calculated the sampling interval (systematic sampling) by dividing the total eligible population estimate by the total number of clusters. A random start value was chosen from a random number table. Clusters to be sampled were identified in each region by adding the sampling interval to the start value, and then to each successive value until the sample was exhausted and 54 clusters were identified. The map of the cluster and household addresses were produced in a sheet so that data collectors could track data collection progress. Every household in a cluster was contacted at least twice before moving on to the next cluster, and all eligible youth and/or young adults were approached for participation in the study.

NON-PROBABILITY SAMPLING

Non-probability sampling is based on selection by non-random means. This can be useful for certain studies, but it provides only a weak basis for generalization.

Accidental sampling (or convenience sampling) involves using what is immediately available (e.g. studying the building you happen to be in, examining the work practices in your firm, etc.). There are no ways of checking to see if this kind of sample is in any way representative of others of its kind, so the results of the study can be applied only to that sample.

Quota sampling is used regularly by reporters interviewing on the streets. It is an attempt to balance the sample interviewed by selecting responses from equal numbers of different respondents (e.g. equal numbers from different political parties). This is an unregulated form of sampling as there is no knowledge of whether the respondents are typical of their parties. For example, Labour respondents might just have come from an extreme left-wing rally.

Theoretical sampling is a useful method of getting information from a sample of the population that you think knows most about a subject. A study on homelessness could concentrate on questioning people living on the street. This approach is common in qualitative research where statistical inference is not required.

Purposive sampling is where the researcher selects what he or she thinks is a 'typical' sample based on specialist knowledge or selection criteria.

Systematic matching sampling is used when two groups of very different size are compared by selecting a number from the larger group to match the number and characteristics of the smaller one.

Snowball sampling is where the researcher contacts a small number of members of the target population and gets them to introduce him or her to others (e.g. of an exclusive club or an underground organization).

Dawn Branley, Judith Covey and Mariann Hardley reported in 2014 on a research project entitled 'Online surveys: investigating social media use and online risk'. The section reproduced here is about the sampling method they used (Branley et al., 2014).

Online surveys have many advantages but they also provide their own unique challenges. By sharing our experiences, we highlight the issues that one may face when recruiting for an online survey and offer our advice on how to overcome these obstacles.

Snowball sampling

Snowball sampling refers to recruiting respondents by asking existing respondents to recommend the study to their acquaintances, that is, friends, family and colleagues. This

(Continued)

(Continued)

technique helps the sample to grow further each time respondents roll out the information to their social network, that is, the numbers grow in size like a rolling snowball hence the term 'snowball sampling'.

We utilized snowball sampling to reach as many potential respondents as possible. This is a particularly effective method when used via social media such as Facebook or Twitter as social media enables respondents to easily and conveniently share the study with everyone in their social circle, for example, by 'sharing' on Facebook or 'Retweeting' on Twitter.

We also searched for social media groups who would be happy to share details of our study on their page. For example, Facebook and LinkedIn have many groups dedicated to research and respondent recruitment. We found that Twitter groups from the local area, or those that share a common interest within the research area, are often happy to share a link to the survey. Similarly, it is worth checking whether your college, university or organization has any social media accounts and if they would be happy to share your survey information. A few retweets (i.e. when another Twitter user reposts your message) can rapidly increase your audience by hundreds or even thousands of people. For example, if just one person retweets your link to their 100 followers (i.e. their social connections on Twitter), and then just 10 per cent of those people retweet to another 100 followers each, you have already reached 1100 additional potential respondents in just two little steps, imagine if the retweets continue to their followers, and their followers and so on.

SAMPLE SIZE

Having selected a suitable sampling method, the remaining problem is to determine the sample size. The first impression is that the bigger the sample size, the more possibility there is of representing all the different characteristics of the population. It is generally accepted that conclusions reached from the study of a large sample are more convincing than those from a small one.

> **Do:** Balance the preference for a large sample against the practicalities of the research resources, that is, cost, time and effort.

If the population is very homogeneous, and the study is not very detailed, then a small sample will give a fairly representative view of the whole. The greater the accuracy required in the true representation of the population, then the larger the sample must be. The amount of variability within the population (technically known as the **standard deviation**) is also significant. Obviously, in order that every sector of a diverse population is adequately represented, a larger sample will be required than if the population were more homogeneous.

> **Do:** If you will use statistical tests to analyse the data, remember that there are usually minimum sample sizes specified from which any significant results can be obtained. The size of the sample should also be in direct relationship to the number of variables to be studied.

A simple method of clarifying the likely size of sample required in a study is to set up a table which cross-references the variability in the population with the number of variables you wish to study. Table 9.1 shows a table for a study of the effect of the number of drinks on driving performance around a course delineated by bollards. Dixon (1987) suggests that for a very simple survey, at least five cases are required in each cell (i.e. $12 \times 5 = 60$). Obviously, if the variables are split into smaller units of measurement (i.e. the number of drinks is increased), then the overall size of the sample must be increased. Dixon also suggests that at least 30 cases are required for even the most elementary kinds of analysis.

Table 9.1 Variables and Variability

Variable A (Values) Number of drinks	Variation in population (standard deviation) Number of bollards collided with		
	1	2	3
1	At least five cases in each of these cells		
2			
3			
4			

SAMPLING ERROR

No sample will be exactly representative of a population. If different samples, using identical methods, are taken from the same population, there are bound to be differences in the mean (average) values of each sample owing to the chance selection of different individuals. The measured difference between the mean value of a sample and that of the population is called the **sampling error**, which will lead to bias in the results. **Bias** is the unwanted distortion of the results of a survey due to parts of the population being more strongly represented than others.

Factors that can lead to sampling error include:

- The use of non-probability sampling
- An inadequate sampling frame
- Non-response by sectors of the sample.

Take it further

Multiple case study selection

When you wish to study several case studies you are faced with the problem of how to choose them. The most common reason for selecting more than one case study is so that several cases can be compared. You will need to know what the characteristics are of the population of possible case studies and devise a sampling frame. Depending on your research objectives you may wish to compare extreme examples, for example, successful and unsuccessful businesses, or wish to compare similar samples, for example, best retirement homes. The selection of case studies will then be based on this decision, using either probability sampling methods or non-probability methods.

Ask yourself

Why do researchers use sampling procedures? What factors must you examine when deciding on an appropriate sampling method?

Usually in order to select a representative sample from a population, but sometimes just to select a manageable number of cases, even if they are not representative. The sorts of factor meant here are the characteristics of the population and practical matters such as location, distribution and number of cases.

What are the two basic types of sampling procedure, and what are the differences between them? When is it appropriate to use them?

This obviously refers to probability and non-probability sampling methods. The main difference is the random and non-random element. You can elaborate on this by explaining the consequences this has. Use your imagination to devise examples of where the different procedures can be appropriately used, for example, snowball sampling techniques when you cannot approach the cases yourself because they belong to a private network.

What are the critical issues which determine the appropriate sample size?

Just read what it says in the chapter above! Mention variability within the population, the number of variables studied and practical issues among other things.

Further reading

Sampling is a big subject in social research, and all research methods textbooks will have a section on it. Here are some books that are entirely devoted to the subject.

Scheaffer, R., Mendenhall, W., Lymann Ott, R. and Gerow, K. (2012) *Elementary Survey Sampling* (7th edn). Boston, MA: Brooks Cole.
Focusing on the practical aspects of survey sampling, this introduction is intended for students in the social sciences, business and natural resources management.

Fink, A. (2003) *How to Sample in Surveys*. Volume 7 of *The Survey Kit*. London: Sage.
Good coverage of target populations and samples, and statistics of sampling. Logical progression through the material with good use of examples.

Emmel, N. (2013) *Sampling and Choosing Cases in Qualitative Research: a Realist Approach*. London: Sage.
This innovative book critically evaluates widely used sampling strategies, identifying key theoretical assumptions and considering how empirical and theoretical claims are made from these diverse methods.

TEN

Data Collection Methods

Data (the plural form of datum) are the raw materials of research. You need to mine your subject in order to dig out the ore in the form of data, which you can then interpret and refine into the gold of conclusions. So, how can you, as a prospector for data, find the relevant sources in your subject?

Although we are surrounded by data, in fact, bombarded with them every day from the television, posters, radio, newspapers, magazines and books, it is not so straightforward to collect the correct data for our purposes. It needs a plan of action that identifies and uses the most effective and appropriate methods of data collection.

> **Do:** Whatever your branch of social science, collecting secondary data will be a must. You will inevitably need to ascertain the background to your research question/problem, and also get an idea of the current theories and ideas. No type of project is done in a vacuum, not even a pure work of art.

Collecting primary information is much more subject-specific. Consider whether you need to get information from people, in single or large numbers, or whether you will need to observe and/or measure things or phenomena. You may need to do several of these. For example, in healthcare you may be examining both the people and their treatments, or in education you may be looking at both the education system or perhaps the building, and the effects on the pupils.

> **Don't:** You are probably wasting your time if you amass data that you are unable to analyse, either because you have too much, or because you have insufficient or inappropriate analytical skills or methods to make the analysis.

I say 'probably' because research is not a linear process, so it is not easy to predict exactly how many data will be 'enough'. What will help you to judge the type of and amount of data required is to decide on the methods that you will use to analyse them. In turn, the decision on the appropriateness of analytical methods must be made in relation to the nature of the research problem and the specific aims of the research project. It should be evident in your overall argument what links the research question/problem with the necessary data to be collected and the type of analysis that needs to be carried out in order to reach valid conclusions.

COLLECTING SECONDARY DATA

All research studies require **secondary data** for the background to the study. Others rely greatly on them for the whole project, for example, when doing a historical study (i.e. of any past events, ideas or objects, even the very recent past) or a nationwide study that uses official statistics.

> **Do:** Be aware that wherever there exists a body of recorded information, there are subjects for study. An advantage of using these kinds of data is that they have not been produced for the specific purposes of social research, and can therefore be the basis of a form of unobtrusive enquiry.

Many of the prevailing theoretical debates (e.g. postmodernism, post-structuralism) are concerned with the subjects of language and cultural interpretation, with the result that these issues have frequently become central to sociological studies. The need has therefore arisen for methodologies that allow analysis of cultural texts to be compared, replicated, disproved and generalized. From the late 1950s, language has been analysed from several basic viewpoints: the structural properties of language (notably Chomsky, Sacks, Schegloff), language as an action in its contextual environment (notably Wittgenstein, Austin and Searle) and sociolinguistics and the 'ethnography of speaking' (Hymes, Bernstein, Labov and many others).

However, the meaning of the term 'cultural texts' has been broadened from that of purely literary works to that of the many manifestations of cultural exchange, be they formal, such as opera, television news programmes, cocktail parties, etc., or informal, such as how people dress or converse. The main criterion for cultural texts is that one should be able to 'read' some meanings into the phenomena. Texts can therefore include tactile, visual and aural aspects, even smells and tastes. They can be current or historical and may be descriptive or statistical in nature. Any of them can be quantitative or qualitative in nature.

Here are some examples of documentary data that come from a wide range of sources:

- Personal documents
- Oral histories
- Commentaries
- Diaries
- Letters
- Autobiographies
- Official published documents
- State documents and records
- Official statistics
- Commercial or organizational documents
- Mass media outputs
- Newspapers and journals
- Maps
- Drawings, comics and photographs
- Fiction
- Non-fiction
- Academic output
- Journal articles and conference papers
- Lecture notes
- Critiques
- Research reports
- Textbooks
- Artistic output
- Theatrical productions – plays, opera, musicals
- Artistic critiques
- Programmes, playbills, notes and other ephemera
- Virtual outputs
- Web pages
- Databases.

Several problems face the researcher seeking historical and recorded data. The main problems are:

- Locating and accessing them
- Authenticating the sources
- Assessing credibility
- Gauging how representative they are
- Selecting methods of interpreting them.

Locating historical data can be an enormous topic. Activities can involve anything from unearthing city ruins in the desert to rummaging through dusty archives in an obscure library or downloading the latest government statistical data from the internet. Even current data may be difficult to get hold of. For instance, much current economic data are restricted and expensive to buy. It is impossible to give a full description of sources, as the detailed nature of the subject of research determines the appropriate source, and, of course, the possible range of subjects is enormous. However, here are some of the principal sources.

Libraries and archives – these are generally equipped with sophisticated catalogue systems that facilitate the tracking down of particular pieces of data or enable a trawl to be made to identify anything which may be relevant. International computer networks can make remote searching possible. See your own library specialists for the latest techniques. Apart from these modernized libraries and archives, much valuable historical material is contained in more obscure and less organized collections, in remote areas and old houses and institutions. The attributes of a detective are often required to track down relevant material, and that of a diplomat to gain access to private or restricted collections.

Museums, galleries and collections – these often have efficient cataloguing systems that will help your search. However, problems may be encountered with searching and access in less organized and restricted or private collections. Larger museums often have their own research departments that can be of help.

Government departments and commercial/professional bodies – these often hold much statistical information, both current and historic.

The internet – rapidly expanding source of information of all types. You can find virtually everything here, if not the actual source material, then at least where to find it.

The field – not all historical artefacts are contained in museums. Ancient cities, buildings, archaeological digs, etc. are available for study *in situ*. Here, various types of observation will be required to record the required data.

Authentication of historical data can be a complex process, and is usually carried out by experts. A wide range of techniques are used, for example, textual analysis, carbon dating, paper analysis, locational checks, cross-referencing and many others. Authentication of modern or current material requires a thorough check of sources.

Don't: Take documents at face value. In other words, they must be regarded as information that is context specific and as data that must be contextualized with other forms of research. They should, therefore, only be used with caution.

Credibility of data refers to their freedom from error or bias. Many documents are written in order to put across a particular message and can be selective with the truth. Much important contextual data can be missing from such documents as reports of spoken events, where the pauses, hesitations and gestures are not recorded.

Do: Assess the degree of representativeness of the documents. This will enable you to make judgements of the generalizability of any conclusions drawn from them.

The wealth of purely statistical data contained in the archives, especially those of more recent date, provides a powerful resource for research into many issues. You will often find, however, that the data recorded are not exactly in the form that you require. For example, when making international comparisons on housing provision, the data might be compiled in different ways in the different countries under consideration. In order to extract the exact data you require, you will have to extrapolate from the existing data.

COLLECTING PRIMARY DATA

This entails going out and collecting information by observing, recording and measuring the activities and ideas of real people, or perhaps watching animals, or inspecting objects and experiencing events. This process of collecting **primary data** is often called survey research.

You should only be interested in collecting data that are required in order to investigate your research problem. Even so, the amount of relevant information you could collect is likely to be enormous, so you must find a way to limit the amount of data you collect to achieve your aims. The main technique for reducing the scope of your data collection is to study a sample, that is, a small section of the subjects of your study, or to select one or several case studies. Most of the data collection methods described below are suitable for qualitative research, the collecting of data is then often combined with ongoing analysis. Some of the methods also lend themselves to quantitative research. The nature of the questions and form of answers sought are the central issue here.

Self-completion questionnaires

Asking questions is an obvious method of collecting both quantitative and qualitative information from people. Using a questionnaire enables you to organize the questions and receive replies without actually having to talk to every respondent. As a method of data collection, the questionnaire is a very flexible tool, but you must use it carefully in order to fulfil the requirements of your research. While there are whole books on the art of questioning and questionnaires, it is possible to isolate a number of important factors to consider before deciding to use a questionnaire.

Before examining its form and content, let's briefly consider why you might choose this form of data collection, and the ways in which you could deliver the questionnaire.

The advantages of self-completion questionnaires:

- They are cheap to administer.
- They are quick to administer.
- They are an easy way to question a large number of cases covering large geographical areas.

- The personal influence of the researcher is eliminated.
- Embarrassing questions can be asked with a fair chance of getting a truthful reply.
- Variability between different researchers or assistants is eliminated.
- They are convenient for respondents.
- Respondents have time to check facts and think about their answers, which tends to lead to more accurate information.
- They have a structured format.
- They can be designed to assist in the analysis stage.
- They are particularly suitable for quantitative data but can also be used for qualitative data.

The disadvantages of self-completion questionnaires:

- They require a lot of time and skill to design and develop.
- They limit the range and scope of questioning - questions need to be simple to follow and understand so complex question structures are not possible.
- Yet more forms to fill in! They can be unpopular, so they need to be as short as possible.
- Prompting and probing are impossible, and this limits the scope of answers and the possibility of getting additional data.
- It is not possible to ascertain if the right person has responded.
- Not everyone is able to complete questionnaires.
- Response rates can be low.

There are two basic methods of delivering questionnaires, personally and by post. The advantages of personal delivery are that you can help respondents to overcome difficulties with the questions, and that you can use personal persuasion and reminders to ensure a high response rate. You can also find out the reasons why some people refuse to answer the questionnaire, and you can check on responses if they seem odd or incomplete. Obviously, there are problems both in time and geographical location that limit the scope and extent to which you can use this method of delivery.

> **Do:** Get personally involved in delivery and collection of questionnaires. This enables you to devise more complicated questionnaires as you will be on hand to explain, remind and encourage.

The rate of response for postal questionnaires is difficult to predict or control, particularly if there is no system of follow-up. The pattern of non-response can have a serious effect on the validity of your sample by introducing bias into the data collected. Mangione (1995, pp. 60–1) rates responses like this:

Over 85% - excellent

70-85% - very good

60-70% - acceptable

50-60% - barely acceptable

Below 50% - not acceptable.

Here are some simple rules for devising a questionnaire. It is not always easy to carry them out perfectly:

- Establish exactly which variables you wish to gather data about, and how these variables can be assessed. This will enable you to list the questions you need to ask (and those that you don't) and to formulate the questions precisely in order to get the required responses.
- Clear instructions are required to guide the respondent on how to complete the questionnaire.
- The language must be unmistakably clear and unambiguous and make no inappropriate assumptions. This requires some clear analytical effort.
- In order to get a good response rate, keep questions simple and the questionnaire as short as possible.
- Clear and professional presentation is another essential factor in encouraging a good response. Vertical format is best, and answers should be kept close to questions.
- Consider how you will process the information from the completed forms. This may influence the layout of the questionnaire, for example, by including spaces for codes and scoring.

It is a good idea to pre-test the questionnaire on a small number of people before you use it in earnest. This is called a pilot study.

> **Do:** If you can, test a pilot study on people of a similar type to those in the intended sample to anticipate any problems of comprehension or other sources of confusion.

It is good practice when sending out or issuing the questionnaire to courteously invite the recipients to complete it, and encourage them by explaining the purpose of the survey, how the results could be of benefit to them and how little time it will take to complete. Include simple instructions on how to fill in the questionnaire. Some form of thanks and appreciation of their efforts should be included at the end. If you need to be sure of a response from a particular person, send a preliminary letter, with a reply-paid response card, to ask if he or she is willing to complete the questionnaire before you send it.

There are basically two types of question:

Closed-format questions - the respondents must choose from a choice of given answers.

Open-format questions - the respondents are free to answer in their own words and style.

The advantages of closed-format questions are:

- They are quick to answer.
- They are easy to code.
- They require no special writing skills from the respondent.

The disadvantages are:

- There is a limited range of possible answers.
- It is not possible to qualify answers.

Types of question can be listed as:

- Single answer (e.g. nationality) – yes/no.
- Multiple answers (e.g. select from a list).
- Rank order (e.g. number items on a list by preference).
- Numerical (e.g. number of miles, age, etc.).
- Lickert style (e.g. rate the extent to which you agree with a statement: strongly agree, agree, undecided, disagree, strongly disagree).
- Semantic differential (e.g. choose from a range of qualities: very good, good, mediocre, poor, very poor).

A **coding frame** is usefully devised and incorporated into the questionnaire design to make coding and data handling simpler and consistent later on during analysis. Responses are assigned a code, usually in the form of a number, which is used for keying the responses into a computer format.

The advantages of open-format questions are:

- They permit freedom of expression.
- Bias is eliminated because respondents are free to answer in their own way.
- Respondents can qualify their responses.

The disadvantages are:

- They are more demanding and time-consuming for respondents.
- They are difficult to code.
- Respondents' answers are open to the researcher's interpretation.
- Coding categories will need to be devised according to the types of response gained. The results of a pilot survey will help to predict these.

Interviews (structured, semi-structured and unstructured)

While questionnaire surveys are relatively easy to organize and prevent the personality of the interviewer affecting the results, they do have certain limitations. They are not suitable for questions that require probing to obtain adequate information, as they should only contain simple, one-stage questions (i.e. questions whose answers do not lead on to further specific questions). It is often difficult to get responses from the complete sample; questionnaires tend to be returned by the more literate sections of the population.

The use of interviews to question samples of people is a very flexible tool with a wide range of applications. Three types of interview are often mentioned:

1 **Structured interview** – standardized questions read out by the interviewer according to an interview schedule. Answers may be closed-format.
2 **Unstructured interview** – a flexible format, usually based on a question guide but where the format remains the choice of the interviewer, who can allow the interview to 'ramble' in order to get insights into the attitudes of the interviewee. No closed-format questions are used.
3 **Semi-structured interview** – one that contains structured and unstructured sections with standardized and open-format questions.

> **Do:** Because of their flexibility, use interviews as a useful method of obtaining information and opinions from experts during the early stages of your research project.

Although suitable for quantitative data collection, interviews are particularly useful when qualitative data is required. There are two main methods of conducting interviews: face-to-face and by telephone.

Face-to-face interviews can be carried out in a variety of situations: in the home, at work, outdoors, on the move (e.g. while travelling). They can be used to question members of the general public, experts or leaders, or specific segments of society, such as elderly or disabled people, ethnic minorities, both singly and in groups. Interviews can be used for a variety of subjects, both general or specific, and even, with the correct preparation, for very sensitive topics. They can be one-off interviews or repeated several times over a period to track developments. As the interviewer, you are in a good position to judge the quality of the responses, to notice if a question has not been properly understood and to encourage the respondent to be full in his or her answers. Using visual signs, such as nods, smiles, etc. helps to get good responses.

Nathalis G. Wamba reported in 2014 on the project 'Participatory action research for school improvement: the Kwithu project'.

He relates how his team managed to get a large amount of data using a mixed methods approach (Wamba, 2014).

After a teacher at Kwithu, a community-based organization in Luwinga serving orphans and vulnerable children, administered an English diagnostic test to a random group of 40 seventh and eighth graders (boys and girls) and discovered that they could hardly read or write, we initiated a participatory action research project involving the school stakeholders, including head teachers, teachers, students, parents, clergy and small business owners, to identify causes for the low academic achievement of children in Luwinga.

We (wherever I use 'we', I refer to myself and Maureen, the Director and Co-Founder of Kwithu) started the research process with our initial meeting with the head teachers of three schools. We interviewed them about the low level of academic performance of Kwithu children who attended their schools. After the initial meeting, we invited them to Kwithu for a community dialogue. 'We want to talk about the education of our children', as Maureen put it on the invitation. We also invited the stakeholders including teachers, students, parents, small business owners, clergy and community leaders. A total of 75 people showed up. 'This is the first time someone invites us to talk about our children', an old man exclaimed.

We started the meeting with an orientation in both English and Tumbuka (the local language), explaining to the participants the purpose of the meeting and what we intended to accomplish. We invited the participants to address two main questions: (1) What are the causes for the low academic achievement of Kwithu children? (2) What are the solutions to these challenges? We divided the participants into five focus groups. The focus group discussions were intended to construct a descriptive account of the primary education situation in the Luwinga ward.

We appointed a recorder and a time keeper to each group and gave the participants 45 minutes to discuss the two questions. We circulated among groups and took notes. After 45 minutes, the groups reconvened and reported to the general assembly what they discussed in their respective groups. We recorded their accounts and wrote them on a flipchart. Participants enumerated several issues including teaching and learning conditions, learners' socioeconomic challenges and physical infrastructure, to name a few. However, when asked about solutions to these challenges, most of the participants, except for the students, mentioned the government as the answer to the problems.

There were several advantages to the focus groups meetings. First, the act of bringing stakeholders together to discuss the crisis in public education in Luwinga ward heightened awareness among the stakeholders with regard to the crisis. This was a crucial first step in a process that would encourage them to act as participants in addressing the challenges. Another positive aspect was that the focus groups were not tightly controlled. Participants could speak in Tumbuka, Chewa if they did not speak English or did not feel comfortable. We were also able to capture how individuals interacted with one another as well as their entrenched political attitudes, which helped us understand the intergroup dynamics. The process ensured that participants were discussing the appropriate topic at hand. It was also cost-efficient and provided us with instant results.

Two weeks later, we invited representatives of the various focus groups who participated in the initial focus group discussions to a follow-up meeting to make sense of what we discussed. Participants recommended that in addition to having a general picture of the challenges encountered by the three schools discussed, specific accounts of individual school were necessary. In response to this suggestion, we organized 'PAR [participatory action research] Studios' that were organized visits to each school. During the school visits, we observed the students, teachers, classrooms, physical infrastructure and surroundings. We carefully and systematically recorded what we saw, heard, smelled, touched and tasted. As Mertler (2006) notes, 'observation can be very useful in certain situations where other forms of data collection simply would not work' (p. 93). Our preference for unstructured observation allowed us flexibility to attend other events taking place simultaneously in the settings. We also asked the head teachers for permission to take pictures. In some instances a head teacher would instruct us to take a picture to capture a particular building, object or space that represented a challenge to education in the school. We also conducted in-depth focus group discussions with stakeholders. We challenged each other's views and sought concrete solutions to school problems rather than leaving such problems to the government to resolve. For most of the participants, the schools belonged to government, non-governmental organizations, church properties or properties of the people who built them.

The interviews, focus group discussions, observations, field notes (logs) including formal and informal conversations with stakeholders, and pictures yielded an impressive amount of data ... that consisted of .... interview transcripts, focus group discussions notes, flipchart notes, observations notes, field notes, pictures and personal logs.

Telephone interviews avoid the necessity of travelling to the respondents and all the problems associated with contacting people personally. Telephone surveys can be carried out more quickly than face-to-face interviews, especially if the questionnaire is short (20–30 minutes at the most). However, you cannot use visual aids to explain questions and there are no visual clues such as eye contact, smiling, puzzled looks between you and the interviewee. Voice quality is an important factor in successful telephone interviews. You should speak steadily and clearly, using standard pronunciation and sounding competent and confident.

For interviewing very busy people, you can pre-arrange a suitable time to ring. Modern communications technology is making it more and more difficult to talk with an actual person on the phone!

> **Do:** Take note that the most important point when you set up an interview is to know exactly what you want to achieve by it, how you are going to record the information and what you intend to do with it.

Although there is a great difference in technique for conducting interviews 'cold' with the general public and interviewing officials or experts by appointment, in both cases the personality and bearing of the interviewer is of great importance. You should be well prepared in the groundwork (i.e. writing letters to make appointments, explaining the purpose of the interview), in presenting the interview (with confidence, friendliness, good appearance, etc.) and in the method of recording the responses (tape recording, writing notes, completing forms, etc.).

There are several types of question that can be used to gain information on facts, behaviour, beliefs and attitudes. Kvale (2008, p. 60) lists nine types:

1 Introducing
2 Follow-up
3 Probing
4 Specifying
5 Direct
6 Indirect
7 Structuring
8 Silence
9 Interpreting.

Interviews can be audio-recorded in many instances in order to retain a full, uninterpreted record of what was said. However, in order to analyse the data, the recording will have to be transcribed.

> **Don't:** Transcription is a lengthy process. Bryman (2012) reckons that five or six hours are required for every hour of speech. Avoid writing down sections of the interview that are irrelevant to the research to avoid a huge amount of paperwork that needs to be analysed.

The main advantage of recording and transcribing interviews is that it makes it easier to check exactly what was said – memories cannot be relied upon! And repeated checking is possible. The raw data are also available for checks against researcher bias and for secondary or different analysis by others. Short cuts to full transcription are either to transcribe only the particularly useful sections of the interviews in full, or to record in note form what was said, similar to notes taken during an interview, perhaps already employing a predetermined coding system.

Example of data collection using interviews and activity logs

Adapted from Tomika W. Greer (2014) Sage Research Methods Case.

As the major project for the qualitative research methods course, I was tasked with performing a qualitative research study. Despite my initial anxieties about the research project, by the end of the first week of the class, I had decided that I would continue to follow my interests and investigate other women whom I could relate to regarding work and family issues. Accordingly, I could narrow down my search for study participants to women in my demographic – married mothers of pre-schoolers who were working full-time outside of the home.

Ultimately, the following questions were used to guide my qualitative research study:

- How do working mothers of preschool-age children accommodate the multiple roles that they play?
- How satisfied are these working moms with the current balance that they have between work and non-work roles?
- What are (or could) these working moms proactively doing to succeed in the multiple roles that they play and achieve the level of balance that they desire?

Given the nature of using the case study methodology and the need to select very specific women to participate in the study, I used a purposive sampling strategy to identify a convenience sample for this study. Convenience samples are selected 'based on time, money, location, availability of sites or respondents, and so on' (Merriam, 1998, p. 63). Given the relatively short time frame to complete this study and a limited geographical area required to conduct face-to-face interviews, I was specifically limited by time and location. Within my own network of women, I identified potential participants who I thought would provide a wealth of rich data for this study and who met all of the following criteria: they were mothers to preschool age children, they were employed outside of the home on a full-time basis and they were married.

I was eager to go beyond relying solely on collecting data using interviews (probably the most used data collection method in qualitative research). My engineering background and analytical orientation persuaded me to think of innovative ways that I could collect qualitative data while appeasing my natural inclination to quantify things.

Consequently, I decided to ask the participants to document their daily activities for a week prior to my interview with them. My plan was to use these activity logs to gain a sense of how they divided their time among their many responsibilities as working mothers.

(Continued)

(Continued)

I also thought that by having them complete the logs, the participants would be cognizant of work-family interactions by the time of our scheduled interviews. Furthermore, I thought that my plan to quantify the qualitative data that they submitted through the activity logs would give us something to talk about or reference during the interviews to spark more rich and accurate dialog. The participants maintained their activity logs according to a Microsoft Excel template that I supplied to them. The activity logs were submitted to me via email prior to the interviews.

I intended for the unstructured interviews to explore the extent to which the mothers had been subjected to role conflict or work-life unbalance and how they dealt with and attempted to minimize those feelings. The unstructured interviews were also used to determine whether the mothers were content with the current balance that they had between paid work and non-work responsibilities and what they were doing to maintain or achieve the balance that they desired.

Each of the interviews lasted between 60 and 90 minutes. I had developed an interview protocol for use in the case that the unstructured conversation was not producing the desired data.

Ultimately, the interviews and the activity logs were the two primary means of collecting data and were used to achieve triangulation of the data. 'Data obtained directly from the statements of individuals should be checked against observed behaviour and various records and documents' (Lincoln and Guba, 1985, p. 31). This triangulation enhances the internal validity of the study (Merriam, 1998). In this study, triangulation was enhanced when the activity logs were used to check the statements given by the participants in the unstructured interviews.

Although the interviews were neither videotaped nor audiotaped, I created a transcript for each of the interviews using my field notes and recollections of my encounters with the participants. Subsequently, a member check was performed for the interviews that I conducted with the second and third participants. The member checks involved me sharing the completed transcripts with the participants and asking them to verify the accuracy of the transcript based on their own recollections of the interviews.

FOCUS GROUPS

Focus groups are a type of group interview, which concentrates in-depth on a particular theme or topic with an element of interaction. The group is often made up of people who have particular experience of or knowledge about the subject of the research, or those who have a particular interest in it (e.g. consumers or customers). It can be quite difficult to organize focus groups due to the difficulty of getting a group of people together for a discussion session.

The interviewer's job is a delicate balancing act. He or she should be seen more as a moderator of the resulting discussion than as a dominant questioner, one who prompts the discussion without unduly influencing its direction. Reticent speakers might need encouragement in order to limit dominant speakers. The moderator should also provide a suitable introduction and conclusion to the session, offering information about the research, the topics, what will happen with the data collected and express thanks to the members of the group.

According to Bryman (2012, pp. 500–3), there are several reasons for holding focus groups:

- To develop an understanding about why people think the way they do.
- Members of the group can bring forward ideas and opinions not foreseen by the interviewer.
- Interviewees can be challenged, often by other members of the group, about their replies.
- The interactions found in group dynamics are closer to the real-life process of sense-making and acquiring understanding.

The common size of group is around 6–10 people. Selection of members of the group will depend on whether you attempt to get a cross-section of people, a proportional membership (e.g. a proportionate number of representatives reflecting the size of each section of the population) or a convenient natural grouping (e.g. just those who show an interest in the subject).

> **Don't:** Although a lot of information is produced in a short time by a focus group, don't think that it will be easy to note down all what is said due to the number of people involved and the heat of the discussion. A clear recording of the discussion will help in this case.

It is important to know not only what was said, but who said it and how. It is therefore best to tape-record the interview and transcribe it later, which can be a lengthy task. Analysis of the data is not easy due to the dual aspects of what people say and how they say it in interaction with the others.

STANDARDIZED TESTS

A wide range of **standardized tests** have been devised by social scientists and psychologists to measure people's abilities, attitudes, aptitudes, opinions, etc. A well-known example of one of these is the IQ or intelligence test. The objective of the tests is usually to measure the abilities of the subjects according to a standardized scale, so that easy comparisons can be made. One of the main problems is to select or devise a suitable scale for measuring the often rather abstract concepts under investigation, such as attitude (e.g. to school meals, military service, capital punishment, etc.).

> **Do:** It is safer to use tried-and-tested standard scales, of which there are several, each taking different approaches according to the results aimed at.

One of the most common standardized tests is the **Lickert scale**, using a summated rating approach. There is also, among others, the Thurlstone scale, which aims to produce an equal interval scale, and the Guttman scale, which is a unidimensional scale where items have a cumulative property.

Here is an example of a Lickert scale so that you get the idea of what it is like:

Strongly agree 1 2 3 4 5 Strongly disagree

The 'questions' are expressed as statements (e.g. the 'Labour Party still represents the workers') and the respondent is asked to ring one of the numbers in the scale 1–5. Another way of expressing the same thing is just to use words:

Strongly agree/tend to agree/neither agree nor disagree/tend to disagree/strongly disagree

at the head of five columns situated to the right of the list of statements, and ask the respondent to tick the column that most reflects his or her opinion. You can use any dichotomous combination you like, such as like/dislike, want/not want, probable/improbable. You just have to be careful that there are gradations of the opinion or feelings, unlike accept/reject, which is either one or the other. As an alternative to five, you can have three or seven stages. (It is best to keep to odd numbers so that you get a middle value.)

You can see that a score is automatically given by the response, so you can easily count the number of different scores to analyse the results.

Do: Take the useful precaution to prevent oversimplification of responses by asking many questions about the same topic, all from different angles.

This form of triangulation helps to build up a more complete picture of complex issues. You can then also weight the results from the different questions – that is, give more importance to those that are particularly crucial by multiplying them by a chosen factor.

DETACHED AND PARTICIPANT OBSERVATION

This is a method of recording conditions, events and activities through looking rather than asking. As an activity, as opposed to a method, observation is of course required in many research situations, for example, observing the results of experiments, the behaviour of models and even observing the reactions of people to questions in an interview. Observation can also be used for recording the nature or condition of objects or events visually, for example, through photography, film or sketching. This is sometimes referred to as **visual ethnography**. The visual materials may be a source of data for analysis, or can be used as a prompt for interviewee reaction.

Observation can be used to record both quantitative and qualitative data. There is a range of levels of involvement in the observed phenomena. Gold (1958) classifies these as follows:

Complete observer – the observer takes a detached stance by not getting involved in the events, and uses unobtrusive observation techniques and remains 'invisible' either in fact or in effect (i.e. by being ignored).

Observer-as-participant – the researcher is mainly an interviewer doing some degree of observation but very little participation.

Participant-as-observer – the researcher engages fully in the life and activities of the observed, who are aware of his/her observing role.

Complete participant – the researcher takes a full part in the social events but is not recognized as an observer by the observed. The complete participant is a covert observer.

> **Don't:** Ignore the possibility that observation can record whether people act differently from what they say or intend.

People can sometimes demonstrate their understanding of a process better by their actions than by verbally explaining their knowledge. For example, a machine operator will probably demonstrate more clearly his or her understanding of the techniques of operating the machine by working with it than by verbal explanation.

Observation is not limited to the visual sense. Any sense (e.g. smell, touch, hearing) can be involved, and these need not be restricted to the range perceptible to the human senses. A microscope or telescope can be used to extend the capacity of the eye, just as a moisture meter can be used to increase sensitivity to the feeling of dampness. You can probably think of instruments that have been developed in every discipline to extend the observational limits of the human senses.

On the one hand, observations of objects can be a quick and efficient method of gaining preliminary knowledge or making a preliminary assessment of its state or condition. For example, after an earthquake, a quick visual assessment of the amount and type of damage to buildings can be made before a detailed survey is undertaken. On the other hand, observation can be very time-consuming and difficult when the activity observed is not constant (i.e. much time can be wasted waiting for things to happen, or so much happens at once that it is impossible to observe it all and record it). Instrumentation can sometimes be devised to overcome the problem of infrequent or spasmodic activity (e.g. automatic cameras and other sensors).

Here are a few basic hints on how to carry out observations:

- Make sure you know what you are looking for. Events and objects are usually complicated and much might seem to be relevant to your study. Identify the variables that you need to study and concentrate on these.
- Getting access is more difficult in closed, as opposed to open, settings. You will need to use friends and other contacts to gain access to organizations, and will invariably have to get clearance for the research from senior management.
- Make sure you can explain clearly what your aims and methods are and how much of a person's time you will be taking up. You may need to negotiate and offer some return (e.g. a short report) for permission to be granted. Be honest.
- Devise a simple and efficient method of recording the information accurately. Rely as much as possible on ticking boxes or circling numbers, particularly if you need to record fast-moving events. Obviously, when observing static objects, you can leave yourself more time to notate or draw the data required. Record the observations as they happen. Memories of detailed observations fade quickly.
- Use instrumentation when appropriate or necessary. Instruments that make an automatic record of their measurements are to be preferred in many situations.
- If possible, process the information as the observations progress. This can help to identify critical matters that need to be studied in greater detail, and others that prove to be unnecessary.
- If you are doing covert observations, use a 'front' to explain your presence, and plan in advance what to do if your presence is discovered, to avoid potentially embarrassing or even dangerous situations! Beware of transgressing the law.
- In overt observation, try to allay worries that you might be a snooping official or inspector by stressing your role as a researcher, your high level of competence and your ability to retain confidentiality.
- Make sure you observe ethical standards and obtain the necessary clearances with the relevant authorities (see Chapter 7).

PERSONAL ACCOUNTS AND DIARIES

This is a method of qualitative data collection. Personal accounts and diaries provide information on people's actions and feelings by asking them to give their own interpretation, or account, of what they experience. Accounts can consist of a variety of data sources: people's spoken explanations, behaviour (such as gestures), personal records of experiences and conversations, letters and diaries. As long as the accounts are authentic, there is no reason why they cannot be used to explain people's actions.

Since the information must come directly from the respondents, you must take care to avoid leading questions, excessive guidance and other factors that may cause distortion. You can check the authenticity of the accounts by cross-checking with other people involved in the events, examining the physical records of the events (e.g. papers, documents, etc.) and checking with the respondents during the account-gathering process. You will need to transform the collected accounts into working documents that can be coded and analysed.

Take it further

Experimental design

The world around us is so complicated that it is often difficult to observe a particular phenomenon without being disturbed by all the other events happening around us. Wouldn't it be useful to be able to extract that part of the world from its surroundings and study it in isolation. You can often do this by setting up an experiment in which only the important factors (variables) that you want to consider are selected for study. Experiments are used in many subject areas, but particularly those that are based on things or the interaction between things and/or people (things include systems or techniques as well as objects or substances).

Generally, experiments are used to examine causality (causes and effects). An experiment manipulates one or more independent variables (that which supplies causes) and measures the effects of this manipulation on dependent variables (those which register effects), while at the same time controlling all other variables. This is used to find explanations of 'what happens if, why, when and how'. It is difficult to control all the other variables, some of which might be unknown, that might have an effect on the outcomes of the experiment.

In order to combat this problem, random sampling methods are used to select the experimental units (the things that are being experimented on, such as materials, components, persons, groups, etc.). This process, called **random assignment**, neutralizes the particular effects of individual variables and allows the results of the experiment to be generalized.

The design of the experiments depends on the type of data required, the level of reliability of the data required and practical matters associated with the problem under investigation. There are many locations where experiments can be carried out, but the laboratory situation is the one that provides the greatest possibilities for control. With this approach, the collection and analysis of data are inextricably linked. The preliminary data on which the experiments are based are used to create new data, which, in turn, can be used for further analysis.

Don't: Fall into the trap to set up an experiment that so simplifies, and even falsifies, the phenomenon extracted from the real world that completely wrong conclusions can be reached.

Checks should be carried out on experiments to test whether the assumptions made are valid. A control group can be used to provide a 'baseline' against which the effects of the experimental treatment may be evaluated. The control group is one that is identical (as near as possible) to the experimental group, but does not receive experimental treatment. For example, in a medical experiment, the control group will be given placebo pills instead

(Continued)

(Continued)

of the medicated pills. As you can see in this example, experiments are not only a matter of bubbling bottles in a laboratory. They can involve people as well as things – only it is more difficult to control the people!

Laboratory and field experiments

What are the significant differences between doing experiments in the contrived setting of a laboratory and those done in a real-life setting? Social science is concerned with what is happening in the real world, so isn't the laboratory the wrong place to do social experiments?

Laboratory experiments have the advantage of providing a good degree of control over the environment, and of studying the effects on the subjects involved. With the aid of some deception, the subjects might not even be aware of what effects they are being tested for. Despite the artificiality of the setting, this can provide reliable data that can be generalized in the real world. However, according to arguments by leading academics (see Robson, 2011, pp. 86–7), the disadvantages of laboratory experiments are that they may:

- Lack experimental realism – the conditions may appear to be artificial and not involve the subjects in the same way as in a realistic setting.
- Lack mundane realism – real-life settings are always much more complicated and ambiguous than those created in a laboratory.
- Lead to bias through demand characteristics – the expectation of the subjects that certain things are demanded of them and their reaction to the knowledge that they are being observed.
- Lead to bias through experimenter expectancy – the often unwitting reactive effects of the experimenters that lead to a biased view of the findings to support the tested hypothesis.

Do: Note that it is not always easy to distinguish between laboratory and field experiments.

Realistic simulations of rooms in a laboratory or the use of normal settings as laboratories for the purposes of experiments make it difficult to know where to draw the line. There may also be a sense of artificiality in a natural setting when people are organized for the purposes of the experiment, or people are just aware that they are subjects of investigation.

In field experiments, planned interventions and innovations are the most useful strategies for natural experiments as they provide possibilities to apply relatively reliable experimental designs, involving control groups and getting information prior to the interventions. External validity (generalizability to the real world) is obviously more easily achieved when the experiments are carried out in normal life settings. Subjects are also more likely to react and behave normally rather than being affected by artificial conditions. In most cases, it is also easy to obtain subjects to take part in the research as they need not make any special effort to attend at a particular time and place. However, the move out of the confined and controllable setting of the laboratory raises some problems:

- Faulty randomization
- Lack of validity
- Ethical issues
- Lack of control.

Internal and external validity

In order for the experiments to be of any use, it must be possible to generalize the results beyond the confines of the experiment itself. For this to be the case, the experiment should really reflect the situation in the real world, that is, it should possess both **internal validity** (the extent to which causal statements are supported by the study) and **external validity** (the extent to which findings can be generalized to populations or to other settings). The level of sophistication of the design and extent of control determines the internal validity of the experimental design. The extent of the legitimate generalizability of the results gives a rating for the external validity of the design.

Ask yourself

When and why might you want to collect secondary data? Give some examples of research topics to illustrate your points.

Two main responses come to mind. First, you need to collect secondary data when you prepare the background for a research project in order to build a basis for the work and, second, when primary data is not available, particularly in the case of historical studies. You can easily devise some examples of topics to illustrate these, and probably think of a few more reasons for collecting secondary data (because they are there! e.g. government statistics).

Devise four really bad questions for a questionnaire and explain what is wrong with them and why. How can they be improved?

There are usually examples of ambiguous or puzzling questions in textbooks about questionnaires. A simple example is 'Do you smoke more than 10 cigarettes in a ... day, week, month, year? – Underline one period'. I can see what the questioner is getting at – the frequency of smoking – but anyone smoking more than 10 a day could underline any of the periods! What about non-smokers? A better version could be: Approximately how many cigarettes do you smoke in a year ... 0, 20, 100, 500, more than 1,000?

Can anyone really do observation in a detached fashion? What can be done to avoid getting involved in the situation being observed?

(Continued)

(Continued)

This brings up the debate about positivism, relativism and realism (see Chapter 1). You can take a stance with particular reference to social science research, and give examples where it might be easier to be a detached observer and not. Obviously, if you need to participate in order to be accepted in the situation studied, it will be more difficult to remain detached. Give examples of how to avoid getting involved. One way is to be a covert observer, where involvement is impossible (though you might still get caught up in the emotions of the actions).

What are the relative advantages and disadvantages of laboratory and field experiments?

The main point here is the control over the variables, which is easier in a laboratory setting. However, when dealing with people, they may behave very differently in an artificial setting so a field experiment might give more reliable results. Anyway, not every phenomenon can be made to happen in a laboratory. Again, it will be useful to illustrate your points with examples. Make as many different advantage/disadvantage comparisons as possible using factors such as the importance of context, complexity, non-repeatability, etc.

Further reading

There are hundreds of books about data collection methods. Your own textbooks will give you plenty of information about these – after all, that is what they are about! You should also consult your **library catalogue** for books that deal specifically with how to do research in your own subject branch of social studies (e.g. management, healthcare, education, etc.).

I do not include general textbooks on social science research methods here, only more specific books about different methods. You should consult your recommended textbooks by looking up the relevant section.

Fowler, F.J. (2013) *Survey Research Methods* (5th edn). London: Sage.
This book goes into great detail into all aspects of the subject of doing surveys. Good on sampling, response rates, methods of data collection – particularly questionnaires and interviews. Use it selectively to find out more about the particular methods you want to use. This book will also be useful later for analysis, and has a section on ethics too.

Aldridge, A. (2001) *Surveying the Social World: Principles and Practice in Survey Research*. Buckingham: Open University Press.
Another comprehensive book – find what you need by using the contents list and index.

Seale, C. (ed.) (2011) *Researching Society and Culture* (3rd edn). London: Sage.
See the first six papers in Part Two.

Fink, A. (2003) *The Survey Kit* (2nd edn). London: Sage.
Nine volumes covering all aspects of survey research! This must be the ultimate.

Here are some books specifically on questionnaires, in order of usefulness:

Peterson, R.A. (2000) *Constructing Effective Questionnaires*. London: Sage.

Gillham, B. (2008) *Developing a Questionnaire* (2nd edn). London: Continuum.

Dillman, D.A. (2014) *Internet, Mail and Mixed-Mode Surveys: the Tailored Design Method* (4th edn). Chichester: Wiley.

Frazer, L. and Lawley, M. (2001) *Questionnaire Design and Administration: A Practical Guide*. Chichester: Wiley.

And a few on interviewing, again in order of usefulness at your stage of work:

Brinkmann, S. (2015) *InterViews: Learning the Craft of Qualitative Research Interviewing* (3rd edn). Thousand Oaks, CA: Sage.

Keats, D.M. (2000) *Interviewing: A Practical Guide for Students and Professionals*. Buckingham: Open University Press.

Jaber, F. and Holstein, J. (2012) *The SAGE Handbook of Interview Research: The Complexity of the Craft*. London: Sage.

Wengraf, T. (2001) *Qualitative Research Interviewing: Biographic, Narrative and Semi-structured*. London: Sage.

And a couple on case studies, the simplest first:

Thomas, G. (2011) *How to do your Case Study; A Guide for Students and Researchers*. London: Sage.

Yin, R.K. (2013) *Case Study Research: Design and Methods* (5th edn). Thousand Oaks, CA: Sage.

Apart from consulting your textbooks, here are some books dedicated to experimental methods. Again, check them under your own subject headings.

Field, A. and Hole, G. (2003) *How to Design and Report Experiments*. London: Sage.

Cohen, L. and Manion, L. (2011) *Research Methods in Education* (7th edn). London: Routledge. Chapter 16 gives a comprehensive explanation about experiments. Most books on research methods have a chapter devoted to experiment design. (Chapter numbers may be different in earlier editions.)

Dean, A., Morris, M., Stufken, J. and Bingham, D. (eds) (2015) *Design and Analysis of Experiments*. London: Taylor and Francis.

Montgomery, D.C. (2008) *Design and Analysis of Experiments* (7th edn). New York: Wiley.

ELEVEN
Quantitative Data Analysis

MANAGING DATA
Raw data

The results of your survey, experiments, archival studies or whatever methods you used to collect data about your chosen subject, are of little use to anyone if they are merely presented as raw data. It should not be the duty of the reader to try to make sense of them, and to relate them to your research questions or problems. It is up to you to use the information that you have collected to make a case for arriving at some conclusions. How exactly you do this depends exactly on what kinds of questions you raised at the beginning of the dissertation, and the directions you have taken in order to answer them.

Types of variable

Just a reminder at this point about the levels of measurement related to variables. Investigate each variable to determine whether it belongs to one of the following types:

Nominal or categorical - a name or a category that cannot be rank-ordered. The simplest of these is a dichotomous variable, that is one that can have only two categories (e.g. male, female).

Ordinal - variables that can be put in rank order (e.g. put in order of size, such as s, m, l, xl in clothing sizes, where the difference between sizes cannot be accurately calculated).

Interval - where the measured interval between variables can be accurately gauged (e.g. the finishing times of a race).

Ratio - where the values are measured and relate to a fixed nought value.

> **Do:** Remember that sorting the variables according to their levels of measures is important since the possible degree of statistical analysis differs for each.

The data you have collected might be recorded in different ways that are not easy to read or to summarize. Perhaps they are contained in numerous questionnaire responses, in hand-written laboratory reports, recorded speech, as series of photographs or observations in a diary. It can be difficult for even you, who has done the collecting, to make sense of it all, let alone someone who has not been involved in the project.

The question now is how to grapple with the various forms of data so that you can present them in a clear and concise fashion, and how you can analyse the presented data to support an argument that leads to convincing conclusions. In order to do this you must be clear about what you are trying to achieve.

CREATING A DATA SET

In order to manipulate the data, it should be compiled in an easily read form. Organizing your data as part of the collection process has already been mentioned in Chapter 8, but further compilation may be needed before analysis is possible. Robson (2011, p. 415) describes three possible ways to enter data into the computer:

Direct automatic entry - data are entered on to a database or other computer readable format as they are collected during the research.

Automatic creation of computer file for import into analysis program - using an optical reading device to read questionnaire responses.

Manual keying-in of data - using the keyboard to convert the collected data into a suitable format for the analysis program, commonly on to a spreadsheet.

> **Do:** Ensure that you use the minimum of steps in the creation of your data sets, as there will be fewer possibilities for errors to creep in. Adding codes to response choices on the questionnaire sheet will simplify the transfer of data.

The use of rows and columns on a spreadsheet is the most common technique. A row is given to each record or case and a column is given to each variable, allowing each cell to contain the data for the case/variable. In the case of IBM Statistical Package for the Social Sciences (IBM SPSS), the type of variable heading each column will need to be defined on entry, for example, integers (whole numbers), real numbers (numbers with decimal points), categories (nominal units, such as gender, of which 'male' and 'female' are the elements). Missing data can either be indicated by a blank cell, or a signal code can be inserted (avoid using 0). You may need to distinguish between genuine missing data and a 'don't know' response.

Accuracy check

It is important to check on the accuracy of the data entry. One way is for two people to do the entry separately and compare the result, although this is a time-consuming method! Alternatively, proofreading, by comparing the entered data with the data set, should uncover mistakes. Use categorical variables wherever possible as the computer program will warn you if you enter an invalid value. Robson (2011, p. 418) also suggests carrying out a frequency analysis on each variable column to highlight 'illegal' or unlikely codes, and box plots for continuous variables to highlight extreme values. Cross-tabulation of the values for two variables will reveal impossible, conflicting or unlikely combinations of values. For large data sets, scattergrams can be used to identify extreme values that could indicate a mistake.

⊗ | **Don't:** Forget to keep copies of the original checked data set, as these are the raw materials for your analysis. You may want to create altered sets for different analytical purposes, for example, with combined variables or simplified values.

ANALYSIS ACCORDING TO TYPES OF DATA

There are several reasons why you may want to analyse data. Some of these are the same as the reasons for doing the study in the first place. You will want to use analytical methods so that you can:

- Measure
- Make comparisons
- Examine relationships
- Make forecasts
- Test hypotheses
- Construct concepts and theories
- Explore
- Control
- Explain.

Quantitative analysis of numerical data

Quantitative analysis deals with numbers and uses mathematical operations to investigate the properties of data. The levels of measurement used in the collection of the data (i.e. nominal, ordinal, interval and ratio) are an important factor in choosing the type of analysis that is applicable, as is the number of cases involved. Statistics is the name given to this type of analysis, and is defined in this sense as:

> The science of collecting and analysing numerical data, especially in, or for, large quantities, and usually inferring proportions in a whole from proportions in a representative sample. (*Oxford Encyclopedic English Dictionary*)

Most surveys result in quantitative data (e.g. numbers of people who believed this or that, how many children of what age do which sports, levels of family income, etc.). However, not all quantitative data originate from surveys. For example, **content analysis** is a specific method of examining records of all kinds (e.g. documents or publications, radio and television programmes, films, etc.).

Do: Note that one of the primary purposes of doing research is to describe the data and to discover relationships among events in order to describe, explain, predict and possibly control their occurrence.

Statistical methods are a valuable tool to enable you to present and describe the data and, if necessary, to discover and quantify relationships. And you do not even have to be a mathematician to use these techniques, as user-friendly computer packages (such as Excel and IBM SPSS) will do all the presentation and calculations for you. However, you must be able to understand the relevance and function of the various **displays** and tests in relationship to your own data sets and the kind of analysis required.

The range of statistical tests is enormous, so only the most frequently used tests are discussed here.

Do: Check with your course description and lecture notes to see which tests are relevant to your studies in order to avoid getting bogged down in unnecessary technicalities.

If you intend to carry out some testing as part of a research project, it is always advisable to consult somebody with specialist statistical knowledge in order to check that you will be doing the right thing before you start. Also, attend a course, usually made available to you at your college or university, in the use of IBM SPSS or any other program you intend to use.

An important factor to be taken into account when selecting suitable statistical tests is the number of cases for which you have data. Generally, statistical tests are more reliable the greater the number of cases. Usually, you need 20 cases or more to make any sense of the analysis, although some tests are designed to work with fewer cases. On this issue always consult the instructions for the particular tests you want to use. It may affect your choice.

PARAMETRIC AND NON-PARAMETRIC STATISTICS

The two major classes of statistics are parametric and non-parametric statistics. You need to understand the meaning of a parameter in order to appreciate the difference between these two types. A **parameter** is a constant feature of a population (i.e. the things or people you are surveying) that it shares with other populations. The most common one is the **'bell'** or **Gaussian** curve of normal frequency distribution. This parameter reveals that most populations display a large number of more or less 'average' cases with extreme cases tailing off at each end, as you can see in Figure 11.1.

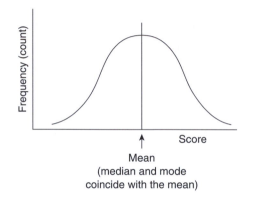

Figure 11.1   A bell or Gaussian curve

For example, most people are of about average height, with those who are extremely tall or small being in a distinct minority. The distribution of people's heights shown on a graph would take the form of the normal or Gaussian curve. Although the shape of this curve varies from case to case (e.g. flatter or steeper, lopsided to the left or right), this feature is so common among populations that statisticians take it as a constant – a basic parameter. Calculations of **parametric statistics** are based on data that conform to a parameter, usually a Gaussian curve.

> **Don't:** Think that all data are parametric. Populations sometimes do not behave in the form of a Gaussian curve.

Data measured by nominal and ordinal methods will not be organized in a curve form. Nominal data tend to be in the dichotomous form of either/or (e.g. this is a cow or a sheep or neither), while ordinal data can be displayed in the form of a set of steps (e.g. the first, second and third positions on the winner's podium). For those cases where this parameter is absent, non-parametric statistics may be applicable.

Non-parametric statistics are tests that have been devised to recognize the particular characteristics of non-curve data, and to take into account these singular characteristics by specialized methods. In general, these types of test are less sensitive and powerful than parametric tests; they need larger samples in order to generate the same level of significance.

STATISTICAL TESTS (PARAMETRIC)

There are two classes of parametric statistical tests: **descriptive statistics**, which quantify the characteristics of parametric numerical data, and **inferential statistics**, which produce predictions through inference based on the data analysed. Distinction is also made between the number of variables considered in relation to each other:

Univariate analysis - analyses the qualities of one variable at a time.

Bivariate analysis - considers the properties of two variables in relation to each other.

Multivariate analysis - looks at the relationships between more than two variables.

Univariate analysis (descriptive)

A range of properties of one variable can be examined using the following measures:

Frequency distribution - usually presented as a table, this simply shows the values for each variable expressed as a number and as a percentage of the total of cases. Alternative ways of presentation are a bar chart, histogram or pie chart, which are easier to read at a glance.

Measure of central tendency - is one number that denotes what is commonly called the 'average' of the values for a variable. There are several measures that can be used:

Arithmetic mean - this is the arithmetic average calculated by adding all the values and dividing by their number. This can be calculated for ordinal, interval and ratio variables.

Mode - the value that occurs most frequently. The only measure that can be used with nominal variables, as well as all the others.

Median - the mid-point in the distribution of values; that is, the mathematical middle between the highest and lowest value. It is used for ordinal, interval and ratio variables.

Normal distribution is when the mean, median and mode are located at the same value. This produces a symmetrical curve. Skewedness occurs when the mean is pushed to one side of the median. When it is to the left, it is known as negatively skewed, and to the right, positively skewed. The curve is lopsided in these cases. If there are two modes to each side of the mean and median points, then it is a bimodal distribution. The curve will have two peaks and a valley in-between.

Measures of dispersion (or variability) - all of the above measures are influenced by the nature of dispersion of the values (how values are spread out or bunched up) and the presence of solitary extreme values. To investigate the dispersion, the following measures can be made:

Range - the distance between the highest and lowest value.

Interquartile range - the distance between the value that has a quarter of the values less than it (first quartile or 25th percentile) and the value that has three-quarters of the values less than it (third quartile or 75th percentile).

Variance - the average of the squared deviations for the individual values from the mean.

Standard deviation - the square root of the variance.

Standard error - the standard deviation of the mean score.

> **Do:** Be aware that these measures do not mean much on their own unless they are compared with some expected measures or those of other variables.

Charts and diagrams

IBM SPSS provides a choice of **display** options to illustrate the measures listed above. The most basic is a summary table of descriptive statistics that gives figures for all of the measures. More graphical options, which make comparisons between variables simpler, are:

Bar graph - this shows the distribution of nominal and ordinal variables. The categories of the variables are along the horizontal axis (x axis) and the values are on the vertical axis (y axis). The bars should not touch each other.

Histogram - a bar graph with the bars touching to produce a shape that reflects the distribution of a variable.

Frequency polygon (or frequency curve) - a line that connects the tops of the bars of a histogram to provide a pure shape illustrating distribution.

Pie chart - this shows the values of a variable as a section of the total cases (like slices of a pie). The percentages are also usually given.

Standard deviation error bar - this shows the mean value as a point and a bar above and below that indicates the extent of one standard deviation.

Confidence interval error bar - this shows the mean value as a point and a bar above and below that indicates the range in which we can be (probabilistically) sure that the mean value of the population from which the sample is drawn lies. The level of confidence can be varied, but it is commonly set at 95 per cent.

Box and whisker plot - this gives more detail of the values that lie within the various percentiles (10th, 25th, 50th, 75th and 90th). Individual values that are outside this range can be pinpointed manually if they are judged to be important.

> **Don't:** Forget that charts and diagrams are far easier to understand quickly by the non-expert than are results presented as numbers.

Bivariate analysis

Bivariate analysis considers the properties of two variables in relation to each other. The relationship between two variables is of common interest in the social sciences, for example: Does social status influence academic achievement? Are boys more likely to be delinquents than girls? Does age have an effect on community involvement? There are various methods for investigating the relationships between two variables.

An important aspect is the different measurement of these relationships, such as assessing the direction and degree of association, statistically termed **correlation coefficients**. The commonly used coefficients assume that there is a linear relationship between the two variables, either positive or negative. In reality, this is seldom achieved, but degrees of correlation can be computed – how near to a straight line the relationship is.

Scattergrams

Scattergrams are a useful type of diagram that graphically shows the relationship between two variables by plotting variable data from cases on a two-dimensional matrix. If the resulting plotted points appear in a scattered and random arrangement, then no association is indicated. If, however, they fall into a linear arrangement, a relationship can be assumed, either positive or negative. The closer the points are to a perfect line, the stronger the association. A line that is drawn to trace this notional line is called the line of best fit or regression line. This line can be used to predict one variable value on the basis of the other.

It is quite possible to get forms of relationships between variables that are not represented in a straight line, for example, groupings or curved linear arrangements. The strength of the scattergrams is that these are clearly shown, thus needing some discussion and possible explanation. For these relationships, statistical tests that assume linearity should not be used.

Contingency tables

Cross-tabulation (contingency tables) is a simple way to display the relationship between variables that have only a few categories. The cells made by the rows show the relationships between each of the categories of the variables in both number of responses and percentages. In addition, the column and row totals and percentages are shown. These can be conveniently produced by IBM SPSS from the data compiled on a matrix. Patterns of association can be detected if they occur. As an alternative, the display can be automatically presented as a bar chart.

The choice of appropriate statistical methods of bivariate analysis depends on the levels of measurement used in the variables. Here are some of the most commonly used:

Pearson's correlation coefficient (r) should be used for examining relationships between interval/ratio variables. The r value indicates the strength and direction of the correlation (how close the points are to a straight line). +1 indicates a perfect positive association and +1 a perfect negative association. Zero indicates a total lack of association.

Spearman's rho (ρ) should be used either when both variables are ordinal, or when one is ordinal and the other is interval/ratio.

Spearman rank correlation coefficient and Kendall's Tau are both used with ordinal data.

Phi (Φ) should be used when both variables are dichotomous (e.g. yes/no).

Cramer's V is used when both variables are nominal and with positive values.

Eta is employed when one variable is nominal and the other is interval/ratio. It expresses the amount of variation in the interval/ratio variable that is due to the nominal variable.

Do: Check with your lecture notes and course guide to see how many of these statistical tests you need to be familiar with.

Statistical significance

As most analysis is carried out on data from only a sample of the population, the question is raised as to how likely is it that the results indicate the situation for the whole population. Are the results simply occasioned by chance or are they truly representative, that is are they **statistically significant**? The process of testing statistical significance to generalize from a sample to the population as a whole is known as **statistical inference**.

The most common statistical tool for this is known as the **chi-square test**. This measures the degree of association or linkage between two variables by comparing the differences between the **observed values** and **expected values** if no association were present, that is those that would be a result of pure chance. This is commonly referred to as the **p value** (p standing for probability). The probability values are sometimes given in reports of quantitative research (e.g. $p = 0.03$ meaning that probability is less than 3 in 100).

A common acceptable maximum p value in social science research is 0.05, but if the researcher wants to be particularly cautious, a maximum of 0.01 is chosen. The value of chi-square is affected by sample size; that is, the bigger the sample, the greater the chance that it will be representative. In addition, for reliable results, the chi-squared calculations require that the minimum expected values of at least 20 per cent of the cells in the contingency table should be greater than 5.

Analysis of variance

The above tests are all designed to look for relationships between variables. Another common requirement is to look for differences between values obtained under two or more different conditions, for example, a group before and after a training course, or three groups after different training courses. There are a range of tests that can be applied depending on the number of groups.

For a single group, say the performance of students on a particular course compared with the mean results of all the other courses in the university, you can use:

Chi-square as a test of 'goodness of fit'.

One-group *t*-test, which compares the means of the results from the sample compared with the population mean.

For two groups, for example comparing the results from the same course at two different universities, you can use:

Two-group *t*-test, which compares the means of two groups. There are two types of test, one for paired scores (i.e. where the same persons provided scores under each condition) or for unpaired scores, where this is not the case.

For three or more groups, for example, the performance of three different age groups in a test, it is necessary to identify the dependent and independent variables that will be tested. A simple test using IBM SPSS is:

ANOVA (analysis of variance). This tests the difference between the means of results gained under different conditions.

One-way analysis of variance is applicable when there is one dependent variable (e.g. an exam mark) and one independent variable (e.g. a new study course) and no matter how many groups or tests are involved. For more complex situations, when more than one independent variable is involved and a single dependent variable, then multiple-way or factorial ANOVA should be used.

Multivariate analysis

Multivariate analysis looks at the relationships between more than two variables.

First, let us look at the effect of a third variable in the relationship between two variables. Elaboration analysis method, devised by Paul Lazarfeld and his colleagues (1972), is a set of techniques that involves a set of steps that has been clearly formulated by Marsh (1982, pp. 84–97) the relationship found in each subgroup with the original relationship.

When presented in tabular form, the initial table (step 1) is called the zero order contingency table, for example, one which shows a significant positive relationship between two variables. However, this may be a spurious result in that the result is actually influenced more by another variable that has not been taken into account. Therefore, a separate table (conditional table) is set up to test the influence of this variable on the two original ones (step 3 above).

If the two tables show a similar significant relationship between the two original variables, this is called replication – the original relationship remains. If neither table shows a significant relationship (zero-order correlation) between the two variables, the original relationship was either spurious, meaning that the test variable actually caused the association between the original variables, or that the test variable is an intervening variable, one that varies because of the independent variable and in turn affects the dependent variable.

If one of the conditional tables demonstrates the association but the other one does not, then it shows a limitation to the association of the original pair of variables, or provides a specification of the conditions under which association occurs.

> **Do:** Use the elaboration method as a good place to start in multivariate analysis. However, its limitation is that it shows what could be happening, but not how and how much the third variable is contributing to the correlation.

You can continue the process of producing tables for fourth and fifth variables, but this quickly becomes unwieldy. It is also difficult to get enough data in each table to achieve significant results. There are better ways to understand the interactions between large numbers of variables and the relative strength of their influence, for example, **regression** techniques such as multiple regression and logistic regression.

Multiple regression

Multiple regression is a technique used to measure the effects of two or more independent variables on a single dependent variable measured on interval or ratio scales, for example, the effect on income due to age, education, ethnicity, area of living and gender. Thanks to computer programs such as IBM SPSS, the complicated mathematical calculations required for this analysis are done automatically. Note that it is assumed that there are interrelationships between the independent variables as well, and this is taken into account in the calculations. The result of multiple regression – the combined correlation of a set of independent variables with the dependent variable – is termed multiple R. The square of this, multiple R2, indicates the amount of variance in the independent variable due to the simultaneous action of two or more independent variables.

Logistic regression

Logistic regression is a development of multiple regression that has the added advantage of holding certain variables constant in order to assess the independent influence of key variables of interest. It is suitable for assessing the influence of independent variables on a dependent variable measured in a nominal scale (for example, whether students' decisions to do a Master's degree were determined by a range of considerations such as cost, future job prospects, level of enjoyment of student life, amount of interest in the subject, etc. (see Field, 2013 for details)). The statistic resulting is an odds ratio (e.g. a student who was interested in the subject was 2.1 times as likely to do a Master's than one who was not, assuming all the other variables were held constant).

Shang-Chun Ma, Ian D. Rotherham and Shang-Min Ma described in 2014 the statistical method they used in their study 'Winning matches in tennis Grand Slam men's singles: a logistic model'.

The study evaluates potential factors determining match wins in tennis Grand Slam men's singles. Their study used a large-scale sample of 9,144 matches (including 845 players) in tennis men's singles Grand Slam tournaments from 1991 to 2008, retrieved from the official open-access website of the Association of Tennis Professionals. It has shown the exceptional value of using regression analysis methods in analysing repeated-measures nature of data (Ma et al., 2014).

Analysis

One dependent variable (match wins) and 21 independent variables were collected to form the regression model. Possible data analysis methods, such as multiple regression and logistic regression, were considered. In this context, multiple regression analysis deals with research problems involving a single metric dependent variable presumed to be related to two or more metric independent variables. For example, if a researcher is concerned about a question such as how well the 'years as a professional' and 'height' predict 'percent of successful first serve', multiple regression is fit for purpose because the dependent variable, percent of successful first serve, is a continuous variable. Logistic regression analysis is similar to multiple regression analysis in that one or more independent variables are used to explain a single-dependent variable. What distinguishes them, however, is that the dependent variable is non-metric. For example, in this case, the outcome variable, winning matches, is a categorical variable because it includes dichotomous situations of 'winning matches' and 'losing matches'. Thus, to suit the particular data scenario, logistic regression analysis was selected. Here, the data analysis approach applied was 'binary' logistic regression because of a dichotomous-dependent variable. If the dependent variable has more than two categories or values, then a 'multinomial' logistic regression must be used. Table 11.1 presents descriptive results by match outcomes.

The issues posed in research data collection and later in modelling match wins were challenging. On the one hand, we retrieved 21 variables regarded as potential predictors. From practical perspective, these were all determinants that constituted a player's performance. Here, for a novice student, he or she may react with a textbook response: deleting variables with multi-co-linearity problems. Multi-co-linearity exists

(Continued)

(Continued)

when two or more independent variables are highly correlated ($r = 0.9$ and above). Nevertheless, our examination of the collected data intended to help answer a question in a real-world context. In this case, it was decided to keep or delete variables relating to multi-co-linearity problems based on both statistical outcomes and more importantly on expert experiences (i.e. from actively engaging in tennis). For example, it is argued that 'age' and 'years of professional experience' can be important factors in determining match outcomes. However, a high correlation was found between age and professional years, signifying multi-co-linearity problems. This indicated that one should be excluded from further analysis. Literature was evaluated to deal with the problem and then develop an argument based on an understanding of tennis as a sport (Ma et al., 2013).

Table 11.1 Descriptive result of match outcomes

Independent Variables (IVs)	Match outcomes (DVs)	
	Wining matches	Losing matches
Age (years)	25.2 (3.4)	25.4 (3.4)
Stature (cm)	184.7 (6.2)	184.2 (6.4)
Mass (kg)	79.3 (6.6)	78.5 (6.7)
Ranking	59.6 (85.9)	93.2 (101)
Years as a professional	6.8 (3.2)	6.6 (3.3)
Aces	8.9 (6.4)	6.6 (5.7)
Double faults	4.2 (3.1)	5.3 (3.4)
% first serve	60.8 (8.3)	58.6 (8.4)
% first serve points won	76.3 (7.9)	66.0 (9.1)
% second serve points won	53.4 (9.8)	43.0 (9.2)
% first serve return points won	33.5 (9.6)	23.4 (9.8)
% second serve return points won	55.9 (9.4)	45.8 (9.9)
% breakpoints converted	47.0 (16)	36.0 (22.8)

On the other hand, at the initial stage of data analysis, we were unaware of the 'repeated-measures' nature of the data whereby a player's performance in one match can influence his performance in other matches. Furthermore, some of the players played more than once over the range of years, suggesting that these observations would not be entirely independent. Reviewers of the initial work from several journals offered this insight. To deal with this problem, a conditional logistic regression model was used to supplement the unconditional logistic regression model. This limits the proposed model's prediction. To improve on the constraints of the limitation, the study by Watts et al. (2012) is relevant.

The variable entry in the hierarchical binominal logistic regression model was made in the order of:

1 Skills and performance
2 Personal characteristics
3 Match characteristics.

The first data entered into the model were for the variable well documented in the literature and the hard-to-intervene variables. Then, the variable of the research concern or easy-to-intervene variable was entered.

Modelling match wins

Through rigorous research design, we found influential determinants of match wins. The findings suggest a model that explains meaningful variance in match outcome and recognized characteristics of winning players from those of losing players. Specifically, a player can improve the chances of winning a match in Grand Slams through higher proportions (e.g. above 60 per cent) of valid first serves, aces, second serve points won, first serves returned, second serves returned and converted and saved break points (skills and performance category). In terms of personal characteristics, players with stature of less than 180 cm height are less likely to win a match than those between 181 and 185 cm. Finally, competitors in Grand Slam men's singles are more likely to win a match in the US Open or Wimbledon than in the French Open. This research established effective guidelines for coaches and professional tennis players in training and preparation for Grand Slam competition.

Path analysis

The detailed effect of the different interrelationships between independent variables on each other and subsequently on the dependent variable is not investigated in multiple regression analysis. Theories about the types and extent of these interrelationships between independent variables and the effect of these on the dependent variable can be tested with path analysis. It requires the researcher to make guesses about how the system of variables works, and then test if these guesses are correct. The path coefficients for pairs of independent variables can be calculated and mapped to show how much changes in each independent variable influence the others and what effect these have on the dependent variable.

Factor analysis

Factor analysis is an exploratory technique used widely in the social sciences to build reliable, compact scales for measuring social and psychological variables. It is used to package information and for data reduction. Although based on complex mathematical calculations (IBM SPSS will do the calculations for you), the idea behind the technique is simple. This is that if a number of variables correlate with each other, they must have something in common. This common thing is called a factor, a 'super-variable' one that encompasses other variables. This simplifies the explanation of the effects of a set of independent variables on a dependent variable.

Factor analysis starts with a matrix of correlations. Large matrices containing numerous variables are notoriously difficult to interpret. Factor analysis makes this easier by identifying clusters of variables that show a high degree of correlation. These clusters can be reduced to a factor. For example, the level of intelligence may be a factor in the exam results of a wide variety of students studying a range of subjects at different educational establishments over years of results. Factors of this type often represent latent (or unobserved) variables – abstract or theoretical constructs that are not directly observable but must be deduced from several other observable variables. Factor analysis is used to examine the relationship between the latent and observed variables.

Multi-dimensional scaling

Multi-dimensional scaling (MDS) is similar to factor analysis in that it reduces data by seeking out underlying relationships between variables. The difference is that MDS does not require metric data, that is data measured on the interval or ratio scale. Many of the data about attitudes and cognition are based on ordinal measurement. By using graphical displays to chart the associations between sets of items (people, things, attitudes, etc.) the strength of association can be easily portrayed. The relationships between three variables can be plotted as a triangle – each point representing a variable and the distance between them representing the strength of association. Points closer together have a higher correlation than those further apart. A similar approach can be used for four variables, although the number of interrelationships (six) means that a three-dimensional display will provide a better picture of the correlation strengths.

Obviously, it is impossible to increase the number of dimensions to match that of the variables, so a two-dimensional map based on a matrix is conventionally used to plot a large number of variables. The stress value can be calculated to gauge the amount of distortion required to reduce the display to two dimensions. The pattern of values distributed on the map is then inspected in order to identify any clusters or arrays that reveal patterns of association.

Cluster analysis

Cluster analysis is a descriptive tool that explores relationships between items on a matrix – which items go together in which order. It measures single link and complete link clustering based on data entered on to a dissimilarity matrix. The result of the analysis is a more closely measured grouping than that achieved visually by MDS (see Bernard, 2012, Chapter 21, for a more detailed explanation). This method does not label the clusters.

Structural equation modelling

Unlike factor analysis, structural equation modelling (SEM) is a confirmatory tool, and has become ever more popular in the social sciences for the analysis of non-experimental data in order to test hypotheses. Its strength is that it provides the opportunity to estimate the extent of error in the model, such as the effects of measurement error. SEM goes a step further than factor analysis by enabling the researcher to test structural (regression) relationships between factors (i.e. between latent variables).

Analysis of variance

Just as ANOVA measured the differences between two variables, the program called MANOVA (multiple analysis of variance) enables you to do many types of analysis of variance with several nominal and interval variables together. It is particularly appropriate when the dependent variable is an interval measure and the predicting variables are nominal. It is also able to detect differences on a set of dependent variables instead of just one.

STATISTICAL TESTS (NON-PARAMETRIC)

Statistical tests built around discovering the means, standard deviations, etc. of the typical characteristics of a Gaussian curve are clearly inappropriate for analysing non-parametric data that do not follow this pattern. Hence, non-parametric data cannot be statistically tested in the ways listed above. Non-parametric statistical tests are used when:

- The sample size is very small
- Few assumptions can be made about the data
- Data are rank-ordered or nominal
- Samples are taken from several different populations.

According to Siegel and Castellan (1988, p. 36), the tests are acknowledged to be much easier to learn and apply, and their interpretation is often more direct than with parametric tests.

Detailed information about which tests to use for particular data sets can be obtained from specialized texts on statistics and your own expert statistical advisor. The levels of measurement of the variables, the number of samples, whether they are related or independent are all factors that determine which tests are appropriate. Here are some tests that you may encounter:

Kolmogorov–Smirnov is used to test a two-sample case with independent samples, the values of which are ordinal.

Kruskal-Wallis test is a non-parametric equivalent of the analysis of variance on independent samples, with variables measured on the ordinal scale.

Friedman test is the equivalent of the above but with related samples.

Cramer coefficient gives measures of association of variables with nominal categories.

Spearman and **Kendall** provide a range of tests to measure association, such as rank-order correlation coefficient, coefficient of concordance and agreement for variables measured at the ordinal or interval levels.

Don't: This is perhaps a good place to warn you that computer statistical packages (e.g. IBM SPSS) will not distinguish between different types of parametric and non-parametric data. In order to avoid producing reams of impressive looking, though meaningless, analytical output, it is up to you to ensure that the tests are appropriate for the type of data you have.

QUANTITATIVE ANALYSIS OF TEXT
Content analysis

Content analysis is an examination of what can be counted in the text. It was developed from the mid-1900s chiefly in America, and is a rather positivistic attempt to apply order to the subjective domain of cultural meaning. A quantitative approach is taken by counting the frequency of phenomena within a case in order to gauge its importance in comparison with other cases. As a simple example, in a study of racial equality, one could compare the frequency of the appearance of black people in television advertisements in various European countries.

Do: Give much importance to careful sampling and rigorous categorization and coding in order to achieve a level of objectivity, reliability and generalizability and the development of theories.

There are five basic stages to this method:

1 Stating the research problem; that is, what is to be counted and why. This will relate to the subject of the study and the relevant contents of the documentary source.
2 Employing sampling methods in order to produce representative findings. This will relate to the choice of publications (e.g. magazine titles), the issues or titles selected and the sections within the issues or titles that are investigated.
3 Retrieving the text fragments. This can be done manually, but computer-based search systems are more commonly used when the text can be digitalized.
4 Quality checks on **interpretation**. This covers issues of:

   - The units of analysis (can the selected stories or themes really be divided from the rest of the text?)
   - Classification (are the units counted really all similar enough to be counted together?)

- Combination of data and formation of '100 per cents' (how can the units counted be weighted by length/detail/authoritativeness and how is the totality of the elements to be calculated?)

5 Analysis of the data (what methods will be used?).

Content frames and coding

This is a preliminary analytical method that tabulates the initial results of content analysis in a content frame. A single publication or article is analysed in order to establish codes that can be used as the basis for the units of measurement to be counted. It is essentially a questionnaire that is filled in by the analyst. A separate content frame is devised to investigate each general question, and each column in the frame is headed by a sub-question that is a component of the general one. The answers to these sub-questions provide the codes that suggest appropriate units of measurement.

Tabulation of results

The numerical data that form the results of a content analysis are most conveniently presented in tabular form. The units of measurement are listed and the number of appearances noted, together with the percentage of the total.

> **Do:** Make checks on the reliability and validity of the use of the content frame and coding. As you must make many personal judgements about the selection and value of the contents of the publications, invite other researchers to check these against your own judgements to check on inter-rater reliability.

What content analysis on its own cannot do is to discover the effects that the publications have on their reader. Other research methods (e.g. questionnaires, interviews, etc.) must be used to gain this type of information. What content analysis can uncover, however, is how the communications are constructed and which styles and conventions of communication are used by authors to produce particular effects. It allows large quantities of data to be analysed in order to make generalizations.

Take it further

Discussion of results

Both spreadsheet and statistical programs will produce very attractive results in the form of charts, graphs and tables that you can integrate into your project report or dissertation

(Continued)

(Continued)

to back up your argument. The important issue is that you have carried out the appropriate analysis related to what you want to demonstrate or test. Explain what data you have collected, perhaps supplying a sample to show their form (e.g. a returned questionnaire), the reasons for doing the particular tests for each section of the investigation, and then present the results of the tests.

Don't: Neglect to explain graphs, tables and other forms of presentation. Do not assume that the reader knows how to read them and that they are self-explanatory in relation to your argument.

Spell out in words the main features of the results and explain how these relate to the parts of the sub-problems or sub-questions that you are addressing. Now draw conclusions. What implications do the results have? Are they conclusive or is there room for doubt? Mention the limitations that might affect the strength of the result, for example, a limited number of responses, possible bias or time constraints. Each conclusion will only form a small part of the overall argument, so you need to fit everything together like constructing a jigsaw puzzle. The full picture should clearly emerge at the end. It is best to devote one section or chapter to each of the sub-problems or sub-questions. Leave it to the final chapter to draw all the threads together in order to answer the main issue of the dissertation.

Do: Computer programs provide you with enormous choice when it comes to presenting graphs and charts. It is best to experiment to see which kind of presentation is the clearest.

Consider whether you will be printing in monochrome or colour, as different coloured graph lines will lose their distinctiveness when reduced to shades of grey. It is also a good idea to set up a style that you maintain throughout the dissertation.

Ask yourself

Univariate analysis essentially describes the properties of one variable. What sorts of description are used?

This is a pretty straightforward question. Refer to the list of descriptive statistics relevant to the properties of one variable, such as frequency distribution, arithmetic mean, etc. You can also mention the ways that these can be displayed, apart from simple numerical statements. You can also expand the answer by suggesting how the descriptions are used to gain understanding of the data.

What does statistical significance mean, and what importance does this have on the usefulness of the results obtained from bivariate analysis?

It is a measure of how much the sample selected is likely to be representative of the population from which it has been drawn. This is obviously important when one wants to make generalizations from the sample to the population. You will need to explain what bivariate analysis is, and mention the chi-square test and explain about probability values. Your textbook will provide you with more information.

Why is multivariate analysis inherently rather complicated? How can these complications be tackled?

Pretty obvious really! Because the interaction of more than two variables is bound to be more complicated than just two. There is also the question of which of the variables are independent and dependent and which are intervening. The second half of the question can be answered by explaining the different statistical tests, such as multiple and logistic regression, path analysis, etc.

Further reading

For a more detailed, though straightforward, introduction to statistics, see:

Foster, L., Diamond, I. and Jeffries, J. (2014) *Beginning Statistics: An Introduction for Social Scientists* (2nd edn). London: Sage.
This book emphasizes description, examples, graphs and displays rather than statistical formula. A good guide to understanding the basic ideas of statistics.

Corder, G. and Foreman, D. (2009) *Nonparametric Statistics for Non-Statisticians: A Step by Step Approach*. Hoboken, NJ: Wiley.
Preece, R. (1994) *Starting Research: An Introduction to Academic Research and Dissertation Writing*. London: Pinter, chapter 7.

For a comprehensive review of the subject, see below. I have listed the simplest text first. The list could go on for pages with ever increasing abstruseness. You can also browse through what is available on your library shelves to see if there are some simple guides there.

Wright, D.B. (2002) *First Steps in Statistics*. London: Sage.
Kerr, A., Hall, H. and Kozub, S. (2002) *Doing Statistics with IBM SPSS*. London: Sage.
Byrne, D. (2002) *Interpreting Quantitative Data*. London: Sage.
Bryman, A. (2001) *Quantitative Data Analysis with IBM SPSS Release 10 for Windows: A Guide for Social Scientists*. London: Routledge.

And for a good guide of how to interpret official statistics, look at part 2 on data archives in:

Seale, C. (ed.) (2012) *Researching Society and Culture* (2nd edn). London: Sage.

TWELVE
Qualitative Data Analysis

Doing research is not always a tidy process where every step is completed before moving on to the next step. In fact, especially if you are doing it for the first time, you often need to go back and reconsider previous decisions or adjust and elaborate on work as you gain more knowledge and acquire more skills. But there are also types of research in which there is an essentially reciprocal process of data collection and data analysis.

Qualitative research is the main one of these. Qualitative research does not involve counting and dealing with numbers but is based more on information expressed in words – descriptions, accounts, opinions, feelings, etc. This approach is common whenever people are the focus of the study, particularly small groups or individuals, but can also concentrate on more general beliefs or customs. Frequently, it is not possible to determine precisely what data should be collected as the situation or process is not sufficiently understood. Periodic analysis of collected data provides direction to further data collection. Adjustments to what is examined further, what questions are asked and what actions are carried out is based on what has already been seen, answered and done. This emphasis on reiteration and interpretation is the hallmark of qualitative research.

> **Do:** Remember that the essential difference between quantitative analysis and qualitative analysis is that with the former, you need to have completed your data collection before you can start analysis, while with the latter, analysis is often carried out concurrently with data collection.

With qualitative studies, there is usually a constant interplay between collection and analysis that produces a gradual growth of understanding. You collect information, you review it, collect more data based on what you have discovered, then analyse again what you have found. This is quite a demanding and difficult process, and is prone to uncertainties and doubts.

Bromley (1986, p. 26) provides a list of 10 steps in the process of qualitative research, summarized as follows:

1 Clearly state the research issues or questions.
2 Collect background information to help understand the relevant context, concepts and theories.
3 Suggest several interpretations or answers to the research problems or questions based on this information.
4 Use these to direct your search for evidence that might support or contradict these. Change the interpretations or answers if necessary.
5 Continue looking for relevant evidence. Eliminate interpretations or answers that are contradictory, leaving, hopefully, one or more that are supported by the evidence.
6 'Cross-examine' the quality and sources of the evidence to ensure accuracy and consistency.
7 Carefully check the logic and validity of the arguments leading to your conclusions.
8 Select the strongest case in the event of more than one possible conclusion.
9 If appropriate, suggest a plan of action in the light of this.
10 Prepare your report as an account of your research.

The strong links between data collection and theory building are a particular feature of qualitative research. Different stress can be laid on the balance and order of these two activities.

Don't: According to grounded theory, the theoretical ideas should develop purely out of the data collected, the theory being developed and refined as data collection proceeds. Don't forget that this is an ideal that is difficult to achieve because without some theoretical standpoint, it is hard to know where to start and what data to collect!

At the other extreme some qualitative researchers (e.g. Silverman, 2015) argue that qualitative theory can first be devised and then tested through data collected by field research, in which case the feedback loops for theory refinement are not present in the process. However, theory testing often calls for a refinement of the theory due to the results of the analysis of the data collected. There is room for research to be pitched at different points between these extremes in the spectrum.

According to Robson (2011, p. 468), the central requirement in qualitative analysis is clear thinking on the part of the analyst, where the analyst is put to the test as much as the data! Although it has been the aim of many researchers to make qualitative analysis as systematic and as 'scientific' as possible, there is still an element of 'art' in dealing with qualitative data. However, in order to convince others of your conclusions, there must be a good argument to support them. A good argument requires high-quality evidence and sound logic. In fact, you will be acting rather like a lawyer presenting a case, using a quasi-judicial approach such as used in an enquiry into a disaster or scandal.

Qualitative research is practised in many disciplines, so a range of methods has been devised to cater for the varied requirements of the different subjects. Bryman (2012, pp. 383–4) identifies the main approaches for collecting data and probing for answers:

Ethnography and participant observation - the immersion of the researcher into the social setting for an extended period in order to observe, question, listen and experience the situation in order to gain an understanding of processes and meanings.

Qualitative interviewing - asking questions and prompting conversation in order to gain information and understanding of social phenomena and attitudes.

Focus groups - asking questions and prompting discussion within a group to elicit qualitative data

Discourse and conversation analysis - a language-based approach to examine how versions of reality are created.

Analysis of texts and documents - a collection and interpretation of written sources.

STEPS IN ANALYSING THE DATA

Qualitative data, represented in words, pictures and even sounds, cannot be analysed by mathematical means such as statistics. So how is it possible to organize all these data and be able to come to some conclusions about what they reveal? Unlike the well-established statistical methods of analysing quantitative data, qualitative data analysis is still in its early stages. The certainties of mathematical formulae and determinable levels of probability are not applicable to the 'soft' nature of qualitative data, which are inextricably bound up with human feelings, attitudes and judgements. Also, unlike the large amounts of data that are often collected for quantitative analysis, which can be readily managed with the available standard statistical procedures conveniently incorporated in computer packages, there are no such standard procedures for codifying and analysing qualitative data.

However, there are some essential activities that are necessary in all qualitative data analysis. Miles and Huberman (2014, pp. 12) suggest that there are three concurrent flows of action:

1 Data reduction
2 Data display
3 Conclusion drawing/verification.

The activity of data display is important. The awkward mass of information that you will normally collect to provide the basis for analysis cannot be easily understood when presented as extended text, even when coded, clustered, summarized, etc. Information in text is dispersed, sequential rather than concurrent, bulky and difficult to structure. Our minds are not good at processing large amounts of information, preferring to simplify complex information into patterns and easily understood configurations.

Do: Use suitable methods to display the data in the form of matrices, graphs, charts and networks, you not only reduce and order the data, but can also analyse it.

PRELIMINARY ANALYSIS DURING DATA COLLECTION

When you conduct field research it is important that you keep a critical attitude to the type and amount of data being collected, and the assumptions and thoughts that brought you to this stage. It is always easier to structure the information while the details are fresh in the mind, to identify gaps and to allow new ideas and hypotheses to develop to challenge your assumptions and biases.

Don't: Raw field notes, often scribbled and full of abbreviations, and tapes of interviews or events need to be processed in order to make them useful. Don't leave these tasks too long as much information will be lost.

The process of data reduction and analysis should be a sequential and continuous procedure, simple in the early stages of the data collection, and becoming more complex as the project progresses. To begin with, one-page summaries can be made of the results of contacts (e.g. phone conversations or visits). A standardized set of headings will prompt the ordering of the information – contact details, main issues, summary of information acquired, interesting issues raised, new questions resulting from these. Similar one-page forms can be used to summarize the contents of documents.

Typologies and taxonomies

As the data accumulate, a valuable step is to organize the shapeless mass of data by building typologies and taxonomies. These are technical words for the nominal level of measurement; that is, ordering by type or properties, thereby forming subgroups within the general category.

Do: Note that even the simplest classification can help you to organize seemingly shapeless information and to identify differences in, say, behaviour or types of people.

For example, children's behaviour in the playground could be divided into 'joiners' and 'loners', or people in the shopping centre as 'serious shoppers', 'window-shoppers', 'passers through', 'loiterers', etc. This can help you to organize amorphous material and to identify patterns in the data. Then, noting the differences in terms of behaviour patterns between these categories can help you to generate the kinds of analysis that will form the basis for the development of explanations and conclusions.

This exercise in classification is the start of the development of a coding system, which is an important aspect of forming typologies. Codes are labels or tags used to allocate units of meaning to the collected data. **Coding** helps you to organize your piles of data (in the form of notes, observations, transcripts, documents, etc.) and provides a first step in conceptualization. It also helps to prevent 'data overload' resulting from mountains of unprocessed data in the form of ambiguous words.

Codes can be used to label different aspects of the subjects of study. Loftland, for example, devised six classes on which to plan a coding scheme for 'social phenomena' (Lofland, 1971, pp. 14–15). These are:

- Acts
- Activities
- Meanings
- Participation
- Relationships
- Settings.

The process of coding is analytical, and requires you to review, select, interpret and summarize the information without distorting it.

> **Do:** Normally, you should compile a set of codes before doing the fieldwork. These codes should be based on your background study. You can then refine them during the data collection.

There are two essentially different types of coding: one that you can use for the retrieval of text sequences, the other devised for theory generation. The former refers to the process of cutting out and pasting sections of text from transcripts or notes under various headings. The latter is a more open coding system that is used as an index for your interpretative ideas, – that is reflective notes or **memos**, rather than merely bits of text.

Several computer programs used for analysing qualitative data (such as NVivo, ATLAS.ti, MAXQDA and others) also have facilities for coding, creating memos, filing and retrieving coded information. They allow codes to be attached to the numbered lines of notes or transcripts of interviews, and for the source of the information/opinion to be noted. This enables a rapid retrieval of selected information from the mass of material collected. However, it does take quite some time to master the techniques involved, so take advice before contemplating the use of these programs.

Pattern coding, memoing and interim summary

The next stage of analysis requires you to begin to look for patterns and themes, and explanations of why and how these occur. This requires a method of pulling together the coded information into more compact and meaningful groupings. Pattern coding can do this by reducing the data into smaller analytical units, such as themes, causes or explanations, relationships among people and emerging concepts, to allow you to develop a more integrated understanding of the situation studied and to test the initial explanations or answers to the research issues or questions. This will generally help to focus later fieldwork and lay the foundations for cross-case analysis in multi-case studies by identifying common themes and processes. Miles and Huberman (2014, p. 81) describe three successive ways that pattern codes may be used:

1   The newly developed codes are provisionally added to the existing list of codes and checked out in the next set of field notes to see whether they fit.
2   The most promising codes are written up in a memo (described below) to clarify and explain the concept so that it can be related to other data and cases.
3   The new pattern codes are tested out in the next round of data collection.

Actually, you will find that generating pattern codes is surprisingly easy, as it is the way by which we habitually process information. However, it is important not to cling uncritically on to your early pattern codes, but to test and develop, and if necessary reject, them as your understanding of the data progresses, and as new waves of data are produced. Compiling memos is a good way to explore links between data and to record and develop intuitions and ideas. You can do this at any time, but it is best done when the idea is fresh!

> **Do:** Remember that memos are written for yourself. The length and style is not important, but it is necessary to label them so that they can be easily sorted and retrieved.

You should continue the activity of memoing throughout the research project. You will find that the ideas become more stable with time until 'saturation' point, that is the point where you are satisfied with your understanding and explanation of the data.

It is a very good idea, at probably about one-third of the way through the data collection, to take stock and seek to reassure yourself and your supervisors by checking:

- The quantity and quality of what you have found out so far
- Your confidence in the reliability of the data
- The presence and nature of any gaps or puzzles that have been revealed
- What still needs to be collected in relation to your time available.

This exercise should result in the production of an **interim summary**, a provisional report a few pages long. This report will be the first time that everything you know about a case will be summarized, and presents the first opportunity to make cross-case analyses in multi-case studies and to review emergent explanatory variables.

Remember, however, that the nature of the summary is provisional and, although perhaps sketchy and incomplete, should be seen as a useful tool for you to reflect on the work done, for discussion with your colleagues and supervisors, and for indicating any changes that might be needed in the coding and in the subsequent data collection work. In order to check on the amount of data collected about each research question, you will find it useful to compile a data accounting sheet. This is a table that sets out the research questions and the amount of data collected from the different, settings, situations, etc. With this you will easily be able to identify any shortcomings.

MAIN ANALYSIS DURING AND AFTER DATA COLLECTION

Traditional text-based reports tend to be lengthy and cumbersome when presenting, analysing, interpreting and communicating the findings of a qualitative research project. Not only do they have to present the evidence and arguments sequentially, they also tend to be bulky and difficult to grasp quickly because information is dispersed over many pages. This presents a problem for you, the writer, as well as for the final reader, who rarely has time to browse backwards and forwards through masses of text to gain full information. This is where certain graphical methods of data display and analysis can largely overcome these problems and are useful for exploring and describing as well as explaining and predicting phenomena. They can be used equally effectively for one case and for cross-case analysis.

Graphical **displays** fall into two categories:

1   Matrices
2   Diagrams.

Matrices (or tables)

Matrices are two-dimensional arrangements of rows and columns that summarize a substantial amount of information. You can easily produce these informally, in a freehand fashion, to explore aspects of the data, and to any size. You can also use computer programs in the form of databases and spreadsheets to help in their production.

> **Do:** You can use matrices to record variables such as time, levels of measurement, roles, clusters, outcomes and effects. If you want to get really sophisticated, the latest developments allow you to formulate three-dimensional matrices.

Diagrams

Diagrams are maps and **networks** used to display data. They are made up of blocks (nodes) that are sometimes connected by links. You can produce these maps and networks in a wide variety of formats, each with the capability of displaying different types of data:

- Flow charts are useful for studying processes or procedures. They are not only helpful in explaining concepts, but their development is a good device for creating understanding.
- Organization charts display relationships between variables and their nature, for example, formal and informal hierarchies.
- Causal networks are used to examine and display the causal relationships between important independent and dependent variables, causes and effects.

These methods of displaying and analysing qualitative data are particularly useful when you compare the results of several case studies because they permit a certain standardization of presentation, allowing comparisons to be made more easily across the cases.

> **Do:** You can display the information on networks in the form of text, codes, abbreviated notes, symbols, quotations or any other form that helps to communicate compactly.

The detail and sophistication of the display can vary depending on its function and on the amount of information available. Displays are useful at any stage in the research process.

Here is an account that Victoria Jupp Kina presented in 2015 of 'analysis and writing up and working your way through the swamp that is your dataset!' Her research was entitled 'Exploring the personal nature of children and young people's participation: a participatory action research study' (Kina, 2015).

Analysis and writing up

This was undoubtedly a daunting stage within the research process. The varied nature of my fieldwork resulted in a wide range of data, including introductory and reflective

(Continued)

(Continued)

evaluation semi-structured interviews, audio recordings of participatory workshops, evaluations completed during workshops with young people and staff, photos from workshop sessions, a participatory evaluation conducted with a group of young people and, not least, my extensive fieldwork diary – that got so long that I had to start a new Microsoft Word document as the programme refused to spell-check any further! However, I soon discovered that the analysis had started long before I officially moved onto this phase of the research and by systematically transcribing the interviews I was able to connect comments made by the participants with events, reflections and challenges that had also been recorded elsewhere. This way the themes and links began to emerge naturally, and I began to be able to map out the findings visually. Although I used NVivo to organize the data, I also worked in the old-fashioned way using a flip chart and markers as I found the physical action of drawing out a map of my main ideas helped to develop my thinking and link my own findings to wider literature. My main challenge during this stage was knowing when to stop – the data analysis process continually led me to explore new paths, to return to the literature with a new eye or to even explore completely new areas of literature that I had not accessed previously. This meant that I spent too long analysing, and therefore, this significantly impacted on the time I had to write up. My suspicion is that this is for two reasons: first, the more I returned to the literature, the more I felt I needed to know in order to ensure I was interpreting my data accurately, and second, the complete fear of putting my thoughts and ideas 'out there' for scrutiny. I think that these feelings are somewhat inevitable within research and particularly within the social sciences where notions of socially constructed understandings of society inform so much of our thinking. So on reflection, I think it is important to roll with these feelings and accept them as an inevitable and valuable part of the research process. Fears of scrutiny tighten our analysis and ensure we have thought about not just what we think but why we think it, so as hard as it may be, try to embrace the feeling. Although I would probably also say that this needs to be balanced out against deadlines, the final year disappeared before I knew it and I regretted not setting clear deadlines for myself to ensure that I did not stagnate. My strategy shifted as my submission date loomed to one of the clear deadlines in which my supervisors took a strong role in ensuring I produced the chapters and kept to task, and I probably should have taken this more structured approach throughout the whole of my final year.

QUALITATIVE ANALYSIS OF TEXTS AND DOCUMENTS

Documentary sources form a large resource of data about society, both historically and of the present. The analysis of the subtleties of text is not a simplistic matter and, as usual in research, there is a wide range of analytical methods that can be applied to documentary sources. Both quantitative and qualitative options are available. Here is a brief summary of the main methods and their characteristics.

> **Do:** Check your course guide and lecture notes to see which are featured as you may not need to know about all of them. If you are going to do some research as part of your assessment, perhaps some of these methods might be applicable to your own project.

Interrogative insertion

By devising and inserting implied questions into a text for which the text provides the answers, the analyst can uncover the logic (or lack of it) of the discourse and the direction and emphasis of the argument as made by the author. This helps to uncover the recipient design of the text – how the text is written to appeal to a particular audience and how it tries to communicate a particular message.

Problem-solution discourse

Problem–solution discourse (PSD) develops interrogative insertion by investigating more closely the implications of statements. Most statements can be read to have one of two implications. The first is the assertion of a fact or a report of a situation, the second is a call for action or a command. This is very commonly found in advertising (e.g. 'Feeling tired? Eat a Mars Bar'). The same, but in a more extended form, is found in reports, instruction manuals, even this SAGE COURSE COMPANION. A full problem–solution discourse will tabulate the results of the analysis of a text under the following categories:

* The situation
* The problem
* The response
* The result and evaluation.

The absence of any of the categories in the report will lead to a sense of incompleteness and lack of logical argument. A negative result and evaluation will result in a feeling of incompleteness and may lead either to an apportionment of blame or to a further round of PSD as a response to the new problem posed by the unsatisfactory outcome. Another way of presenting the analysis of PSD is to devise a network in the form of a decision tree that traces the problems and the possible solutions with their implications (very often grouped in threes, and assessed according to desirability, suitability, etc.).

> **Don't:** Forget that each person involved in the same situation will perceive the problems and solutions differently according to their standpoint and values. Their judgements and attitudes will be revealed by this type of analysis.

Membership categorization

Membership category analysis (MCA) is a technique that analyses the way people, both writers and readers, perceive commonly held views on social organization, how people are expected to behave, how they relate to each other and what they do in different social situations. Examples of these are the expected relationships between parents and their children, the behaviour of members of different classes of society or the roles of different people in formal situations. Most of these assumptions are not made explicit in the text. By highlighting what is regarded as normal, assumptions and pre-judgements may be revealed and an understanding of typical characterization can be gained.

The category is the label for the unit being considered. Every person can be categorized in many different ways, but the label chosen brings with it certain expectations (e.g. a factory worker, an executive, a parent). Category modifiers provide some additional meaning to the category (e.g. hard-working parent, militant trade unionist). A membership category device (MCD) is the label given to a particular grouping of categories into a unit, for example parents and children are grouped to make the MDC 'family', a bride-to-be and her friends celebrating before the wedding form a 'hen party'.

Standardized relational pairs are expected to perform in particular ways with each other, such as the employee will behave with deference to the boss, the parents will look after their children. The type of expected behaviour is called a category-bound activity. The reader will tend to group people mentioned into membership categories unless it is indicated otherwise, for example, parent and child will be expected to belong to the same family, a bride and groom are a wedding couple.

Rhetorical analysis

As I am writing this book, a national election campaign is in full swing. All the politicians are trying to give the impression that they should be believed, and harness the vocabulary and structure of spoken and written language to bolster this impression – clearly demonstrating the use of rhetoric. Rhetorical analysis uncovers the techniques used in this kind of communication.

Rhetoric is used to aim at a particular audience or readership. It may appeal to, and engender belief in, the target audience, but is likely to repel and undermine the confidence of others. For example, a racist diatribe will encourage certain elements on the far-right but repel others.

Any type of partisan writing will contain clear credibility markers, signals that indicate the 'rightness' of the author and the 'wrongness' of others. Typical markers in this kind of text are:

- Correct moral position
- Alliance with oppressed groups
- Privileged understanding of the situation
- Deconstruction of alternatives as unbelievable.

Even in apparently non-partisan writing, such as scientific reports, where the author is de-personalized, rhetorical techniques are used to persuade the reader about the 'rightness' of the conclusions. Markers to look for are:

- Objectivity
- Methodical practice
- Logicality
- Circumspection.

> **Do:** Remember that it is impossible to avoid the use of rhetoric in writing. This form of analysis will reveal the effect of the rhetoric used.

If rhetoric is used purposely to target a message or convince an audience, one should be become even more aware of the techniques used in order to uncover the hidden arguments and suggestive language employed.

Semiotics

Semiotics is the 'science of signs'. This approach is used to examine other media (e.g. architecture and design) as well as written texts. Semiotics attempts to gain a deep understanding of meanings by the interpretation of single elements of text rather than to generalize through a quantitative assessment of components. The approach is derived from the linguistic studies of Saussure, in which he saw meanings being derived from their place in a system of signs. Words are only meaningful in their relationship with other words, for example, we only know the meaning of 'horse' if we can compare it with different animals with different features.

This approach was further developed by Barthes and others to extend the analysis of linguistic-based signs to more general sign systems in any sets of objects:

> semiotics as a method focuses our attention on to the task of tracing the meanings of things back through the systems and codes through which they have meaning and make meaning. (Slater, 1998, p. 240)

Hence the meanings of a red traffic light can be seen as embedded in the system of traffic laws, colour psychology, codes of conduct and convention, etc. (which could explain why in China a red traffic light means 'go'). A strong distinction is therefore made between denotation (what we perceive) and connotation (what we read into) when analysing a sign. Bryman (2012, p. 295) lists the most important terms that are used in semiotics, summarized as follows:

Sign - a signal denoting something. This consist of a signifier and signified.

Signifier - that which performs as a vehicle for the meaning.

Signified - what the signifier points to.

Denotative meaning - the obvious functional element of the sign.

Connotative meaning - a further meaning associated with a particular social situation.

Sign function - an object that denotes a certain function.

Polysemy - the term that indicates that signs can be interpreted in different ways.

Code or sign system - the generalized meaning instilled in a sign by interested parties.

Discourse analysis

Discourse analysis studies the way that people communicate with each other through language within a social setting. Language is not seen as a neutral medium for transmitting information; it is bedded in our social situation and helps to create and recreate it. Language shapes our perception of the world, our attitudes and identities. While a study of communication can be broken down into four elements (sender, message code, receiver and channel), or alternatively into a set of signs with both syntactical (i.e. orderly or systematic) organization and semantic (i.e. meaningful and significant) relationships, such simplistic analysis does not reflect the power of discourse.

It is the triangular relationship between discourse, cognition and society that provides the focus for this form of analysis (van Dijk, 1994, p. 122). Two central themes can be identified: the interpretative context in which the discourse is set, and the rhetorical organization of the discourse. The former concentrates on analysing the social context, for example, the power relations between the speakers (perhaps due to age or seniority) or the type of occasion where the discourse takes place (a private meeting or at a party). The latter investigates the style and scheme of the argument in the discourse, for example, a sermon will aim to convince the listener in a very different way from a lawyer's presentation in court.

Post-structuralist social theory, and particularly the work of the French theorist Michel Foucault, has been influential in the development of this analytical approach to language. According to Foucault (1972, p. 43), discourses are 'practices that systematically form the objects of which they speak'. He could thus demonstrate how discourse is used to make social regulation and control appear natural.

Take it further

Hermeneutics

This is not a method for the uninitiated, but it may be useful to know about it, especially if you are reading some research that has been based on this method. Modern hermeneutics is derived from the techniques used to study sacred texts, especially the Bible. It is based on the principles of interpretivism in that it aims to discover the meanings within the text while taking into account the social and historical context in which it was written. Weber's concept of *Verstehen* is closely linked with this approach.

> **Don't:** Ignore the fact that this form of analysis requires a deep knowledge of the relevant culture and language in order to understand the symbolic references contained in the text.

Phillips and Brown (1993, pp. 1558–67) identify three stages in the process, referred to as 'moments':

1 **The social-historical moment** – this stage involves the investigations into the context in which the text is written, produced and read, what it refers to, who it is aimed at and who wrote it and why.
2 **The formal moment** – this stage consists of an examination of the structure and formal qualities of the text, using several possible methods such as semiotics or discourse analysis.
3 **The interpretation-reinterpretation moment** – in this stage the first two 'moments' are synthesized.

Ask yourself

What are the first steps in analysing qualitative data that you can undertake during data collection? Describe some of the techniques involved.

Apart from making one-page summaries, the process of classification through the generation of typologies and taxonomies forms an important part of analysis that can feed back into subsequent data gathering. After explaining what this involves, you can then go on to discuss the activities of pattern coding and memoing, giving examples of the sorts of code you might use in a particular type of research.

Describe three different qualitative methods of analysing text.

This is a pretty straightforward question to answer. You just need to select three of the several methods described in this chapter, for example, rhetorical analysis or

(Continued)

(Continued)

problem-solving discourse. You will probably need to refer to your textbook to find enough information for a longer answer. Include a discussion of the contexts in which each is suitable for use, and some comparison of their relative merits would provide more evidence of your knowledge and understanding.

Is it possible to maintain a completely neutral role when analysing qualitative data?

I think a politician's answer is probably the best here – 'yes and no'! You will need to stand back every now and again to consider your position in relation to the issues being examined. Keeping a detached attitude to the data will ensure that accusations of bias can be rebutted, but there is no way of getting away from the fact that you will need to make many personal judgements as to the relative significance of factors, in the absence of rigorous methods of measurement.

Further reading

As you would expect with this big and complex a subject, there are a myriad of books dedicated to explaining all aspects of qualitative data analysis. All the textbooks on social research methods will have sections on qualitative analysis. In the list below, I have tried to explain a bit about the individual book and how it may be of use to you. I have ordered them in what I think is going from simplest to most sophisticated.

Robson, C. (2011) *Real World Research: A Resource for Social Scientists and Practitioner-Researchers* (3rd edn). Oxford: Blackwell.
A brilliant resource book, and should be used as such. Good for getting more detailed information on most aspects of data collection and analysis.

David, M. and Sutton, C. (2004) *Social Research: The Basics*. London: Sage.
See chapter 16 to start with.

Bryman, A. (2012) *Social Research Methods* (4th edn). Oxford: Oxford University Press.
Another fantastic book on all aspects of social research. Perhaps it is your set textbook. Part 3 is about qualitative research.

Flick, U. (2009) *An Introduction to Qualitative Research* (4th edn). London: Sage.
Part 4 of the book is dedicated to analysing verbal data, with practical advice on documentation, coding, interpretation and analysis. Part 5 is about observation and ethnography, including visual data. The second half of the book is dedicated to analysing verbal, visual data, with practical advice on documentation, coding, interpretation and analysis. Be selective in picking out what is relevant to you, as a lot of it will not be.

Seale, C. (ed.) (2012) *Researching Society and Culture* (2nd edn). London: Sage.
This edited book has chapters by various authors, each on one aspect of research. See those on qualitative analysis, choosing whatever is appropriate for your study.

For a really comprehensive, though incredibly dense and rather technical guide to qualitative data analysis, refer to:

Miles, M., Huberman, A. and Saldaña, J. (2013) *Qualitative Data Analysis: An Expanded Sourcebook*. London: Sage.
This has a lot of examples of displays that help to explain how they work, but is technically sophisticated so you might find it difficult initially to understand the terminology in the examples.

Your library catalogue will list many more. Try a search using key words, such as data analysis, with management, education (or whatever your particular subject is), to see if there are specific books dedicated to your particular interest. And a few more books if you don't find what you want in the above.

Silverman, D. (2015) *Interpreting Qualitative Data* (5th edn). London: Sage.
A fantastic range of topics covered here, with interesting sections on why talk matters in part 2.

Holliday, A. (2007) *Doing and Writing Qualitative Research*. London: Sage.
A general guide to writing qualitative research aimed at students of sociology, applied linguistics, management and education.

Schwandt, T. (2007) *The Sage Dictionary of Qualitative Enquiry* (3rd edn). Thousand Oaks, CA: Sage.
To help you understand all the technical jargon.

Coffey, A. and Atkinson, P. (1996) *Making Sense of Qualitative Data: Complementary Research Strategies*. London: Sage.

PART III

WRITING UP YOUR RESEARCH

THIRTEEN
Presenting Data Graphically

A picture is worth a thousand words, so goes the saying, and there is an element of truth in this, but only if the picture is a true reflection of the data. The best way to present data is in graphical form, which can provide a compact list of the results, describe the data according to some criteria of measurement or bring them into relationship with other data. In the previous chapters on data collection and analysis, various ways of presenting data have been mentioned in the text. This chapter illustrates examples of a wide selection of these graphics, and provides some advice on their features and how to use them appropriately.

In general, in order to present data effectively in graphics, you have to do several things at once to make sure that it:

1   Accurately illustrates the data
2   Presents the data as simply as possible
3   Uses colour to clarify the message
4   Is consistent across comparative presentations.

Graphics should be used to stimulate thinking by enabling the interpretation of data. You can use them effectively to reduce the amount of textual explanation when describing trends, relationships and comparisons. It is, of course, important to use the right type of graphic to portray your ideas. As a rule you should ensure that each graphic has a heading and that the components are labelled and the data sources are indicated.

> **Do:** Before you start devising a graphic, write down in words exactly what you are aiming to communicate. Then, when completed, check that it is doing just that.

With all graphics, you should devise a title or caption that provides enough detail that the reader can understand the content without needing to consult the accompanying text. Number them too – tables are usually numbered separately from other graphics and pictures – entitled 'figures'. In longer texts such as dissertations, you will need to provide a list of tables and figures with their page numbers at the beginning with the contents list. You can use the 'insert caption' facility in your word-processor to make this simple.

TABLES

These are used to cross reference a list of variables or other factors (usually down the left hand column) with a list of values or descriptions (usually distributed along the top line). Tables can be used both for quantitative and qualitative data. They are a very versatile presentation method and are primarily used to reduce the data into a manageable form that can be easily reviewed and understood – particularly necessary when analysing a mass of qualitative data.

Tables are an effective way of presenting quantitative data when:

- The single variable is measured at different points (in time or space).
- The data set contains relatively few numbers.
- Precise variable values must be presented.

Because most people find it easier to identify patterns in numerical data by reading down a column rather than across a row, it is best to put the values in the columns. If there is a pattern in the values, for example, a bunching or progression, make this clear by ordering them in such a way as to make this clear. Don't make the tables too complex by introducing numerous columns. Split it into two or more tables to make them easy to read. Present the values in their most simple format. This may mean rounding up values to avoid the use of decimal places (e.g. £3.7 million rather than £3,685,638) or using scientific notation (e.g. 5.412×10^{-2} rather than 0.05412). See Table 13.1 as an example.

Table 13.1   Membership of case studies by occupation category

	Case study 1	Case study 2	Case study 3	Case study 4	Total
Production	10	18	3	26	57
Administration	14	21	25	11	71
Sales	7	4	2	23	36
Finance	4	2	16	5	27
Total	35	45	46	65	191

Indicate the source of the data being used, whether they are data found in the literature or generated by yourself in your research. There is a wide range of automatic computer-based formatting choices available, using various combination of lines and shading. Experiment with these to choose the one that presents the data most clearly. It is important to distinguish between the variables and the data, so the top row and first column should be distinctive.

But tables are not only used to display quantitative data – they are really useful for qualitative data in the form of concepts, variables in the form of words, events, etc. These tables are often referred to as matrices. Here, precision is not the aim, but clarification is. The best way to reduce the mass of formless data into intelligible form is to tabulate it – showing relationships and qualities of the variables under consideration (see Table 13.2).

Table 13.2 Self-build skills in nine case studies

TASKS.... INITIATION AND DESIGN PHASE	grade of difficulty	PET	NVT	GL	DU	LTM	DCH	HOL	FUS	BA
Investigation of situation, inception	low	R	P	P	P	P	P	P	R	P/R
formulation of brief	med	R	P/R	P	P	D/P	P	P	P/R	P/R
source land	low	R	P	P	P	P	P	P	P/R	P/R
survey site	high	P	P	N	P	P/R	P	P	P	P
design site layout	med	P	P	N	T	D	P	P	P/D	P
design house plan layout	high	P/R	P/R	P	P	D	P	P	D	P
3D house design	high	P	P	P	P	P/D	P	P	D	P
construction design	high	P	P	P	P	P	P	P	D/P	P
structural design	high	P	P	N	P	P	P	P	P	P
planning and building regs applications	high	P	P	P	P	P	P	P	P	P
costing and programming	high	R	P	P	P	P	P	P	P	P
find funds	med	R	P	T	P	T	P	P	P	P/R
find self-builders	low	R	T	P	T	T	P	P	R	R/P
select self-builders	med	R	R	P	T	R/P	P	P	R	R/P
select professionals	low	R	P	P	P	R/P	P	P	P/R	P/R

Key: skill requirement

R   required skill of self-builders

D   deskilling of task to reduce skill requirement

T   training provided to instil skill required

P   professional person allocated to task

N   no requirements for skill and task within the scope of the project

Key: skill difficulty grade

LOW   no particular skills, though some instructions necessary

MEDIUM   basic skills requiring limited training and practice

HIGH   sophisticated skills requiring extended training and practice

> ✓   **Do:** If you are comparing several case studies, you can combine the matrices to make meta-matrices displays that amalgamate and contrast the data from each case.

For example, a case-ordered meta-matrix does this by simply arranging case matrices next to each other in the chosen order to enable you simply to compare the data across the meta-matrix. The meta-matrix can initially be quite large if there are a number of cases. A function of the analysis is to summarize the data in a smaller matrix, giving a summary of the significant issues discovered. Following this a contrast table can also be devised to display and compare how one or two variables perform in cases as ordered in the meta-matrix.

> ✕   **Don't:** Leave the interpretation of the graphic to the reader. Always refer to the graphic in your text and explain what it shows.

Contingency table

A contingency table is used to analyse and record the relationship between two or more categorical variables. Contingency tables will normally have as many rows as there are categories. As a simple way to display the frequency distribution of the variables resulting from survey data, it provides a basic picture of the inter-relation between two variables. Contingency tables are also used as part of the output from Chi-square statistical tests, which test the statistical significance of the differences between the expected frequencies with actual ones resulting from a survey. Table 13.3 is a simple example of a contingency table.

Table 13.3   Contingency table

	Right-handed	Left-handed	Total
Males	43	9	52
Females	44	4	48
Totals	87	13	100

CHARTS

Charts are used to plot data in two dimensions using a so-called x-axis in the horizontal dimension and y-axis in the vertical dimension to display the range of values. The known values go on the x-axis and the measured values on the y-axis. Grid lines are commonly used in order to make the individual values clear to read. There are a range of charts that are suitable for a variety of data sets. These are explained below.

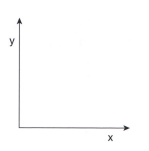

Figure 13.1 X-axis and y-axis

Line chart or graph

These are used to show the movements or trends in one or more data sets over time. The x-axis is used to measure the time equal intervals, for example, years, months, etc. Line graphs may consist of straight lines between points or curved segments that interpolate the values between measured points. You can even use line charts to extrapolate beyond known data values (i.e. make a forecast of future trajectories). By comparing different data sets on one graph; that is, producing two or more lines, you can compare trends and perhaps detect similarities between these. If the area below the line is coloured to emphasize change in values, it is called an area chart.

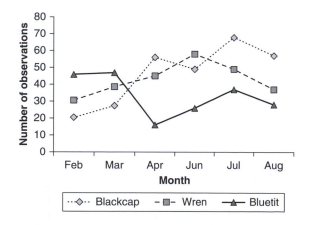

Figure 13.2 Multiple line graph

Don't: Start the y-axis scale at a value above 0 as this can give the wrong impression of the extent of the movement up and down. This is also relevant for bar charts. ⊗

Bar chart

These can be arranged in a variety of ways, with vertical or horizontal bars, single or multiple, which should start at zero on the y-axis, and can measure positive as well as negative values on the y-axis. They are used to show the relationship between the data's values in terms of the bar lengths. As with graphs, it is very important that the bars are correctly drawn with the scale shown – including the zero point. They are good for presenting small amounts of data over a nominal or interval scale. If the labels of the variables are long, it may be more convenient to use horizontal bars so the labels can more easily be read.

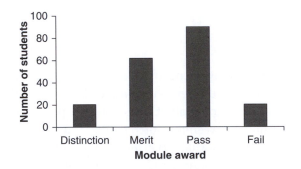

Figure 13.3   Bar chart. Average publication sales per week per kiosk

Multiple columns or bars can be used to present data for several variables. For clarity, do not overlap the bars. It is normal that the different data sets are measured at the same scale, even though different scales are sometimes used (one measured on the left y-axis and the other on the right y-axis). If you choose the latter, ensure that the message you want to get across is still clear and that the different scales do not add confusion.

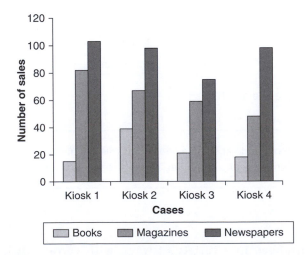

Figure 13.4   Multiple bar chart. Average weekly publication sales per kiosk

Stacked and segmented bar chart

These charts divide the bar into sections of different data categories so they can show the values of each category within the total as well as the total and be compared across time. They can either be arranged to show real values (stacked) or show percentage proportions of the totals (segmented). It is easier to perceive relative to the measurements on the bars, than as segments of a circle, so they tend to give a more accurate picture than pie charts.

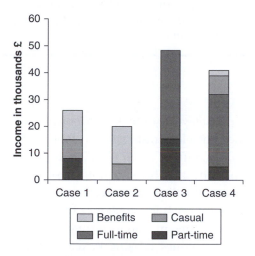

Figure 13.5 Stacked bar chart. Family incomes

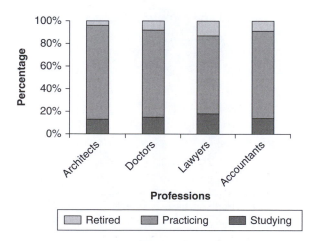

Figure 13.6 Segmented bar chart. Professional stages

Histogram

A histogram has bars that touch at the sides and is used to display the frequency or proportion of cases that fall within defined intervals or columns. The bars on the histogram can be of varying width depending on the range of the measurement, and typically display continuous data. They are useful for larger sets of data points. A histogram can also be expressed in the form of an area chart (including stacked and with total) where the segmented columns are replaced by a coloured area under a line showing the totals.

> **Do:** Note that a bar graph is not the same as a histogram. On a histogram, the width of the bar varies according to the range of the x-axis variable (e.g. 0-2, 3-10, 11-20, 20-40 and so on) and the area of the column indicates the frequency of the data. With a bar graph, it is only the height of the bar that matters.

Pie chart

This is a familiar way to display the different proportions of elements that add up to the total. There is no time element in this – it represents the state at a particular moment. They are only suitable when there are few segments (not more than about six) and it is important that these are not too slim to gauge the proportion. Because the segments are difficult to measure, they only provide an approximate impression of the relative values. It is a good idea to use shades of the same colour if the items are related, and different colours if they are unrelated, for example, fall into completely different categories. It helps the reader if the sections start at 12.00 o'clock and go clockwise, showing the values in order of magnitude, largest first.

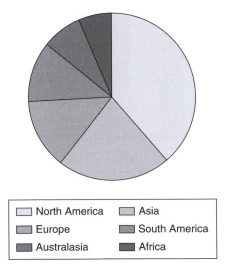

North America	Asia
Europe	South America
Australasia	Africa

Figure 13.7 Pie chart. Proportion of world's millionaires

> **Don't:** Use 3D versions of pie charts, they are difficult to read however much they resemble an attractive cake! Use exploded views with caution - best to emphasize just one segment.

Scatter plot chart

These are used to show correlation between two data sets. This chart type has two dependent variables: One is plotted along the x-axis, the other along the y-axis; the independent variable is the intersection of both dependent variables, realized as a data point in the diagram. It conveys an overall impression of the relationship between two variables. The way that the plots (or dots) are arranged can indicate whether there is some kind of a relationship between two variables. Statistical programs use these to display lines of regression, which show the mid-line between the points if they tend to bunch into a roughly linear fashion.

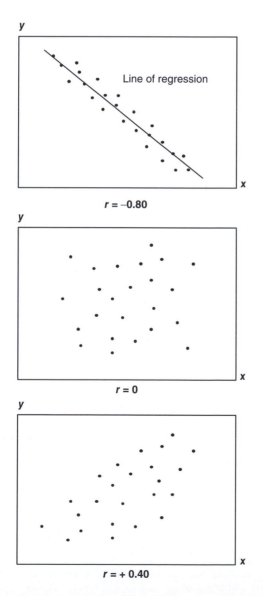

Figure 13.8   Scatter plot charts showing different degrees of relationship

Error bar and box and whisker charts

Some data present variability in their measurements because they cannot be accurately measured.

Charts with error bars are used to represent the variability of data and depict error or uncertainty in a reported measurement. They give a general idea of the range of values presented in the measurements and how far from the reported value the true (error free) value might be. Charts with box and whisker plots show the same thing but emphasize their quartiles by a box shape and lines (whiskers). Outliers (values that are exceptionally at extreme ends of the scale) may be plotted as individual points.

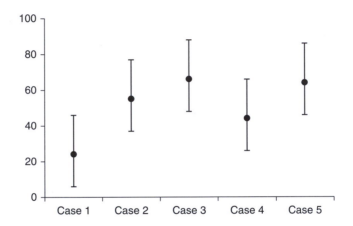

Figure 13.9 Error bar chart

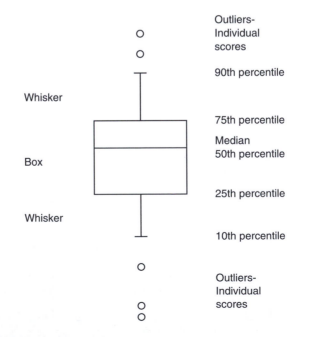

Figure 13.10 Whisker and box plot

Pictogram

These are used to present data in a non-technical way for the general reader. Instead of bars on the charts, some form of relevant pictorial representation is used, for example, lines of cars, people, etc. It is best to use repeated images in a line to represent the amounts rather than the same image in different sizes, as the increase in size is in two dimensions making the area the measure rather than a line.

Venn diagram

This is an arrangement of overlapping circles, each circle representing a variable. It is used to plot how the variables relate to each other, overlapping one or more of each other to various degrees when they share properties. You can use the size of the circles to indicate the values of the variables.

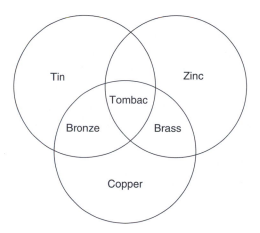

Figure 13.11   Venn diagram. Alloys of tin, zinc and copper

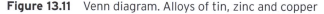

Do: Always label the diagrams clearly and specify the units of measurement on the x- and y-axis. Show gridlines to help interpretation. Always use appropriate rounding of numbers on the axes.

Radar chart

This spider's web of a chart displays multivariate data in more than three quantitative variables represented on axes starting from the same point. A radar chart is also called, unsurprisingly, a spider chart, web chart, but also polar chart, star chart or star plot. The relative position and angle of the axes is of no consequence, but the shape of the plots give a quick impression of the balance between the various values.

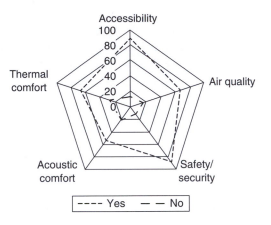

Figure 13.12   Radar chart. Perceived improvements after a building renovation

Word cloud

This is an interesting way to visualize the frequency distribution of words with textual data. The data can be in the form of written material, speech and thought expressed in words. Although not exactly measurable, it does provide an attractive way to represent the comparative importance of words or thoughts in a graphic manner. Word clouds can be a useful way to quickly analyse open-ended comments from surveys, and have the advantage that they are easily understood by the reader. You can download free word cloud programs from the internet.

Figure 13.13   Word cloud. Of the introduction to this chapter

DIAGRAMS

Diagrams provide a really big range of choices for displaying and analysing data, particularly qualitative data and the relationships between variables. I cannot cover all of these in detail, but here as a summary is a taxonomy tree diagram to show the main types of diagrammatic displays.

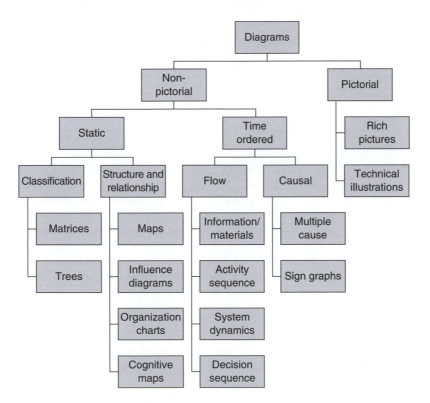

Figure 13.14   Taxonomy tree diagram of types of diagram

I will briefly describe some of the types of diagram that I think will be most useful to you, and provide some indication of what they are like and what they are used for.

Maps

There are two main types of map:

- Geographical maps
- Conceptual maps.

Geographical maps can be used to enable spatial analysis, or identify locations and extents of single features. They are usually based on accurately scaled geographic maps that are coloured in or annotated to present the desired information. However, distorted maps called cartograms have been used to show comparative values by proportional area sizes, for example, showing relative population densities – only useful if you can still recognize the map for what it was originally. Another cartogram made familiar during the recent parliamentary elections is one that depicts the location of each area returning one member of parliament (ward) with the same size tile, coloured according to the party of the winning candidate. This distorts the map, as the areas are actually all different sizes.

⊗ | **Don't:** Forget that most people will try to interpret a map without reading the notes or the scale.

There are three main ways to display geographical data on maps:

- Colour shading maps – this is the most common type, and is especially appropriate for showing standardized data such as rates, densities or percentages. How you use colour is an important factor in presenting these maps. Use shades of the same colour if values of the same variable are shown, for example, density of doctors per area, but use different colours if displaying categorical variables, for example, different underlying rocks types in a geological map.
- Proportional symbol maps – these use symbols that are proportional in size to the values they represent, such that the biggest symbol will fall in the area with the highest value. Symbols can include circles, bars or objects indicating what is being measured. This type of map is better for count data.
- Dot maps – individual events or groups of events are marked with a dot, allowing users to see distribution patterns such as clusters. A famous use of this technique was by Dr John Sow, who mapped cholera deaths in an outbreak in London in 1854 and was able to show that they were concentrated around a particular water pump.

⊗ | **Don't:** Use white for any of the areas of the map – except to represent missing data.

Conceptual maps are entirely different. These are not based on physical geography at all, but consist of an arrangement on paper of concepts, ideas, organizations, etc. that show their structure or relationships with each other. Concept maps are usually hierarchical in arrangement, with the subordinate concepts stemming from the main concept or idea. Think first what issue or concept you aim to clarify, and start with writing this down. Then decide on the subordinate concepts that connect and relate to your main idea and rank them; most general, inclusive concepts come first, then link to smaller, more specific concepts. When you have written these down in an arrangement on the page, connect them with lines and arrows to create links, perhaps adding words to give meaning to them. These lines can link adjacent concepts but can also link those further apart, showing connections across the system.

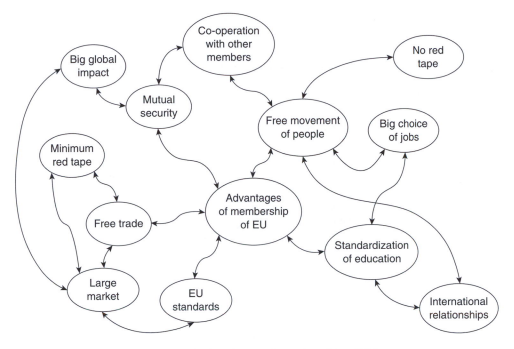

Figure 13.15   Conceptual map of advantages of membership of EU

Networks

Most of these consist of a series of boxes or blobs that contain words depicting what they represent, and lines that link them. The position of the blobs, either in relation to each other, adjacent, overlapping or even contained within another, is often a significant feature of the diagram. The lines are also important, indicating links or lines of influence or even cause. They sometimes have arrows to indicate the direction of flow, or causal effect.

Flow/process chart

This is used to illustrate the steps and sometimes decision in a process. These are often used to guide decision making in a structured fashion, for example, fault finding in a car engine. They are sometimes also called decision trees. There is a convention to follow about the shape of the boxes.

- Lozenge shape for the beginning and end
- Rectangle for an action
- Circle for a constant

- Parallelogram for an input
- Diamond for a decision.

Lines with arrowheads show the direction of the flow or decision making.

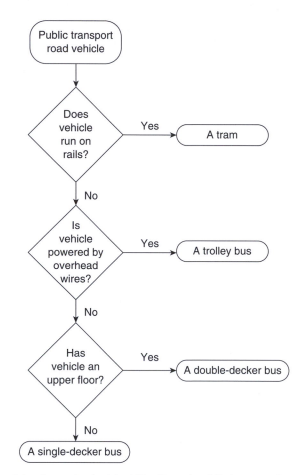

Figure 13.16 Decision tree chart – identification of public transport road vehicles

Organization chart

This displays relationships between variables and their nature, for example, formal and informal hierarchies. The most familiar of these is perhaps those that illustrate the hierarchy of a company from the bosses down to the operatives. Although this is likely to be pyramidical in appearance, this is not the case for all organizations, particularly informal ones. The convention is to start with the most senior or most responsible roles at the top, and work down to those further 'down the line' Lines between roles indicate the paths of responsibility. Informal organizations might appear to be arranged more in a network.

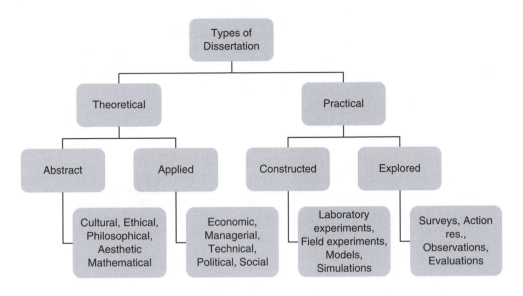

Figure 13.17 Organization chart. Types of dissertation

Causal network

This is used to examine and display the causal relationships between important independent and dependent variables, showing causes and effects. Here, the direction of the arrowheads at the end of the connecting lines is important, as it shows the direction of the causal effect. Actually, the lines may be read as meaning 'contributes to' 'enables' and other less definitive terms. It is a good idea to label the lines to indicate these. Lines can go in both directions between two variables indicating a feedback loop. The phrases should describe variables rather than things, for example, level of income, rather than just income. The network should be read sequentially – that is, there is a time element involved.

Time-ordered displays

These record a sequence of events in relation to their chronology. A simple example of this is a project programme giving names, times and locations for different kinds of task. The scale and precision of timing can be suited to the subject. Events can be of various types, for example, tasks, critical events, experiences, stages in a programme, activities, decisions, etc.

Some examples of types of time-ordered displays are:

- **Events lists or matrices** - showing a sequence of events, perhaps highlighting the critical ones, and perhaps including times and dates.
- **Activity records** - showing the sequential steps required to accomplish a task.
- **Decision models** - commonly used to analyse a course of action employing a matrix with yes/no routes from each decision taken.

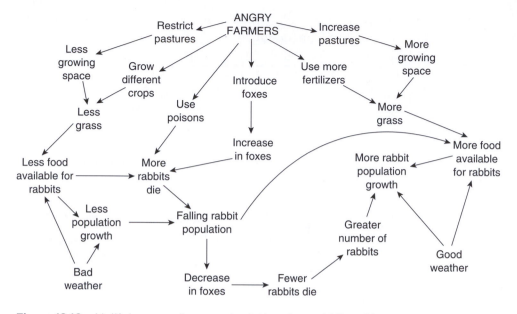

Figure 13.18   Multiple cause diagram of solutions to a rabbit problem

Conceptually ordered displays concentrate on variables in the form of abstract concepts related to a theory and the relationships between these. Examples of such variables are motives, attitudes, expertise, barriers, coping strategies, etc. They can be shown as matrices or networks to illustrate taxonomies, content analysis, cognitive structures, relationships of cause and effect or influence. Some examples of conceptually ordered displays are:

- **Conceptually or thematically clustered matrix** – these help to summarize the mass of data about numerous research questions by combining groups of questions that are connected, either from a theoretical point of view or as a result of groupings that can be detected in the data.
- **Taxonomy tree diagram** – these can be used to break down concepts into their constituent parts or elements.
- **Cognitive map** – this is a descriptive diagrammatic plotting of a person's way of thinking about an issue. It can be used to understand somebody's way of thinking or to compare that of several people.
- **Effects matrix** – this plots the observed effects of an action or intervention. It is a necessary precursor to explaining or predicting effects.
- **Decision tree modelling** – this helps to make clear a sequence of decisions by setting up a network of sequential yes/no response routes.
- **Causal models** – these are used in theory building to provide a testable set of propositions about a complete network of variables with causal and other relationships between them, based on a multi-case situation. A preliminary stage in the development of a causal model is to develop causal chains, linear cause-and-effect lines.

Role-ordered displays show people's roles and their relationships in formal and informal organizations or groups. A role defines a person's standing and position by assessing his/her behaviour and expectations within the group or organization. These may be conventionally recognized positions (e.g. judge, mother, machine operator) or more abstract and situation-dependent (e.g. motivator, objector). People in different roles tend to see situations from different perspectives – a strike in a factory will be viewed very differently by the management and the workforce. A role-ordered matrix will help to systematically display these differences or can be used to investigate whether people in the same roles are unified in their views.

Partially ordered displays are useful in analysing 'messy' situations without trying to impose too much internal order on them. For example, a context chart can be designed to show, in the form of a network, the influences and pressures that bear on an individual from surrounding organizations and persons when making a decision to act. This helps us to understand why a particular action was taken.

Case-ordered displays show the data of cases arranged in some kind of order according to an important variable in the study. This allows you to compare cases and note their different features according to where they appear in the order.

Do: Ensure your graphic is clear and unambiguous. To achieve this you may need to do several iterations of your first attempt to arrange the different elements of the graphic in order to simplify it.

Take it further

How about going into three dimensions? By this I do not mean making a 3D version of a 2D graphic so that it looks smart, but to actually think spatially and draw what is essentially a 3D model. Not easy, but can be a useful way to depict the relationship between more than two variables.

For example, the relationships between words or concepts in a text corpus or data set may be visualized in a 3D cluster diagram or scatter plot. Although you could sketch this out by hand using a 3D graph, using the NVivo software makes this much easier and enables the visualization to be interactive, and the whole diagram may be rotated in a number of directions and zoomed in and zoomed out for increased insight. This is very useful for judging the relative positions of the clusters. When it is exported, though, it is a static 2D image (that visually emulates 3D).

You could try SketchUp, the simple to use free 3D drafting program to invent your own 3D presentation. I could see that wire diagrams depicting the movement of people through a multi-storey building could be depicted this way.

(Continued)

(Continued)

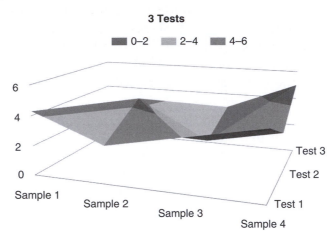

Figure 13.19   3D surface chart. Seconds taken to break samples types in strength test

Ask yourself

You want to predict the future likely movement in the average house price in a particular area of a town on the basis of data collected of house sale prices over the last 10 years. What is the best way to do this graphically?

You would have to calculate the average house price for each of the 10 years, and use a line graph to plot the annual price according to the year. Then extend the trajectory of the line into the future years. This will be a very speculative way to predict the future if you do not take into account the reasons for the price/rises falls during those years. If you have discovered the reasons for the price changes, for example, gentrification, large-scale job losses in the area, etc., you might be able to include these explanations in the graph and speculate as to the future conditions in the area that could affect the prices.

You have collected over 1,000 answers to the question 'what political party will you vote for in the next general election?'. What is the best way to display this data?

It really depends on what you want to reveal about the data. You could simply devise a table to show the number of voters for each party – pretty raw data! If you do some descriptive statistical analysis, then the choice of presentation is much wider. Refer to Chapter 11 for the possible outputs from descriptive analysis.

You are looking into the organizational aspects of a care home for the elderly. What sort of diagrams could you use to display these?

There are several diagrams that would be useful to illustrate different aspects of the organization. Structural and relationship diagrams could reveal the management structure, lines of responsibility, control systems. Flow diagrams, such as information/material flow diagrams and activity sequence diagrams could show how the work is organized. Technical illustrations, such as building plans can reveal the spatial organization of the care home. You will probably need to be more precise in your research questions to limit the scope of the enquiry to the time you have to do the project.

Further reading

Evergreen, S. (2014) *Presenting Data Effectively: Communicating Your Findings for Maximum Impact*. Thousand Oaks, CA: Sage.

Chapman, M. and Wykes, C. (1996) *Plain Figures*. London: The Stationery Office.

Few, S. (2004) *Show Me the Numbers*. Oakland, CA: Analytics Press.

Ehrenberg, A.S.C. (1982) *A Primer in Data Reduction*. Chichester: John Wiley and Sons.

Freeman, J.V., Walters, S.J. and Campbell, M.J. (2008) *How to Display Data*. Oxford: Wiley-Blackwell.

Harder, C. (1999) *Serving Maps on the Internet: Geographic Information on the World Wide Web*. ebrandedbooks.com

Tufte, E.R. (1990) *Envisioning Information*. Cheshire, CN: Graphics Press.

Tufte, E.R. (2001) *The Visual Display of Quantitative Information*. Cheshire, CN: Graphics Press.

Wallgren, A., Wallgren, B., Persson, R., Joyner, U. and Haaland, J. (1996) *Graphing Statistics and Data: Creating Better Charts*. London: Sage.

There don't seem to be any more useful books specifically concentrating on presenting data through graphs, diagrams, etc., though every research methods textbook will give advice and examples of relevant techniques for presentation related to particular research methods. You can explore these yourself in any of the books you have to hand – for example, Bryman, *Social Research Methods*; Robson, *Real World Research*; Miles and Huberman, *Qualitative Data Analysis*; Cohen and Manion, *Research Methods in Education* and any others.

Here is a useful internet site that will provide you with more information and ideas:

38 Tools For Beautiful Data Visualisations | DBi

www.dbi.io/uk/blog/38-tools-for-beautiful-data-visualisations/
Lots of different programs, some free to help you make attractive diagrams.

Look up Google: *research methods*, and then click on *images*.

This will lead you to a huge array of ideas for illustrating your data and results.

FOURTEEN

Writing Up a Dissertation or Research Project

Your dissertation is probably your first lengthy piece of independent writing. The big question when faced with such a task is how to structure the work so that it forms an integral whole. The structure will provide a guide to the reader, as well as providing a framework for you to fill in as you are writing it. In academic-type writing, the aim is not to tell a story as one might in a novel, but to set up an argument to support a particular view, analysis or conclusion. In fact, argument will pervade all that you write – you will be trying to persuade the reader that what you have done is worthwhile and based on some kind of intellectual process.

> **Do:** Whatever the subject of the enquiry, there has to be a focus, a central issue that is being considered. You should be able to define this quite clearly when you prepare your proposal, by explanation and persuasion.

The body of the dissertation will then revolve around this focal point, perhaps considering it from different perspectives, or examining causes or finding explanations for the situation. At the end you will have to come to some conclusions, and this is where argument is required. You will need to base these conclusions on evidence, and you should produce some reasoned argument about how this evidence leads to your conclusions.

WHEN TO START WRITING UP

> **Don't:** Sit down in front of a blank computer monitor with the task of writing a 20,000 word dissertation. This is a daunting prospect and one to be avoided. It is not difficult to avoid being faced with this situation.

The trick is to gradually amass a collection of notes, observations and data on the issues relevant to your study, which you can then use as a basis for your first draft. This way, you will have started writing your dissertation without even realizing it!

To lessen the anguish of starting writing up late on in the programme, it helps to build up your first draft from an early stage. To be able to do this you will need to prepare a structure for the dissertation as soon as you are clear with what you will be doing. You can devise this in outline after you have done some background reading and completed your proposal. The structure will then provide a framework into which you can insert your text. Don't expect either the framework or the text to be the final version. Both will need refining and revising as your work and understanding progresses. Luckily, word processors make revision very quick and easy.

The issue of writing style should be considered at this point. As a dissertation is an academic piece of work, generally a more formal style is adopted. This, at its extreme, avoids the personal pronoun, I, altogether.

> **Do:** It is a good idea to raise the issue of style when you discuss your work with your tutor. There may be some indications given in the assignment details - you should read these carefully anyway for instructions on what is expected of you.

FRAME AND FILL

The framework for your dissertation is most easily created by making a list of possible chapter or section headings. Consult your proposal and plan of work for indications of what these may be. At the very simplest level, the divisions may be like this:

- Introduction
- Background
- The main issues
- Research methods
- The research actions and results
- Conclusions.

This assumes that you will use the background reading to clarify the main issues of your research; that you will use one or several research methods to delve more deeply into these issues; that this will produce some data or results that you will present and analyse; and that you will be able to draw some conclusions from this analysis in relation to the main issues explained in point 3. This is a conventional format and can be applied to a study in almost any subject. There are other, unconventional, ways of organizing a dissertation. If you do want to use an unusual structure or even want to develop your own, it is best to discuss this with your supervisor to check that it will be acceptable. The main thing is that you can set up a convincing overall argument that leads from your intentions to your conclusions.

Once you have the main framework, you can elaborate on the contents of each section by inserting sub-headings indicating the aspects that you want to cover in each. Just use your current knowledge and a bit of imagination at first to suggest relevant sub-headings. This will help to establish the thread of your argument. You will be able to reorder, expand or change these as you progress. An example of sub-headings is given below:

Dissertation sub-headings

- Introduction
- The main aims of the dissertation
- A short summary of the context of the study
- The main problems or issues to be investigated
- The overall approach to the project
- A short description of the structure of the dissertation
- Background
- Aspects of the subject investigated
- Historical and current context
- Evidence of problems or contentious issues
- Current debate – comparison of different opinions or approaches
- Shortcomings in the level of knowledge
- The main issues
- A summary of the main problem or issue and how it can be divided into different aspects or sub-problems
- First aspect/sub-problem described and analysed
- Second aspect/sub-problem described and analysed
- Third aspect/sub-problem described and analysed
- Research methods
- General approach to investigation (philosophy?)
- Alternative methods discussed
- Selection and description of methods related to aspects/sub-problems (experiment, survey, modelling, accounts, archival analysis, case study, historical, etc.)
- Selection of samples or case studies (if you are doing a survey or choosing particular examples for detail study), pilot study

- Methods of presentation of results (e.g. charts, graphs, diagrams, spreadsheets, mathematical calculations, commentaries, etc.)
- Analytical methods used (statistical tests – specify which ones, comparisons, coding, systems analysis, **algorithms**, models, diagramming, etc.)
- Research actions and results
- Description of actions taken (use a heading for each type of action, for example: questionnaires, interviews, observations, textual analysis, etc.), possibly related to the different aspects/sub-problems
- Results of actions (give account of data collected from each of the actions above), again, possibly related to the different aspects/sub-problems
- Conclusions – conclusions drawn from sets of data in relation to the main issues (this can be separated into sections for each aspect/sub-problem
- Overall conclusions of the dissertation.

I have kept the sub-headings as general as possible so that you can apply these or something equivalent in the context of your subject. You will have to use your imagination and judgement to assess if this arrangement actually suits what you want to do. Devise your own sequence if you like, but note the overall pattern of identifying issues from background study, the definition of how you will investigate these, and how you will present the information gained and how this will be analysed to enable you to come to conclusions.

Don't: You don't have to start writing your text at the beginning and continue to the end.

Use what notes you have got so far and insert them where they are relevant in order to fill in the framework. If you have the notes already written on computer, then you can simply copy and paste them in a rough order under the appropriate headings and sub-headings. If you have recorded them on paper, now is the time to transfer them into the word processor. You will thus quickly have several pages of (very) rough draft.

However, be warned. Even though it might look pretty impressive, the text will be no more than a series of raw notes, completely unedited, disjointed and incomplete. But it will provide a solid basis for working on to produce a first draft.

MARSHALLING YOUR NOTES AND DRAFTING YOUR TEXT

You will probably be told what the overall length of your dissertation is required to be. If not, find out by asking your tutor, or consult previous dissertations written in your course. You need to know this in order to determine how long each section should be to get a balanced result. As a guide, 5,000 words are equivalent to about 25 double-space typed pages. Taking the above six-chapter arrangement, a balanced proportion of content might be as follows:

Introduction – 5%. This serves as a guide to the dissertation for the reader.

Background – 20%. A review of the literature and information about the context of the study.

The main issues – 10%. The main points or problems arising from the background that your research will tackle.

Research methods – 10%. A description of the steps you will take and techniques you will use to investigate the main issues. Reasons for using these methods must also be included.

The research actions and results – 35%. A record of what you did and what results came out of your investigations. You might split this into two or three sections if you are investigating two or three different issues.

Conclusions – 15%. An interpretation of the results in the light of the main issues.

The remaining 5% will be ancillary matter such as the abstract or summary, list of contents, bibliography, etc.

Now you will be ready to start inserting your notes into your structure. How do you get the right notes in the right place? This is where your retrieval techniques will be put to the test. Assuming that your framework gives you enough indication of what you are looking for, search through your notes by key word or subject. If you do this on the computer, you will be shown a selection of relevant notes, from which you can choose what you think is suitable for that section. You can do this manually with notes on paper. Other useful search parameters may be date or author.

For the introduction, just insert your proposal for now. You will be able to use this, suitably edited, when you have finished the rest of the writing, to explain the nature of the dissertation. You will add more later to explain the structure of the dissertation.

Your proposal will indicate the sorts of area that your background study will need to cover. There are likely to be several aspects of the subject that need looking at, for example, historical precedents, conflicting opinions, political/financial/organizational/social aspects, etc.

> **Do:** At this stage you will need to define the limits of your study clearly – you only have a short time to complete it, so keep it manageable.

REVISIONS

The nice thing about using a word processor is that you can easily change things after you have written them. This takes off the pressure of getting everything right first time – something that is impossible to do anyway. Once your work is on paper, then you can review it, get a second opinion on it and discuss it. You cannot do these if it is still all in your head. Hence the importance to get on with writing as soon as possible.

You don't have to finish the dissertation or even a section of it before you revise it. You can use the process to accumulate your written material, adding to the latest version as the information comes in or as you get the writing bug. Regularly reviewing what you have done so far and to what quality will keep you aware of how far you have progressed and what still needs to be done. It also enables you to break down the work into small sections – revising, altering and expanding sections as your understanding develops. The text will thus evolve as a series of small steps that should need no drastic revision at the last moment.

> **Do:** Regard the making of revisions to be an integral part of the process of doing a dissertation. You will of course have to include some time for this in your time plan.

Revising can be done at different levels. The more general levels are concerned with getting the structure and sequence right. Revision might entail moving around headings and blocks of text. Apart from the content of the text, you may want to try out different page layouts and formatting. At a more detailed level, you might look at the sequence of paragraphs: Does each concentrate on one point? Do they follow each other in the right sequence? At the most detailed level you will be looking at grammar, punctuation, vocabulary and spelling.

I find that it is much easier to review what I have written when it is printed out on paper rather that reading it from the screen – I can get a better overview of the layout, length of sections and line of the argument. If your eyesight is good, decrease the font size (perhaps to 8 point) before printing, both to save paper and to make it easier to have an overall view of the work. You will quickly spot gaps, dislocations in the sequence and imbalances in the length of sections.

It is important to keep track of your revisions – make sure you know what the latest one is! The best way is to save your revision as a new file, clearly labelled with a revision number (e.g. Chapter 3/1, 3/2, etc.). You will thus be able to go back to a previous revision if you change your mind or want to check on some detail. Most word-processing programs also provide a facility for keeping track of revisions.

COMING TO CONCLUSIONS

The whole point of collecting data and analysing them is so that you can come to some conclusions that answer your research questions and achieve the aims of your dissertation project.

Don't: Panic! The trouble with this part of the dissertation is that it inevitably comes near the end of your project, when you are probably tired from all the work you have already done, when your time is running out, when you have pressures from other commitments such as revision and exams. Let alone all the other things you want to get in before your undergraduate days are over.

To compound it all, the coming to conclusions is a demanding and creative process that requires a lot of clear thinking, perception and meticulous care. All the previous work will be devalued if you do not sufficiently draw out the implications of your analysis and capitalize on the insights that it affords. You cannot rely on the reader to make inferences from your results. It really is up to you to explain vividly how the results of your analysis provide evidence for new insight into your chosen subject and answer the particular research questions that you posed at the beginning of the dissertation.

Do: The main point I want to make is that you should allocate some time for this process, and not underestimate its importance.

Ideally, you will have the research question(s) at the forefront of your mind throughout your time working on your dissertation. However, this is not always possible as you grapple with learning new techniques, methods and the problems of organizing your data collection and analysis. However, you must come back to your research question(s) regularly in order to ensure that you are keeping to the intentions of the project, and will end up with relevant material in order to be able to suggest answers to the questions.

Coming to conclusions is a cumulative process. It is unlikely that the problem you have chosen is simple, with questions raised that can be answered with a simple yes or no. Even if they can, you will be required to describe why it is one or the other and make an argument to support your case. Normally, you will find that the questions have several sub-questions, and even these can be broken down into components requiring separate investigation. Throughout the analysis part of your work you will be able to make conclusions about these fragments of the main issues. The skill is to gather these up at the end in the concluding chapter to fit them together into a 'mosaic' that will present the complete picture of the conclusion to the entire dissertation.

Do: Just as you should be able to summarize the main problem that your dissertation addresses in one or two sentences, so you should be able to state the conclusion equally briefly.

This belies the complexities that lie in-between. You can picture your dissertation as having a continuous thread of argument running through it. The beginning and end of the argument is fat and tightly woven but, in-between, the separate strands fan out, become twisted and frayed as different aspects are investigated, but manage to weave together before reaching the end.

> **Do:** The secret to success lies in the sound construction of your argument. Spend some time to review its integrity.

Take it further

Once you have finished writing up and got your mark, or even before, why not consider getting your work, or some of it, published? This does not have to be in a top-line refereed journal – it would have to be a really significant piece of research to qualify for this. There are plenty of other opportunities to share the results of your investigations. Professional and trade journals are always on the lookout for interesting articles, especially when something new is revealed. Newsletters, local interest groups where you could give a talk, and even blogs and websites provide opportunities to engage with the public. After all, all your hard work should be rewarded with some recognition, and the best way to get that is to let other people know about it!

Ask yourself

How much time should I reserve in the project programme for writing up?

More than you think! You will not be able to do it all in one go. You must leave time for your supervisor to comment on your drafts and time for corrections and revisions. If you are including illustrations, these can take a lot of time to compile and refine, particularly if they involve sophisticated graphics. The secret is to get writing from early on in the project, and keep writing! That way you will build up a body of text, even though it might be in rather rough draft form, which you can refine to produce the final report. And don't forget that the formatting, printing and binding takes time too.

How can I check that the sequence and nature of contents are easy and interesting for the reader to understand?

Reading student dissertations can be a sleep inducing activity! A well-constructed, clearly written, well-illustrated and logically argued report is a really welcome object on the pile. First, make sure that you have clearly stated, unambiguous research questions at the beginning of the dissertation, and that you have answered them at the end. Everything in-between should lead from question to answer. Don't include loads of raw data. The reader will be interested in the analysis and interpretation. Do pay attention to the attractiveness of the

(Continued)

(Continued)

presentation – there is plenty of scope using word processors. Check on the logical sequence of chapters – it is best if they obviously relate to the different questions, and include relevant illustrations that are referred to in the text. And do cut out unnecessary waffle!

> What is the best way to work with my tutor to get the best out of his or her expertise in presenting research reports?

You will be normally allocated a specific supervisor to guide you through the process of your research. I am sure that you have consulted him or her at the beginning of the project in order to ensure that your proposal is sound, and later on when issues arose during the research work. Now that you are near the end, you should keep your supervisor informed of your progress and programme of work. Although he or she will probably not want to see every chapter as it is completed, it is important that you submit a draft of the complete dissertation or thesis to him or her well before the final deadline so that you can be given advice on the structure and contents. That information will help to answer the previous question. Remember – supervisors are not there to egg you on – it is you who should do the running!

Further reading

Here are some books on writing reports and dissertations.
Thody, A. (2006) *Writing and Presenting Your Research*. London: Sage.
This gives a huge range of ideas of ways to present your research across a wide range of disciplines.

Becker, H. (2008) *Writing for Social Scientists: How to Start and Finish Your Thesis, Book, or Article* (2nd edn). Chicago, IL: University of Chicago Press.
This has become a lifesaver for writers in all fields, from beginning students to published authors.

Swetnam, D. and Swetnam, R. (2000) *Writing Your Dissertation* (3rd edn). Oxford: How to Books.
This book gives you the confidence, tools and techniques to produce a first-class dissertation.

You can quickly get into deep water on the subject of thinking and argument. I would recommend the following to start with:
Pirie, M. (2015) *How to Win Every Argument* (2nd edn). London: Bloomsbury.
A witty and infectious book. A guide to using – and indeed abusing – logic in order to win arguments.

Brink-Budgen, R. (2000) *Critical Thinking for Students: Learn the Skills of Critical Assessment and Effective Argument* (3rd edn). Oxford: How To Books.
This book is a must if you want to find out how to develop your own arguments and evaluate other people's. Specifically, you will need to look at others' assumptions and their use of evidence. Learn how to spot, and rectify, weaknesses of your own.

Thouless, R.H. (1974) *Straight and Crooked Thinking* (rev. edn). London: Pan Books.
Old, but still entertaining and thought provoking.

PART IV

SUCCEEDING IN YOUR RESEARCH PROJECT*

Written in collaboration with David McIlroy.

This section will help you to profit from your lectures and seminars, get the best out of your reading and note taking and construct your essays efficiently.

The guidance given here for the longer written assignments will give you a framework on which to base your writing. If the written work is based on research that you have carried out, for example, in a dissertation, then you will need to consult the material in the rest of this book for assistance during the research project. Finally, the overall aim of the section is to point you to the keys for academic and personal development. The twin emphases of academic development and personal qualities are stressed throughout. By giving attention to these factors you will give yourself the toolkit you will need to excel in your studies.

FIFTEEN

How to Get the Most out of your Lectures and Seminars

Best quality learning is facilitated when it is set within an overall learning context. Your tutors will provide the context in which you can learn, but it is your responsibility to realize this.

> **Do:** Find your way around your study programme and locate the position of each lecture within this overall framework.

USE OF LECTURE NOTES

If you can, do some preliminary reading before you enter a lecture. Sometimes, lecture notes are provided in advance (e.g. electronically). If so, print these out and read them. Otherwise use the notes if they are provided at the beginning of the lecture. Supplement these with your own notes as you listen. This will make it easier to learn material the second time round.

> **Don't:** Overdo it! You are more likely to maintain preliminary reading for a lecture if you set modest targets.

Mastering technical terms

Most subjects require technical terms and the use of them is unavoidable. However, when you have heard a term a number of times it will not seem as daunting as it initially was. Below are some hints to help in mastering the terms you hear in lectures.

- Read lecture notes before the lectures.
- List any unfamiliar terms.
- Read over the listed terms until you are familiar with their sound.
- Try to work out meanings of terms from their context.
- Write out a sentence that includes the new word (do this for each word).
- Meet with other students and test each other with the technical terms.
- Jot down new words you hear in lectures and check out the meaning soon afterwards.

> **Do:** Feel how your confidence greatly increases when you begin to follow the flow of arguments that contain technical terms, and more especially when you can freely use the terms yourself in speaking and writing.

Developing independent study

The issues raised in lectures are pointers to provide direction and structure for your extended personal study. Your aim should invariably be to build on what you are given, and you should never think of merely returning the bare bones of the lecture material in a coursework essay or exam.

> **Do:** Note that it is always very refreshing to a marker to be given work from a student that contains recent studies that the examiner has not previously encountered.

Note-taking strategy

Note taking in lectures is an art that you will only perfect with practice and by trial and error. The problem will always be to try to find a balance between concentrating on what you hear and making sufficient notes that will enable you to comprehend later what you have heard. Don't become frustrated if you do not understand or remember everything you have heard.

> **Do:** Go to your lectures, and by making some attempt to attend to what you hear, you will already have a substantial advantage over those students who do not attend.

Guidelines for note taking in lectures

Develop the note-taking strategy that works best for you. Find a balance between listening and writing. Make some use of optimal shorthand (e.g. a few key words may summarize a story).

- Too much writing may impair the flow of the lecture.
- Too much writing may impair the quality of your notes.
- Some limited notes are better than none.
- Good note taking may facilitate deeper processing of information.
- It is essential to 'tidy up' notes as soon as possible after a lecture.
- Reading over notes soon after lectures will consolidate your learning.

Developing the lecture

Lectures are often criticized for being just 'passive learning'. Some lecturers work to devise ways of making a lecture more interactive. For example, they make use of interactive handouts or pose questions during the lecture and form small discussion groups during the session. You can ensure that you are not merely a passive recipient of information by taking steps to develop the lecture yourself.

Here is a list of suggestions to help you take the initiative in developing the lecture content:

- Try to interact with the lecture material by asking questions.
- Highlight points that you would like to develop in personal study.
- Trace connections between the lecture and other parts of your study programme.
- Bring together notes from the lecture and other sources.
- Restructure the lecture outline into your own preferred format.
- Think of ways in which aspects of the lecture material can be applied.
- Design ways in which aspects of the lecture material can be illustrated.
- If the lecturer invites questions, make a note of all the questions asked.
- Follow up on issues of interest that have arisen out of the lecture.

> **Do:** You can contribute to this active involvement in a lecture by engaging with the material before, during and after it is delivered.

HOW TO MAKE THE MOST OF SEMINARS

> **Don't:** Seminars are often optional in a degree programme and sometimes poorly attended because they are underestimated. So, don't miss them!

Lectures do play an important role in an academic programme, but seminars have a unique contribution to learning that will complement lectures. For example, they can:

- Identify problems that you had not thought of.
- Clear up confusing issues.

- Allow you to ask questions and make comments.
- Help you develop friendships and teamwork.
- Enable you to refresh and consolidate your knowledge.
- Help you sharpen motivation and redirect study efforts.
- Be an asset to complement other learning activities.

Although private study is essential for personal learning and development, you will diminish your learning experience if you neglect seminars. If seminars were to be removed from academic programmes, then something really important would be lost. But, as with most things, a bit of effort will make a lot of difference to the benefits gained. Here is how you can benefit from seminars:

- Do some preparatory reading.
- Familiarize yourself with the main ideas to be addressed.
- Make notes during the seminar.
- Make some verbal contribution, even a question.
- Remind yourself of the skills you can develop.
- Trace learning links from the seminar to other subjects/topics on your programme.
- Make brief bullet points on what you should follow up on.
- Read over your notes as soon as possible after the seminar.
- Continue discussion with fellow students after the seminar has ended.

In seminars you will hear a variety of contributions, and different perspectives and emphases. You will have the chance to interrupt and the experience of being interrupted! You will also learn that you can get things wrong and still survive! It is often the case that when one student admits that he or she does not know some important piece of information, other students quickly follow on to the same admission in the wake of this. If you can, learn to ask questions and not feel stupid. Do speak yourself, even if it is just to repeat something that you agree with. You can also learn to disagree in an agreeable way.

If you are required to give a presentation, here are a few useful hints to make it less stressful and more successful:

- Have a practice run with friends.
- If using visuals, do not obstruct them.
- Check out beforehand that all equipment works.
- Space out points clearly on visuals (large and legible).
- Time talk by visuals (e.g. five slides for a 15-minute talk = 3 minutes per slide).
- Make sure your talk synchronizes with the slide on view at any given point.
- Project your voice so that all in the room can hear.
- Inflect your voice and do not stand motionless.
- Spread eye contact around audience.
- Avoid twin extremes of fixed gaze at individuals, and never looking at anyone.
- It is better to fall a little short of time allocation than run over it.
- Be selective in what you choose to present.
- Map out where you are going and summarize the main points at the end.
- Links in learning and transferable skills.

When you progress from shallow to deep learning you develop the capacity to make connecting links between themes or topics and across subjects. This also applies to the various learning activities such as lectures, seminars, fieldwork, computer searches and private study.

Take it further

Just about every college and university provides online advice on how to make the best of your lectures and seminars, so look up on your own site and see what there is on offer. You can see what else there is on other university sites by simply making a search with the key words 'study skills lectures and seminars'.

Ask yourself

By attending seminars, what skills can I develop, or improve on that I can use across my study programme?

A couple of examples of key skills are the ability to communicate and the capacity to work within a team. These are skills that you will be able to use at various points in your course (transferable), but you are not likely to develop them within the formal setting of a lecture. By entering actively into discussions you will increase your self-confidence, and be encouraged to clarify your thoughts and arguments about the topics discussed.

How do seminars connect with my learning activities and my assessments?

Seminars are devised to expand on the information imparted in lectures, and to provide the opportunity for you to enquire further into the aspects that you do completely understand. They provide a good forum for discussing issues with your fellow students and provide feedback on your progress to your lecturers. The seminars are also a good opportunity to explore with your tutor exactly what is required of your assignments and how they will be assessed.

What should you do if you get confused by all the technical jargon in the lectures?

Don't be afraid to ask your lecturer to explain the concept or terms if you don't understand. Lecturers rarely object to being interrupted during their presentation in order to explain something more fully or in a different way. After all, that is what the lectures are for! If you notice that you do not understand some words only after the lecture, look up the concepts in a dictionary, encyclopedia (even Wikipedia) or glossary – often found at the end of textbooks (this one included).

Further reading

These issues are also covered in books on studying in general, which cover all the aspects of getting organized, lectures and seminars, and effective learning and communication skills:

Cottrell, S. (2006) *The Study Skills Handbook* (2nd edn). Basingstoke: Palgrave.
This bestselling author helps you develop the skills you need to improve your grades, build your confidence and plan for the future you want.

McIlroy, D. (2003) *Studying at University: How to Be a Successful Student*. London: Sage.
An astute compilation of the university experience, made easily accessible to the reader, and lightened by the ability of a good storyteller.

Turner, J. (2002) *How to Study*. London: Sage.
The aim of this guide is to help you along the study route, not by claiming there is only one right way to do things but by building awareness of different approaches, attitudes and strategies.

Evans, K. and King, D. (2006) *Studying Society: The Essentials*. London: Psychology Press.
This introductory text combines study skills and research methods to provide you with an invaluable guide to the techniques, practical skills and methods of study that will enable you to achieve success in your academic course and become an effective 'student of society'.

SIXTEEN

How to Get the Best out of Reading and Note Taking

For any type of research you will have to do a lot of reading in order to find out about the subject you want to investigate. As you find the books, articles, web pages, etc. you probably wonder what to do with them. In fact, if there are many references, you might get worried: 'How am I going to read all this lot?' There are so many interesting publications accessible, so the first step that you should take is to determine whether the data included in a document, book or other source are appropriate to your research subject or not. If not, discard them, and if you want you can make a note of it for later reading. If you decide that the source contains information relevant to your project, then you should follow a systematic and consistent approach to dealing with this information, in order to get the best out of it as quickly as possible. Not only do you need to read the contents, but you have to record what is relevant in such a way that you can easily store and retrieve it when you need it to write your report, dissertation or thesis.

READING

Since you are likely to be dealing with masses of written sources, you have to acquire the appropriate technique for reading their contents in a limited time. That means being able to home in on sections that are relevant to your interests. Reading text quickly is not easy.

Don't: Think you have to read a book or article from cover to cover. You will rarely find an entire book or other publication that centres neatly on your chosen subject.

Reading systematically to fully understand a textbook demands a lot of effort and may be time-consuming and not really necessary. So there are different techniques for reading and when faced with a publication:

1   Skimming. This involves looking quickly through the book and reading only things like contents, headings, introductions and conclusions. This is a quick and efficient way of familiarizing yourself with a publication and is useful if you wish to check whether a written report is relevant, or wish to find particular information or ideas quickly.
2   Scanning. This is a very rapid search for some important point. It may be a page number, a title or a key word. The essential thing is that you deliberately ignore everything except the one item for which you are scanning. You use scanning when you look up a number in the telephone directory.
3   Reading to understand. This involves detailed study of a chapter, passage or article in order to absorb all the major facts and ideas. You may read it more than once, and take notes to summarize what you have read.
4   Word-by-word reading. Very occasionally, you actually need to read every word extremely carefully; for example, when reading an exam question or following a set of instructions.
5   Reading for pleasure. This is the reading you do to relax and enjoy, as with a novel.

There are short cuts to locate the part or passage of the text that interests you and this will enable you to develop ways of using your reading time more effectively. If it is a book, the first place to look is in the contents at the beginning of the book. You obviously will have to know in advance what sort of issues are important to you, so that you can use the chapter or section headings to identify which pages to refer to. To get even more precision in your search, consult the index at the back for key words, then look at the pages mentioned to see if what is there is useful. If it is a scholarly paper, then there may be a few key words at the beginning that could attract your attention, and then the abstract will give you a very convenient summary of the main aspects of the paper.

> **Do:** Looking at a publication online means that you can use the search facility on your computer to find key words or concepts within the text.

Another way to look at reading is to consider it to be in four analytical stages:

Stage 1

Try to gain some quick impression of what the book is about; what question or questions the author is trying to answer; how the book is structured; and whether, in fact, the questions tackled and the answers put forward are relevant to your needs. You can do this by glancing over the cover or jacket, the preface (if any), the list of contents and the index. Try then to gain an overall impression of the book and its structure.

Stage 2

If you decide that the book or article is relevant to your research subject, then you must formulate the question or questions that you hope will be answered in the publication. This enables you to locate the required information and will save you time and effort, as you cannot afford to go on reading aimlessly through the book. In addition, at this stage you must adopt an active and analytical attitude.

Stage 3

After formulating the main question or questions, you must review the publication to look for answers to your questions. This involves locating the parts where your questions are dealt with. You must then look for the answers or conclusions that the author has drawn, and also at how the author arrived at them. You will also look at arguments and evidence put forward to support the views expressed and you will make an attempt to assess the validity of the evidence and the structure of the argument which utilizes such evidence. There are, however, cases where conclusions are unsupported, arguments or evidence are non-existent, or sometimes there is no conclusion at all.

Stage 4

Supposing that you have extracted the relevant information from the written report, you must now record your data in note form, so that later you can retrieve them and use them easily at the appropriate stage. The different ways of doing this are explained later in this chapter.

Do: Be aware of how you are going to read a text before you begin. Your reading method should be decided by the type and detail of information that you require from the text. A conscious decision before reading or scanning can save you much time by avoiding inappropriate techniques, resulting in too much or too little information being extracted.

MAKING NOTES

The only way to keep track of your survey of the literature is to make and keep notes on what you have read. Through doing this you can pick out the main points of interest from the papers, books, etc. and keep them for future use in your review and your subsequent research. But what notes should you make and how should you organize them?

There are a number of topics that you will wish to record. Here is a short list of the main ones you will probably include:

- Terminology and definitions of technical terms and concepts
- Theories and theoretical positions taken
- Main issues and problems addressed
- Types of research methods used to collect and analyse data
- Leading thinkers in the subject, and comparisons of their approaches
- Interesting case studies
- Significant historical events and developments
- Geographical locations and contexts relevant to the research
- Specific social conditions and situations.

In fact, anything that you find interesting and useful in the subject studied and related to your project.

Do: Before making these notes, the most important thing is to devise a system for recording, storing and retrieving them so that they become a useful resource, and not just a pile of jottings randomly stuffed away in a folder.

The two main ways you can do this are either on paper or on a computer. For small projects and short reviews, you can probably manage with the paper approach, but for anything more ambitious, you will need to do this electronically.

Don't: Quote long passages from the text in your notes. It is best to use your own language to record the information you need – it forces you to think about what you are writing! Short quotations can be useful if they provide a good summary of an approach or idea.

The on-paper approach involves writing the notes on sheets of paper or cards, being careful to record the bibliographic details (author, date, title of publication, publisher etc. – see Chapter 7 on referencing) for each note or set of notes. You will also need to keep the notes on the various topics separated, so that you can collate them when you are writing the review. As you can imagine, this way of recording your notes can quickly become unwieldy. The problem arises when you want to find, for example, all the notes that refer to a particular concept or issue, requiring a search through all your notes unless you have specifically ordered them under those headings as you wrote them. Also, compiling the list of references in the required format is laborious.

The computer-based approach presents no limits to the scale of your note management. Although you can devise your own database, it is best to use a dedicated referencing program, such as ProCite, EndNote, Zotero (and many others which you can compare on Wikipedia), which ensures that you record all the required information and also deals with citations and lists of references automatically. It is probably best if you use the program supported by your college or university so that you can get training or help when necessary. These programs provide templates for your notes so that you remember to include the full reference, key words and other useful data that are used to sort the notes when you want to retrieve them. For example, if you want to retrieve all your notes on a particular topic – just insert the key word and they will instantly appear, ready to copy and paste into a first draft of the paper you are writing. The list of cited references will also be generated in any format that you wish.

Take it further

As with other study skills, just about every university library provides online advice on how to read and make notes. Just search using the key words: academic writing, note taking, and you will have a big choice of, usually very practical, advice. Also, if you have not already done so, do investigate the computer programs that take all the hard work out of referencing.

Ask yourself

This is a task rather than a set of questions. Put your reading skills to the test by reading an article in different ways. Select, from the information you have collected about your subject, any article or research paper that you have not yet read but that you think might contain useful information. Now read it in the following ways:

1. First skim the text and write down very briefly the main points of the information offered. Remember to first check the contents or abstract, the main headings and perhaps part of the last paragraph about conclusions. Do not write down more than 20 words, but make sure that they are quite precise and organized in a coherent way so that you will easily understand your notes at a later date.
2. Next, select two main concepts that you are interested in and that seem to be featured prominently in the article (perhaps they are mentioned in the title). Scan the text and note what is written about these two concepts.
3. Now take just one section headed by a subtitle and read it carefully, making detailed notes on all the major issues and facts. You should have about 10 short notes to cover the information properly.
4. Finally, read the last paragraph(s) very carefully indeed. What are the main conclusions and why are they important, or perhaps they are not? What effect do they have on your thinking about your subject? You could express this as personal notes to remind you of the significance of this article in some aspect of your work.

The other type of reading – reading for pleasure – you can practise without needing it to be the subject of an exercise!

Further reading

For more detailed consideration of these issues, try these books.

Burns, T. and Sinfield, S. (2012) *Essential Study Skills: The Complete Guide to Success at University* (3rd edn). London: Sage.
Really useful sections on reading and taking notes ... the bread and butter of student life.

Godfrey, J. (2010) *Reading and Making Notes (Pocket Study Skills)*. London: Palgrave Macmillan.
This guide focuses on a single crucial aspect of study, giving you step-by-step guidance, handy tips and clear advice on how to approach the important areas that will continually be at the core of your study ethic. The guides are in a small pocket format – not much bigger than a wallet – which can easily slip into a pocket or bag.

(Continued)

(Continued)

Godfrey, J. (2013) *How to Use Your Reading in Your Essays (Palgrave Study Skills)*.
    London: Palgrave Macmillan.
From the same series as the above.

Here is where you can get information about reference management software. Check
what is available on your college/university network before you make an expensive decision to buy a program yourself. There are also free versions available. Information on the
various referencing programs can be obtained directly from their websites. The comparisons can be seen on Wikipedia by searching for 'comparison of reference management
software'.

SEVENTEEN
How to Write Great Essays

In essay writing, one of your first aims should be to get your mind active and engaged with your subject. Tennis players like to go out on to the court and hit the ball back and forth just before the competitive match begins. In the same way you can warm up for your essay by tossing the ideas to and fro within your head before you begin to write. This will allow you to think within the framework of your topic, and this will be especially important if you are coming to the subject for the first time. Make a list of the main points that occur to you and put them in a logical order if possible – you can easily change these later. You can also add further points as they occur to you while you write.

FINDING MAJOR QUESTIONS

When you are constructing a draft outline for an essay or project, you should ask what is the major question or questions you wish to address. It is useful to make a list of all the issues that spring to mind that you may wish to tackle. Which are the most interesting and address the most important issues? The ability to design a good question is an art form that should be cultivated, and such questions will allow you to impress your assessor with the quality of your thinking.

> **Do:** If you construct your ideas around key questions, this will help you focus your mind and engage effectively with your subject. Your role will be like that of a detective - exploring the evidence and investigating the findings.

LISTING AND LINKING THE KEY CONCEPTS

All subjects will have central concepts that can sometimes be usefully labelled by a single word. Course textbooks may include a glossary of terms and these provide a direct route to the beginning of efficient mastery of the topic. The central words or terms are the essential raw materials that you will need to build upon. Ensure that you learn the words and their definitions, and that you can go on to link the key words together so that in your learning activities you will add understanding to your basic memory work.

> **Do:** It is useful to list your key words under general headings if that is possible and logical. You may not always see the connections immediately but when you later come back to a problem that seemed intractable, you will often find that your thinking is much clearer.

AN ADVERSARIAL SYSTEM

In higher education, students are required to make the transition from descriptive to critical writing. Think of the critical approach as like a law case that is being conducted in a courtroom, where there is both a prosecution and a defence. Your concern should be for objectivity, transparency and fairness. No matter how passionately you may feel about a given cause, you must not allow information to be filtered out because of your personal prejudice. An essay is not to become a crusade for a cause in which the contrary arguments are not addressed in an even-handed manner. This means that you should show awareness that opposite views are held and you should at least represent these as accurately as possible. The challenge will be to present these in a balanced way and come to some conclusions based on what you have found out.

> **Do:** Your role as the writer is like that of the judge in that you must ensure that all the evidence is heard, and that nothing will compromise either party.

STRUCTURING AN OUTLINE

It is a basic principle in all walks of life that structure and order facilitate good communication. Therefore, when you have the flow of inspiration in your essay you must get this into a structure that will allow the marker to recognize the true quality of your work. For example, you might plan for:

- An introduction
- Three main headings (each of these with several subheadings)
- A conclusion.

In an introduction to an essay you have the opportunity to define the problem or issue that is being addressed and to set it within context. You can also provide a brief guide to the reader on the structure of your essay. Resist the temptation to elaborate on any issue at the introductory stage. The introduction should be written last, as you do not really know what you are introducing before you have actually written it!

Break down the main part of the essay into sections that address the main questions or major issues separately. Use the main points that you drafted out at the beginning. You can then deal with detailed matters under subheadings. Don't forget to include secondary conclusions for each section.

In the conclusion you should aim to tie your essay together in a clear and coherent manner. It is your last chance to leave an overall impression in your reader's mind. This is your opportunity to identify where the strongest evidence points or where the balance of probability lies. The conclusion to an exam question often has to be written hurriedly under the pressure of time, but with an essay (course work) you have time to reflect on, refine and adjust the content to your satisfaction. Do not underestimate the value of an effective conclusion.

Once you have drafted this outline you can then easily sketch some material under the main headings and subheadings, after which you will be well prepared for devising the main conclusion and the introduction.

> **Do:** Develop a good structure that will help you to balance the weight of each of your arguments against each other, and arrange your points in the order that will facilitate the fluent progression of your argument.

REST YOUR CASE: EVIDENCE, CITATIONS AND QUOTES

It should be your aim to give the clear impression that your arguments are not based entirely on hunches, bias, feelings or intuition. In exams and essay questions it is usually assumed (even if not directly specified) that you will appeal to evidence to support your claims. Therefore, when you write your essay you should ensure that it is liberally sprinkled with citations and evidence. By the time the assessor reaches the end of your work, he or she should be convinced that your conclusions are evidence-based. A fatal flaw to be avoided is to make claims for which you have provided no authoritative source.

Do: Give the clear impression that what you have asserted is derived from recognized sources (including up-to-date sources). It also looks impressive if you spread your citations across your essay rather than compressing them into a paragraph or two at the beginning and end.

It is sensible to vary the expressions used so that you are not monotonous and repetitive, and it also aids variety to introduce researchers' names at various places in the sentence (not always at the beginning). It is advisable to choose the expression that is most appropriate. For example, you can make a stronger statement about reviews that have identified recurrent and predominant trends in findings as opposed to one study that appears to run contrary to all the rest. Some examples of how you might introduce your evidence and sources are provided below:

According to O'Neil (1999) …

Wilson (2009) has concluded that …

Taylor (2011) found that …

It has been claimed by McKibben (2014) that …

Appleby (2001) asserted that …

A review of the evidence by Lawlor (2004) suggests that …

Findings from a meta-analysis presented by Rea (2014) would indicate that …

Don't: Forget that credit is given for the use of caution and discretion when this is clearly needed.

Although it is desirable to present a good range of cited sources, it is not judicious to present these as a 'patchwork quilt' – that is, you just paste together what others have said with little thought for interpretative comment or coherent structure. It is a good general point to aim to avoid very lengthy quotes – short ones can be very effective. Aim at blending the quotations as naturally as possible into the flow of your sentences. Also, it is good to vary your practices – sometimes use short, direct, brief quotes (cite page number as well as author and year), and at times you can summarize the gist of a quote in your own words. In this case you should cite the author's name and year of publication but leave out quotation marks and page number.

Do: Use your quotes and evidence in a manner that demonstrates that you have thought the issues through, and have integrated them in a manner that shows you have been focused and selective in the use of your sources.

In terms of referencing, practice may vary from one discipline to the next, but some general points that will go a long way in contributing to good practice are:

- If a reference is cited in the text, it must be included in the list of references at the end of the essay (and vice versa).
- Names and dates in the text should correspond exactly with the list in the References or **Bibliography**.
- The list of References or Bibliography should be in alphabetical order by the surname (not the initials) of the author or first author.
- Any reference you make in the text should be traceable by the reader (readers should clearly be able to identify and trace the source).

Take it further

An essay is a mini-dissertation, just as a paragraph is a mini-essay. Carefully analyse whatever you are reading for the structure of the writings, from the small scale to the large. You will notice, if what you are reading is well constructed, that each paragraph introduces a topic or theme, considers it in some way and then comes to some kind of conclusion. This should be the same in sections of essays (headed by headings), chapters of longer works, whole essays, dissertations and theses, and informative books. Novels and poetic writing can and do break this rule with impunity!

Ask yourself

I find it difficult to limit the length of my essays and keep them within the maximum word count allowed. What can I do?

It is one of the disciplines of academic writing (and journalism) to adhere to the permitted word count. So this is an important aspect of the assignment and should not be ignored. If you tend to write too much, check on the following.

- Have you repeated anything (sometimes with copying and pasting notes you can duplicate them in different parts of the essay) or written about the same thing but in a different way? Cut out the repeats.
- Have you included material that is not essential to your argument? Leave it out. Reviewing the contents of your argument is a good test at the same time of its soundness.
- Have you been too florid in your sentence construction or descriptions? Keep sentences short. With careful consideration you will be able to cut down on words without losing the meaning.

I never seem to have enough to write about, so my essays are too short. What can I do?

You probably need to read more about the subject you have to write about. Every subject has been studied by other people who have unearthed all sorts of new and

(Continued)

(Continued)

interesting facts and theories. Use the words in the essay title as key words in internet and bibliographic searches to find more information. You will need to spend time doing this, so don't leave it to the last minute. Reading and making sense of the literature also takes time, especially if you have to use it for writing a piece of your own. Do cite the literature you have consulted to ensure that the reader appreciates the efforts you have gone to to be informed.

> I have loads of ideas but never know where to start on an essay, so keep putting off writing. What can I do to get started?

I know what it is like to be able to think and discuss a subject, but find the discipline of it getting down on paper to be almost unsurmountable. The horror of the empty page! The trick is to trick yourself! Don't try to start writing the text, just jot down a few ideas on the essay subject as they come to you, in any order. That should not be too difficult. You might then be able to elaborate a bit on some or all of them. Then think, how could these fragments be organized into some sort of order? You could even put them on separate bits of paper to make swapping them round easier. Once you have arranged them – hey presto – you have started!

Further reading

There are loads of books on advice for students for different aspects of study. I have picked a range of books that will provide more information than was possible in the short summary above.

Here are some comprehensive books on writing skills and writing essays.

Copus, J. (2009) *Brilliant Writing Tips for Students (Pocket Study Skills)*. Basingstoke: Palgrave.
Tips on punctuation, style, grammar and essay structure and succinct and practical guidance on the most common areas of concern in written work.

Greetham, B. (2013) *How to Write Better Essays (Palgrave Study Skills)*. Basingstoke: Palgrave.
This teaches you how to analyse the question and break down difficult terms and concepts, brainstorm effectively and generate your own ideas, evaluate and criticize arguments, express your thoughts coherently and develop your own style of writing, and plan and structure your essay from introduction to conclusion.

Redman, P. and Maples, W. (2013) *Good Essay Writing: A Social Sciences Guide* (4th edn). London: Sage.
The authors focus on answering key questions you will face when preparing essays – What do tutors look for when marking my essay? What kind of skills do I need as I progress through my course? How can I avoid inadvertent plagiarism? What are the protocols for referencing?

Glossary

Accidental sampling   Also called convenience sampling. A non-random sampling technique that involves selecting what is immediately available; for example, studying the building you happen to be in or examining the work practices of your firm.

Action research   Small-scale interventions in the functioning of the real world in order to make a close examination of the effects of such an intervention.

Algorithm   A process or set of rules used for calculation or problem solving, especially using a computer. These can be expressed graphically or, more often, as a mathematical formula. An example is a formula that summarizes the interior conditions that lead to the feeling of climatic comfort, with factors such as air temperature, humidity, air movement, amount of clothing, etc.

Area sampling   See cluster sampling.

Argument   A type of discourse that not only makes assertions but also asserts that some of these assertions are reasons for others. Argument is often based on the rules of logic in order to provide a solid structure.

Authentication   Checking on historical data to verify whether they are authentic. Typical techniques used are textual analysis, carbon dating, paper analysis, cross-referencing, etc.

Bell curve   See Gaussian curve.

Bias   The unwanted distortion of the results of a survey due to parts of the population being more strongly represented than others.

Bibliography   A list of key information about publications. These can be compiled on particular subjects or in relation to a particular piece of academic work. There are standard systems for compiling bibliographies (e.g. the Harvard system). Libraries usually compile their own bibliographies to guide students to literature in their particular subject.

Bivariate analysis　Considers the properties of two variables in relation to each other.

Case study design　Intensive investigation into one or a few cases in order to generate a test theory, using both inductive and deductive reasoning.

Categorization　Involves forming a typology of objects, events or concepts. This can be useful in explaining what 'things' belong together and how.

Causal statements　These make an assertion that one concept or variable causes another – a 'cause and effect' relationship. This can be deterministic, meaning that under certain conditions an event will inevitably follow, or if the outcome is not so certain, probabilistic, meaning that an event has a certain chance (which may be quantifiable) of following.

Chi-square test　Measures the degree of association or linkage between two variables by comparing the differences between the observed values and expected values if no association were present, that is those that would be a result of pure chance.

Citation　A reference to a source of information or quotation given in a text. This is usually in abbreviated form to enable the full details to be found in the list of references.

Class　A set of persons or things grouped together or graded or differentiated from others. Classes can be formed by collection or division. Classes can be divided into subclasses to form a hierarchy.

Closed-format questions　Where the respondent must choose from a choice of given answers.

Cluster sampling　Selection of cases in a population that share one or some characteristics but are otherwise as heterogeneous as possible (e.g. travellers using a railway station). Also known as area sampling when random segments are chosen from a large area of population distribution.

Coding　The application of labels or tags to allocate units of meaning to collected data. This is an important aspect of forming typologies and facilitates the organization of copious data in the form of notes, observations, transcripts, documents, etc. It helps to prevent 'data overload' resulting from mountains of unprocessed data in the form of ambiguous words. Coding of qualitative data can form a part in theory building. Codes can also be allocated to responses to fixed-choice questionnaires.

Coding frame　A list of codes that is used to categorize the answers to questionnaire questions in order to facilitate analysis.

Comparative research　Examines two or more cases to highlight differences and similarities between them, leading to a better understanding of social phenomena and their theoretical basis. Suitable for both qualitative and quantitative methodologies.

Concepts General expressions of a particular phenomenon, or words that represent an object or an idea. These can be concrete (e.g. dog, cat, house) or abstract, that is, independent of time or place (e.g. anger, marginality, politics). We use concepts to communicate our experience of the world around us.

Constructionism The belief that social phenomena are in a constant state of change because they are totally reliant on social interactions as they take place. Even the account of researchers is subject to these interactions, therefore social knowledge can only be interdeterminate.

Content analysis An examination of what can be counted in a text. Developed from the mid-1900s chiefly in America, it is a rather positivistic attempt to apply order to the subjective domain of cultural meaning. A quantitative approach is taken by counting the frequency of phenomena within a case in order to gauge its importance in comparison with other cases.

Control Having the ability to determine the influences on variables in a phenomenon, for example in an experiment. The crucial issue in control is to understand how certain variables affect one another, and then be able to change the variables in such a way as to produce predictable results. Not all phenomena can be controlled as many are too complex or not sufficiently understood.

Correlation coefficient The measure of a statistical correlation between two or more variables. There are many types, the 'Pearsonian *r*' being the most common.

Correlation research Describes the measure of association or the relationships between two phenomena. In order to find meaning in the numerical data, the techniques of statistics are used. What kind of statistical tests are used to analyse the data depends very much on the nature of the data. This form of quantitative research can be broadly classified into relational studies and prediction studies.

Critical realism A non-empirical (i.e. realist) epistemology that maintains the importance of identifying the structures of social systems, even if they are not amenable to the senses. This will enable the structures to be changed to ameliorate social ills.

Cross-sectional design Research that often uses survey methods, and surveys are often equated with cross-sectional studies. It entails the collection of quantitative or qualitative data on more than one case, generally using a sampling method to select cases, collected at a single point in time in order to examine patterns of association between variables.

Cross-tabulation (contingency tables) A way to display the relationship between variables that have only a few categories. The cells made by the rows show the relationships between each of the categories of the variables in both number of responses and percentages. In addition, the column and row totals and percentages are shown

Deduction   The inferring of particular instances from a general law (i.e. the 'theory then research' approach).

Descriptive statistics   A method of quantifying the characteristics of parametric numerical data; for example, where the centre is, how broadly data are spread, the point of central tendency, the mode, median and means. These are often explained in relation to a Gaussian (bell) curve.

Diagram   A data display in the form of a two dimensional map or network. It is made up of blocks (nodes) that can be connected by links.

Discourse   Communication in the form of words as speech or writing or even attitude and gesture.

Discourse analysis   Studies the way people communicate with each other through language in a social setting, where language is not seen as a neutral medium for transmission of information, but is loaded with meanings displaying different versions of reality.

Display   A graphical form of showing data and the interrelationships between variables. Two main forms are matrices and networks.

Ecological validity   The extent to which the findings are applicable to people's everyday, natural social settings.

Empiricism   Knowledge gained by sensory experience (using inductive reasoning).

Epistemology   The theory of knowledge, especially about its validation and the methods used. Often used in connection with one's epistemological standpoint; that is, how one sees and makes sense of the world.

Ethics   The rules of conduct in research. In this book, particularly about conduct with other people and organizations, aimed at causing no harm and providing, if possible, benefits.

Ethnography   An approach used to uncover the shared cultural meanings of the behaviour, actions, events and contexts of a group of people, using an insider's perspective, studied in its natural setting. The focus of the research and detailed research questions emerge and evolve in the course of the involvement. Data collection is usually in phases over an extended time.

Ethnomethodology   The theoretical basis for conversation analysis, which studies how talk and social interaction generate social order.

Evaluation   Making judgements about the quality of objects or events. Quality can be measured either in an absolute sense or on a comparative basis.

Evaluation research   A design that is concerned with the critical assessment of real-life interventions in the social world.

Expected value   The frequency expected based on a null hypothesis, that is if no association were present so would be a result of pure chance.

Experience   Actual observation or practical acquaintance with facts or events that results in knowledge and understanding.

Experimental research   A design in which the research strives to isolate and control every relevant condition that determines the events investigated, so as to observe the effects when the conditions are manipulated. Comparisons are made between results from a control group not exposed to the treatment and an experimental group that is.

Explanation   An attempt to describe how and why things work. One of the common objectives of research.

External reality   Acceptance of the reliability of knowledge gained by experience to provide empirical evidence.

External validity   The extent to which findings can be generalized to populations or to other settings.

Falsification   The process by which a hypothesis is rejected as a result of true observational statements that conflict with it.

Fixed designs   A design strategy that calls for a tight pre-specification at the outset and is commonly equated with a quantitative approach. The designs employ experimental and non-experimental methods.

Flexible designs   A design strategy that evolves during data collection and is associated with a qualitative approach, although some quantitative data may be collected. The designs employ, among other things, case study, ethnographic and grounded theory methods.

Focus group   A type of group interview which concentrates in-depth on a particular theme or topic with an element of interaction. The group is often made up of people who have particular experience or knowledge about the subject of the research, or those who have a particular interest in it (e.g. consumers or customers).

Gaussian curve   A graph showing a normal frequency distribution of a population, often known as the 'bell curve'.

Generality   The assumption that there can be valid relationships between the particular cases investigated by the researcher and other similar cases in the world at large.

Generalizability   Refers to the results of the research and how far they are applicable to locations and situations beyond the scope of the study. Especially in qualitative research, there may well be limits to the generalizability of the findings.

Grounded theory   Emphasizes the continuous data collection process interlaced with periodic pauses for analysis. The analysis is used to tease out categories in the data on which the subsequent data collection can be based. This process is called 'coding'. This reciprocal procedure continues until these categories are 'saturated' (i.e. the new data no longer provide new evidence). From these results, concepts and theoretical frameworks can be developed resulting in a gradual emergence and refinement of theory.

Hypothesis   A theoretical statement that has not yet been tested against data collected in a concrete situation, but which it is possible to test by providing clear evidence for support or rejection.

Hypothetico-deductive method   Synonymous with scientific method. Progress in scientific thought via the four-step method of: (1) identification of a problem; (2) formulation of a hypothesis; (3) practical or theoretical testing of the hypothesis; and (4) rejection or adjustment of the hypothesis if it is falsified.

Indicator   A phenomenon that points to the existence of a concept.

Induction   The inference of a general law from particular instances. Our experiences lead us to make conclusions from which we generalize.

Inferential statistics   Statistical analysis that goes beyond describing the characteristics of the data and the examination of correlations of variables in order to produce predictions through inference based on the data analysed. Inferential statistics are also used to test statistically based hypotheses.

Informed consent   Consent given by participants taking part in a research project based on having sufficient information about the purposes and nature of the research and the involvement required.

Interim summary   A short report prepared about one-third of the way through data collection in qualitative research in order to review the quantity and quality of the data, confidence in their reliability, the presence and nature of any gaps or puzzles that have been revealed, and to judge what still needs to be collected in the time available.

Internal reliability   The degree to which the indicators that make up the scale or index are consistent.

Internal validity   The extent to which causal statements are supported by the study. In an experiment it is a measure of the sophistication of the design and extent of control. The values of data gained should genuinely reflect the influences of the controlled variables.

Inter-observer consistency   The degree to which there is consistency in the decisions of several 'observers' in their recording of observations or translation of data into categories.

Interpretation   An integral part of the analysis of data that requires verification and extrapolation in order to make out or bring out the meaning.

Interpretivism   The recognition that subjective meanings play a crucial role in social actions. It aims to reveal interpretations and meanings. This standpoint recognizes the 'embedded' nature of the researcher, and the unique personal theoretical stances upon which each person bases his or her actions. It rejects the assertion that human behaviour can be codified in laws by identifying underlying regularities, and that society can be studied from a detached, objective and impartial viewpoint by the researcher. Attempts to find understanding in research are mediated by our own historical and cultural milieu.

Interrogation   Data gained by asking and probing (e.g. information about people's beliefs motivations, etc.).

Interval (level of measurement)   The use of equal units of measurement, but without a significant zero value (e.g. the Fahrenheit or Centigrade temperature scales).

Levels of abstraction   The degree of abstraction of a statement based on three levels – theoretical, operational and concrete, the last being the least abstract.

Levels of measurement (or levels of quantification)   The four different types of quantification, especially when applied to operational definitions, namely nominal, ordinal, interval and ratio.

Library catalogue   Bibliographic details of items in a library. The databases are now usually accessed by computer as online public access catalogues (OPACs).

Lickert scale   A format for asking attitude questions using a summated rating approach that indicates the intensity of feeling a subject has about a topic.

Longitudinal design   Consists of repeated cross-sectional surveys to ascertain how time influences the results.

Matrices   Two-dimensional arrangements of rows and columns that summarize substantial amounts of information. They can be used to record variables such as time, levels of measurement, roles, clusters outcomes, effects, etc. Latest developments allow the formulation of three-dimensional matrices.

Measurement   Records of amounts or numbers (e.g. population statistics, instrumental measurements of distance, temperature, mass, etc.).

Measurement validity   The degree to which measures (e.g. questions on a questionnaire) successfully indicate concepts.

Memos   Short analytical descriptions based on the developing ideas of the researcher reacting to the data and development of codes and pattern codes. Compiling memos is a good way to explore links between data and to record and develop intuitions and ideas.

Model (a) A term used to describe the overall framework that we use to look at reality, based on a philosophical stance (e.g. postmodernism, post-structuralism, positivism, empiricism, etc.).

(b) A simplified physical or mathematical representation of an object or a system used as a tool for analysis. It may be able to be manipulated in order to obtain data about the effects of the manipulations.

Multi-stage cluster sampling An extension of cluster sampling, where clusters of successively smaller size are selected from within each other. For example, you might take a random sample from all UK universities, then a random sample from subjects within those universities, then a random sample of modules taught in those subjects, then a random sample of students doing those modules.

Multivariate analysis Looks at the relationships between more than two variables.

Networks Maps or charts used to display data, made up of blocks (nodes) connected by links. They can be produced in a wide variety of formats, each with the capability of displaying different types of data (e.g. flow charts, organization charts, causal networks, mind maps, etc.).

Nominal (level of measurement) The division of data into separate categories by naming or labelling.

Non-parametric statistics Statistical tests devised to recognize the particular characteristics of data that do not conform to a parameter.

Non-probability sampling Sampling based on non-random selection. This relies on the judgement of the researcher or section by accident and cannot be used to make generalizations about the whole population.

Null hypothesis A statistically based hypothesis tested by using inferential statistics. A null hypothesis suggests no relationship between two variables.

Objectivism The belief that social phenomena and their meanings have an existence that is not dependent on social actors. They are facts that have an independent existence.

Observation Records, usually of events, situations or things, of what you have experienced in your own senses, perhaps with the help of an instrument (e.g. camera, tape recorder, microscope, etc.).

Observed value A value which is the result analysis of the data gathered.

Ontology A theory of the nature of social entities that is concerned with what there exists to be investigated.

Open-format questions Questions that the respondents are free to answer in their own words and style.

Operational definition   A set of actions that an observer should perform in order to detect or measure a theoretical concept. Operational definitions should be abstract; that is, independent of time and space.

Operationalization (of a hypothesis)   Breaking down the hypothesis into its components to make it testable, from the most abstract to the most concrete expressions by defining in turn concepts, indicators, variables and values.

Order   The condition in which things are constituted, in an organized fashion, that can be revealed through observation.

Ordinal (level of measurement)   Ordering data by rank without reference to specific measurement (i.e. more or less than, bigger or smaller than).

Parameter   A constant feature of a population that it shares with other populations. The most common one is the 'bell' or 'Gaussian' curve of normal frequency distribution.

Parametric statistics   Statistical calculations based on data that conform to a parameter, usually a Gaussian curve.

Parsimony   The economy of explanation of phenomena, especially in formulating theories.

Participant   Someone who takes part in a research project as a subject of study. This term implies that the person takes an active role in the research by performing actions or providing information.

Participation   Data gained by experiences that can perhaps be seen as an intensified form of observations (e.g. the experience of learning to drive a car tells you different things above cars and traffic than just watching).

Phenomenology   A philosophy or method of enquiry based on the premise that reality consists of objects and events as they are perceived or understood in human terms.

Pilot study   A pre-test of a questionnaire or other type of survey on a small number of cases in order to test the procedures and quality of responses.

Plagiarism   The taking and use of other people's thoughts or writing as your own. This is sometimes done by students who copy out chunks of text from publications or the internet and include it in their writing without any acknowledgement of its source.

Population   A collective term used to describe the total quantity of cases of the type that is the subject of the study. It can consist of objects, people and even events.

Positivism   The application of the natural sciences to the study of social reality. An objective approach that can test theories and establish scientific laws. It aims to establish causes and effects.

Postmodernism   A term applied to a wide-ranging set of developments in critical theory, philosophy, architecture, art, literature and culture, which are generally characterized as either emerging from, in reaction to, or superseding, modernism. In sociology, postmodernism is described as being the result of economic, cultural and demographic changes (related terms in this context include 'post-industrial society' and 'late capitalism'). It is attributed to: (1) factors that have emerged from the service economy; (2) the importance of the mass media; and (3) the rise of an increasingly interdependent world economy.

Post-structuralism   Any of various theories or methods of analysis, including deconstruction and some psychoanalytic theories that deny the validity of structuralism's method of binary opposition and maintain that meanings and intellectual categories are shifting and unstable.

Prediction studies   These aim to foretell the outcome of a phenomenon on the basis of previous experience – one of the common objectives of research.

Primary data   Data gained by direct, detached observation or measurement of phenomena in the real world, undisturbed by any intermediary interpreter.

Probability sampling   Sampling based on random selection. These techniques give the most reliable representation of the whole population from which predictions can be made about the population.

Problem area   An issue within a general body of knowledge or subject from which a research project might be selected.

Proportional stratified sampling   A sampling method used when cases in a population fall into distinctly different categories (strata) of a known proportion of that population.

Proposition   A theoretical statement that indicates the clear direction and scope of a research project.

Purposive sampling   A sampling method where the researcher selects what he or she thinks is a 'typical' sample based on specialist knowledge on selection criteria.

p value   The result of the chi-square test which measures the degree of association between two variables (e.g. $p = 0.03$ meaning that probability of association is less than 3 in 100)

Qualitative data   Data that cannot be accurately measured and counted, and are generally expressed in words rather than numbers. These kinds of data are therefore descriptive in character, and rarely go beyond the nominal and ordinal levels of measurement.

Qualitative research   Relies heavily on language for the interpretation of its meaning, so data collection methods tend to involve close human involvement and a creative process of theory development rather than testing.

Quantification (of concepts)   Measurement techniques used in association with operational definitions.

Quantitative data   Data that can be measured, more or less exactly. Measurement implies some form of magnitude, usually expressed in numbers. Mathematical procedures can be applied to analyse the data. These might be extremely simple, such as counts or percentages, or more sophisticated, such as statistical tests or mathematical models.

Quantitative research   Relies on collecting data that are numerically based and amenable to such analytical methods as statistical correlations, often in relation to hypothesis testing.

Quota sampling   An attempt to balance the sample by selecting responses from equal numbers of different respondents. This is an unregulated form of sampling as there is no knowledge of whether the respondents are typical of their class.

Random assignment   Random sampling methods used to select the experimental units (the things that are being experimented on, e.g. materials, components, persons, groups, etc.) in order to combat the problem of unknown variables. This process neutralizes the particular effects of individual variables and allows the result of the experiment to be generalized.

Ratio (level of measurement)   A scale with equal units of measurement and containing a true zero equal to nought, that is the total absence of the quantity being measured.

Rationalism   Knowledge gained by reasoning (using deductive reasoning).

Realism (particularly social realism)   This maintains that structures do underpin social events and discourses, but as these are only indirectly observable they must be expressed in theoretical terms and are thus likely to be provisional in nature. This does not prevent them being used in action to change society.

Reasoning   A method of coming to conclusions by the use of logical argument.

Regression   A statistical technique for using the values of one variable to predict the value of another, based on information about their relationship.

Relational studies   An investigation of possible relationships between phenomena to establish if a correlation exists and, if so, its extent. The information about relationships between concepts form the bedrock of scientific knowledge, and explain, predict and provide us with a sense of understanding of our surroundings.

Relativism   The stance that implies that judgement is principally dependent on the values of the individuals or society and the perspectives from which they make their judgements. No universal criteria can be 'rationally' applied, and an understanding of decisions made by individuals or organizations can only be gained through knowledge of the historical, psychological and social backgrounds of the individuals.

Reliability   The degree to which the results of research are repeatable. This is based on: stability – the degree to which a measure is stable over time; internal reliability – the degree to which the indicators that make up the scale or index are consistent; and inter-observer consistency – the degree to which there is consistency in the decisions of several 'observers' in their recording of observations or translation of data into categories.

Replicability   Whether the research can be repeated and whether similar results are obtained. This is a check on the objectivity and lack of bias of the research findings. It requires a detailed account of the concepts used in the research, the measurements applied and methods employed.

Research question   A theoretical question that indicates a clear direction and scope for a research project.

Research problem   A general statement of an issue meriting research. It is usually used to help formulate a research project and is the basis on which specific research questions, hypotheses or statements are formed.

Sample   The small part of a whole (population) selected to show what the whole is like. There are two main types of sampling procedure – random and non-random.

Sampling error   The differences between the random sample and the population from which it has been selected.

Sampling frame   A complete list of cases in a population.

Scattergram   A type of diagram that graphically shows the relationship between two variables by plotting variable data from cases as dots on a two-dimensional matrix.

Scientific method   The foundation of modern scientific enquiry. It is based on observation and testing of the soundness of conclusions, commonly by using the hypothetico-deductive method. The four-step method is: (1) identification of a problem; (2) formulation of a hypothesis; (3) practical or theoretical testing of the hypothesis; and (4) rejection or adjustment of the hypothesis if it is falsified.

Secondary data   Data that have been subject to interpretation by others, usually in the form of publications.

Semiotics   The 'science of signs'. This approach is used to examine other media (e.g. visual communication and design) as well as written texts. It attempts to gain a deep understanding of meanings by the interpretation of single elements of a subject rather than to generalize through a quantitative assessment of components.

Semi-structured interview   One that contains structured and unstructured sections with standardized and open-format questions.

Sense of understanding   A complete explanation of a phenomenon provided by a wider study of the processes that surround, influence and cause it to happen.

Simple random sampling   A sampling method used to select cases at random from a uniform population.

Simple stratified sampling   A sampling method that recognizes the different strata in a population in order to select a representative sample.

Snowball sampling   A sampling method where the researcher contacts a small number of members of a target population and gets them to introduce him/her to others.

Stability   The degree to which a measure is stable over time.

Standard deviation   The amount of variability within the population expressed as the square root of the variance.

Standardized tests   Devised by social scientists and psychologists to establish people's abilities, attitudes, aptitudes, opinions, etc. The objective of the tests is usually to measure in some way the abilities of the subjects according to a standardized scale so that easy comparisons can be made.

Statement   An assertion based on a combination of concepts.

Statistical inference   The process of using a test of statistical significance to generalize from a sample to a population.

Statistical significance   A measure of how much statistical results are simply occasioned by chance or how truly representative they are of a population. An example of a test is the chi-square test.

Structuralism   A method of analysing phenomena, as in anthropology, linguistics, psychology or literature. It is chiefly characterized by contrasting the elemental structures of the phenomena in a system of binary opposition.

Structured interview   Interviews that use standardized questions read out by the interviewer according to an interview schedule. Answers may be closed-format.

Subject   The participant in a research project. The term implies a passive role in the project; that is, things are done to the subject in the form of a test or an experiment.

Sub-problem   A component of a main problem, usually expressed in less abstract terms to indicate an avenue of investigation.

Symbol   A sign used to communicate concepts in the form of natural or artificial language.

Symbolic interactionism   A sociological perspective that examines how individuals and groups interact, focusing on the creation of personal identity through interaction with others. Of particular interest is the relationship between individual action and group pressures. This perspective examines the idea that subjective meanings are socially constructed, and that these subjective meanings interrelate with objective actions.

Systematic sampling   A sampling method that selects samples using a numerical method, for example, the selection of every 10th name on a list.

Systematic matching sampling   A sampling method that is used when two groups of very different size are compared by selecting a number from the larger group to match the number and characteristics of the smaller one.

Theory   A system of ideas based on interrelated concepts, definitions and propositions with the purpose of explaining or predicting phenomena.

Theoretical sampling   The selection of a sample of the population that the researcher thinks knows most about the subject. This approach is common in qualitative research where statistical inference is not required.

Triangulation   Comparing results from the use of more than one method to collect data.

Univariate analysis   Analyses the qualities of one variable at a time.

Unstructured interview   A flexible format interview, usually based on a question guide but where the format remains the choice of the interviewer, who can allow the interview to 'ramble' in order to get insights into the attitudes of the interviewee. No closed-format questions are used.

Validity of argument   The property of an argument to draw conclusions from premises correctly according to the rules of logic.

Validity of research   The degree to which the research findings are true.

Value   The actual unit or method of measurement of a variable. These are data in their most concrete form.

Variable   The component of an indicator that can be measured.

Visual ethnography   Observation used for recording the nature or condition of objects or events visually, for example, through photography, film or sketching.

References

Alldred, P. and Gillies, V. (2002) 'Eliciting research accounts: re/producing modern subjects?', in M. Mauthner, M. Birch, J. Jessop and T. Miller (eds), *Ethics in Qualitative Research*. London: Sage, pp. 148–65.

Bernard, H.R. (2000) *Social Research Methods: Qualitative and Quantitative Approaches*. Thousand Oaks, CA: Sage.

Bernard, H.R. (2012) *Social Research Methods: Qualitative and Quantitative Approaches* (2nd edn). Thousand Oaks, CA: Sage.

Blaxter, L., Hughes, C. and Tight, M. (2010) *How to Research* (4th edn). Buckingham: Open University Press.

Booth, W.C., Colomb, G.G. and William, J.M. (2008) *The Craft of Research* (3rd edn). Chicago, IL: University of Chicago Press.

Branley, D., Covey, J. and Hardey, M. (2014) 'Online surveys: investigating social media use and online risk'. London: Sage, doi: http://dx.doi.org/10.4135/9781 44627305013514666.

Bromley, D.B. (1986) *The Case-Study Method in Psychology and Related Disciplines*. Chichester: Wiley.

Bryman, A. (2012) *Social Research Methods* (4th edn). Oxford: Oxford University Press.

Cleary, S., Simmons, L., Cubilla, I., Andrade, E. and Edberg, M. (2014) 'Community sampling: sampling in an immigrant community'. London: Sage, doi: http://dx.doi.org/10.4135/9781446273050145295519.

Cohen, L. and Manion, L. (2011) *Research Methods in Education* (7th edn). London: Routledge.

Dixon, B.R. (1987) *A Handbook of Social Science Research*. New York: Oxford University Press.

Duncombe, J. and Jessop, J. (2002) '"Doing rapport" and the ethics of "faking friendship"', in M. Mauthner, M. Birch, J. Jessop and T. Miller (eds), *Ethics in Qualitative Research*. London: Sage, pp. 107–22.

Field, A. (2013) *Discovering Statistics Using IBM SPSS for Windows: Advanced Techniques for the Beginner* (4th edn). London: Sage.

Foucault, M. (1972) *The Archaeology of Knowledge*. London: Tavistock.

Glaser, B. and Strauss, A. (1967) *The Discovery of Grounded Theory: Strategies for Qualitative Research*. Chicago, IL: Aldine.

Gold, R. (1958) 'Roles in sociological fieldwork', *Social Forces*, 36: 217–23.

Greer, T. (2014) 'Example of data collection using interviews and activity logs'. London: Sage, doi: http://dx.doi.org/10.4135/9781446273050145 56457.

Guba, E. and Lincoln, Y. (1989) *Fourth Generation Evaluation*. Newbury Park, CA: Sage.

Hacking, I. (ed.) (1981) *Scientific Revolutions*. Oxford: Oxford University Press.

Harré, R. (1972) *The Philosophies of Science*. Oxford: Oxford University Press.

Hughes, J.A. and Sharrock, W.W. (1997) *The Philosophy of Social Research* (3rd edn). Harlow: Longman.

Kerlinger, F. (1970) *Foundations of Behavioral Research*. New York: Holt, Rinehart & Winston.

Kina, V. (2015) 'Exploring the personal nature of children and young people's participation: a participatory action research study'. London: Sage, doi: http://dx.doi.org/10.4135/9781446273050145 56457.

Kvale, S. (2008) *Doing Interviews*. Thousand Oaks, CA: Sage.

Lazarfeld, P., Pasanella, A. and Rosenberg, M. (eds) (1972) *Continuities in the Language of Social Research*. New York: Free Press.

Leedy, P. and Ormrod, J. (2012) *Practical Research: Planning and Design* (10th edn). London: Collier Macmillan.

Lofland, J. (1971) *Analysing Social Settings: A Guide to Qualitative Observation and Analysis*. Belmont, CA: Wadsworth.

Ma, S-C., Rotherham, I. and Ma, S-M. (2014) 'Winning matches in tennis grand slam men's singles: a logistic model'. London: Sage, doi: http://dx.doi.org/10.4135/9781446273050135 16575.

Mangione, T. (1995) *Mail Surveys: Improving the Quality*. Thousand Oaks, CA: Sage.

Marsh, C. (1982) *The Survey Method: The Contribution of Surveys to Sociological Explanation*. London: Allen and Unwin.

Mertler, C.A. (2006) *Action Research: Teachers as Researchers in the Classroom*. Los Angeles: CA, Sage.

Miles, M.B. and Huberman, A.M. (2014) *Qualitative Data Analysis: An Expanded Sourcebook* (3rd edn). London: Sage.

Miller, T. and Bell, L. (2002) 'Consenting to what? Issues of access, gatekeeping and "informed" consent', in M. Mauthner, M. Birch, J. Jessop and T. Miller (eds), *Ethics in Qualitative Research*. London: Sage, pp. 53–69.

Open University (1993) *An Equal Opportunities Guide to Language and Image*. Milton Keynes: Open University.

Phillips, N. and Brown, J. (1993) 'Analyzing communications in and around organizations: a critical hermeneutic approach', *Academy of Management Journal*, 36: 1547–76.

Preece, R. (1994) *Starting Research: An Introduction to Academic Research and Dissertation Writing*. London: Pinter.

Quine, W.V.O. (1969) *Ontological Relativity and Other Essays*. New York: Columbia University Press.

Reynolds, P.D. (1977) *A Primer in Theory Construction*. Indianapolis, IN: Bobbs-Merrill.

Robson, C. (2011) *Real World Research: A Resource for Social Scientists and Practitioner-Researchers* (3rd edn). Oxford: Blackwell.

Seale, C. (ed.) (1998) *Researching Society and Culture*. London: Sage.

Seale, C. (ed.) (2004) *Researching Society and Culture* (2nd edn). London: Sage.

Seale, C. and Filmer, P. (1998) 'Doing social surveys', in C. Seale (ed.), *Researching Society and Culture*. London: Sage, pp. 125–45.

Siegel, S. and Castellan, N. (1988) *Nonparametric Statistics for the Behavioral Sciences* (2nd edn). New York: McGraw-Hill.

Silverman, D. (2015) *Interpreting Qualitative Data: Methods for Analysing Qualitative Data* (5th edn). London: Sage.

Silverman, D. (1998) 'Research and social theory', in C. Seale (ed.), *Researching Society and Culture*. London: Sage.

Slater, D. (1998) 'Analysing cultural objects: content analysis and semiotics', in C. Seale (ed.), *Researching Society and Culture*. London: Sage.

Swales, J. and Feak, C. (2000) *English in Today's Research World: A Writing Guide*. Michigan: University of Michigan Press.

van Dijk, T.A. (1994) 'Discourse and cognition in society', in C. Crowly and D. Michell (eds), *Communication Theory Today*. Cambridge: Polity Press. pp. 107–26.

Wamba, N. (2014) 'Participatory action research for school improvement: the Kwithu project'. London: Sage, doi: http://dx.doi.org/10.4135/978144627305 014528626.

Williams, E. (2015) 'Analysing public disposal behaviour: observational research', London: Sage, doi: http://dx.doi.org/10.4135/9781446273050 14554894.

Williams, M. and May, T. (1996) *Introduction to the Philosophy of Social Research*. London: UCL Press.

Index